Just Be Love

Messages on the Spiritual
and Human Journey

David Schroeder, LMSW, CPC

Love is not for in the thought of Love.
Love is found in the awareness, I Am Love.

ISBN: 978-1-64467-262-4   (Paperback Edition)
ISBN: 978-1-64467-263-1   (E-book Edition)

Some characters and events in this book are fictitious. Any similarity to real persons, living or dead, is coincidental and not intended by the author.

Book Ordering Information

Phone Number: 347-901-4929 or 347-901-4920
Email: info@globalsummithouse.com
Global Summit House
www.globalsummithouse.com

Printed in the United States of America

Dedication

Just Be Love is dedicated to my beloved master and brother, Jesus, also known by his birth name, Yeshua ben Joseph, and his soul name, Lord Sananda. I am extremely grateful for my experiences with you and your unwavering love and compassion toward me. Through and because of you, Jesus, the inspiration and messages in writing *Just Be Love* came to be. I am blessed beyond measure.

Just Be Love is also dedicated, to all those who have touched my life through their expressions of love and friendship. I thank you all for the experiences, lessons and gifts. This book is my gift of love and appreciation to each of you.

Lastly, *Just Be Love* is dedicated to those who seek a greater wisdom and practice of love. This book is my gift to you as well. Your desire and willingness to read these messages is your gift to me.

Contents

Acknowledgments

I wish to thank the following people for their time, effort, and feedback on this book. I am very grateful for your willingness to aid with completing this manuscript. Your belief in my writing is love without measure.

Kelly Epperson Simmons: Much gratitude Kelly, with your coaching and some editing of my words. Your insights brought more life and clarity to this work.

Stephanie Larson: You challenged me in many ways. You offered confidence about the book's inspiration and potential.

Patricia McShane-Gearhart: I am in much gratitude Patricia for your time, heart and unwavering commitment in editing this challenging manuscript. Your suggestions brought life to this book. I am blessed beyond measure dear soul sister, for your love and confidence in this books message.

Linda Missad: Much appreciation Linda, for your suggestions and editing expertise. Your work provided improved clarity to the books content. Thank you for your time and commitment to the books message.

Terese Schroeder: Thank you my dear, for your love and gentle ways in helping me to improve the wording and meanings. Your willingness to share how my words touched you and your excitement for my effort with this project kept me motivated and focused. Terese, such a blessing and soulful love you are.

Susan Mavity: Gratitude Sue for your loving friendship and your gentle presence of confidence as I would share with you the books content.

John Schroeder: For always believing in me and for your curiosity as to what I was writing. For your words of praise about how this book touched you. Your perspective and honest feedback helped improve the clarity of my writing.

Introduction

Just Be Love explores the many aspects of love from both our human and spiritual perspective. This book offers messages on love that are not only familiar to us, but also that are at times mysterious, hidden and paradoxical. *Just Be Love* weaves my insights on love with the teachings and wisdom of spiritual masters, poets and authors of many traditions. These spiritual masters, through their open hearts and minds, understood and mirrored the essence of Divine Love, while living their human experience. They recognized and demonstrated that we are spiritual beings first and foremost, while living the human experience. I believe Divine Love is: *The unconditional love and acceptance of the spirit in all that exists.*

Throughout this book I offer examples of what I call Divine love and its relationship to human love. The book is written in two parts. Part One is dedicated to exploring the dynamic of the human knowing and the expression of love. It also explores how our life experiences cause us to forget we are love and worthy. Part Two describes the dynamic and expression of Divine love as I've come to experience and understand it. It also offers means for us to remember we are love as we experience life through our higher and wiser perspective and knowing.

Please know that we cannot really comprehend the energy of Divine love totally. Our human minds limit us by our experiences and perspective, so we humanize the Divine through our thoughts, beliefs and language to comprehend a Source that is incomprehensible to us. I acknowledge there will be words I use that will not describe the totality of our Source.

I write *Just Be Love* as a sojourner like you; for I too struggle with the experience of love. While in my mother's womb, I was impacted by complications of Rh factor, a condition of conflicting blood types between mother and baby. Sixty-two years ago, doctors were just beginning to understand how to treat this complication. The condition caused me to be born nearly dead. Since I wasn't breathing, I required a total blood transfusion. As a result of the lack of oxygen to my brain, I have severe hearing loss and some learning challenges. I have thrived to this day, due to the love, patience and care of my parents, siblings and many others. Through my human hardships and heartaches, I've come to realize and honor the many people and experiences that have been my teachers, providing opportunities for me to more deeply love myself and enhance my self-worth. They have taught me about acceptance, compassion, forgiveness and letting go.

Like many of you, I struggled while growing up to fit in, both in my family and with my peers. I had growing pains, wrong turns and lost dreams. In my adult years, I've been divorced, and lost a dear woman, lover and friend to an aneurysm. I've had relationships that became broken and have acknowledged that they taught me even more about love, commitment and life. I've had endearing and evolving friendships, which also helped me understand more about love, life and myself. I've lost jobs and walked away from a few as well. I've realized the mistakes I have made as a parent while helping to raise two resilient sons, Andy and Ryan. I've come to understand unconditional love more deeply by interacting with my grandkids.

I have moments of fear and doubt, and I've even lost myself a few times along the way. I've struggled with writing this book. Several times I wanted to give up on the writing process. One morning while shaving, I was in a moment of doubt about my writing and just wanting to end the project. I suddenly felt as if I was being pulled so strongly, that I needed to sit down. I ended up sitting on the closest thing to me—the toilet—as the pull literally put me on my butt. I heard a voice from deep within me say, "You are to write this book—no need to doubt yourself or give up on the process. Just continue being open and willing; it will all fall into place as intended."

As you read these pages, please know that I'm not an expert on the concept of love. I struggle with its mystery. I have challenges with the giving and receiving of it, and experience times of misunderstanding loves divine intent. I've hurt people I love, and I've been hurt too. I've discovered when to let go of love and when to fight for it. I've struggled with the yearning for my higher divine self and to know myself as love. I've come to accept that life is a process, and that our soul is always creating, expanding and renewing. As humans, we too are meant to create, expand and renew in perspective, and ways of understanding and living our earthly journey.

Such is the journey and lessons of *Just Be Love*. As a counselor and coach, I've helped people remember the love that they are, despite their traumas and feelings of unworthiness. I've helped couples overcome the barriers they've created to love by giving them tools to remove those barriers, enabling them to move toward loving themselves and each other more deeply. I've also helped individuals and couples love themselves enough to step out of painful relationships. A part of love is letting go, for an aspect of love is to set yourself and the others free for the highest good of all. Love turns and returns everything to God. God is love, and love is God.

I invite you on a journey to *Just Be Love*, in which we will weave in and out of the spiritual and human realms, providing the opportunity to remember the love that we are. We will explore the mystery of love and the array of meanings it holds. Humanity's concept of love has a profound impact on our relationship with our self, with others and with God, however we define God. Since the dawn of human existence, these concepts of love have impacted human consciousness and evolution. Please note in this book: I refer to God also as: Divine, Source, Creator or the Holy One

This book is not intended to provide instructions on how to love and be loved; rather, my hope is that it will challenge and expand your perceptions of love and open your heart, to be love—to give and receive love more freely and fully. It's my belief that the soul comes to Earth, seeking to expand itself to greater capacities of love.

Some of the concepts of love we explore may be new to you. Certain chapters may take you to your untouched spiritual and emotional depths. This might create struggles or become unsettling to the parts of you that only know love from your current perspective. As I wrote this book, I too had unsettling times, and my perspective was challenged. This is natural and expected as our soul journeys through human life. Love calls us to wrestle with ourselves at times, in order to expand our awareness and break us free from limiting beliefs about ourselves and what real love is. If you experience a shift in belief while reading this book, or a time after, use gentleness in your self-reflection; deeper knowing is raising your consciousness. Remember to nurture and pace yourself as needed.

In my journey and yearning for love, I've become aware that to experience the Divine, is to know love. To experience love is to have the awareness of the Divine. I believe one main purpose of the soul, as it experiences itself in human form, is to experience Divine love. In the experience of God's love, we come to an awareness of knowing ourselves as love. I believe an open heart and a trained mind create this knowing.

Martin Luther King Jr. said it well, *"I believe the unnamed truth and unconditional love will have the final word in reality."* There is an unnamed truth that we struggle to recognize and embrace. The basis of this truth is grounded in unconditional love and acceptance. *Just Be Love* offers you the opportunity to explore and embrace this unnamed truth; through unconditional love and acceptance of yourself and your life experiences. There is a good chance as you read this book, you will see yourself in these pages.

This is good and as it should be, for I am you and you are me. We are both the student and the teacher, so life and our experiences are reflecting themselves to us by way of being mirrors to each other.

Some of the book's content has come through messages from my beloved teacher and friend, Yeshua/Jesus. A mystical experience I had with Jesus in the spring of 2010 and the years that followed provided much of the inspiration to write this book. These pages are my perceptions and interpretations of the messages. It is not my intention to change your view; I only ask that you be open to consider the content. Of course, you alone decide what feels appropriate for you.

1

The Sun, the Cloud, Jesus and Me

For it was not into my ear you whispered, but into my heart. It was not my lips you kissed, but my soul. —Judy Garland

In the spring of 2010, I made my yearly retreat of solitude to a place called Christ in the Wilderness, located in northwest Illinois. On the second evening I was on a bluff, overlooking the Mississippi River. There, I had a profound experience with my master teacher, Jesus.

While I was enjoying the sunset, the sun began to disappear behind a cloud. The cloud's outer edges lit up like a string of white-orange lights. I knew I was in for an experience. I surrendered and opened to the vison before me. As the sun went down further, a thin area of the cloud's right side lit up in a bright orange-white glow and an opening appeared like a portal into a cave. Scenes began unfolding before me in this opening. A short stone pillar appeared with a baby lying on top of it. Then I saw a young man dressed in a robe, with long, slightly curly hair, and a beard, walking on a path. A temple was in the background. The portal in this cloud then began to slowly close like a theater curtain. I closed my eyes and asked, "What do you want me to know?"

A gentle voice replied from the cloud, *"Just Be Love."* I knew this was the voice of Jesus. I held out my arms and opened my heart to the message presented to me, as tears came.

I stopped in the retreat center's chapel on the way back to my cabin. Its construction of Native American decor. There, I sat in silence and reflected on what I had experienced.

Back in my cabin I began to write. I glanced at the clock; it showed 8:11 p.m. I thought, "Wow, this is amazing," as I recalled Lee Carroll's book, *The Twelve Layers of DNA,* channeled by Kryon.

As I was reviewing his book, Kryon explains twelve layers of our DNA: The eighth layer of our DNA is about the cave of creation and the quantum state. The eleventh layer is about the wise divine feminine. It is a God layer within the human being and is the powerful energy of compassion. In numerology, which is one of the oldest sciences in the world, eight is the symbol for the cosmic Christ; the totality of the universe, associated with prosperity. It also is related to infinity, being in the flow; as one circle of the figure eight weaves into the other, two parts seamlessly merge to create the whole. Eight is the mirror as one circle reflects the other circle. Eleven is a master number and is about intuition, spirituality, patience and equality. It's a portal or gateway; it's about illumination and higher consciousness. What Kyron was explaining in Carroll's book, was much of what I had experienced with Jesus.

I believe there is a connection to my experience and the meaning of these numbers. The cave I saw in the cloud was the cave of creation; the energy of love which is the foundation of creation. Through this cave of creation, a portal was opened to me and Jesus (the cosmic Christ), asked that I remember who I am. He offered me the gift of returning to my infinite I AM Presence. I was opened to a higher awareness of love and transcendence. With his gentle statement of *"Just Be Love,"* Jesus was asking me to awaken more fully, become one with the energy of Divine love and offer this message to others.

2

Just Be Love

Love is, above all, the gift of oneself. —Jean Anouilh

L ove is the great yearning and mystery of the human condition. Just as there are many questions about love, there are also many ways that love is defined. There can be many questions and many definitions as to what love is truly about. There are many definitions of the word love. As I have come to understand it, love is the absence of fear. It is the conscious awareness, acknowledgement and acceptance of the unity and oneness with all that is. Love is knowing ourselves as love, and freely love and accept who we are. Love is also going beyond oneself for the benefit of another.

In the English language love is a noun, and more importantly, love is a verb, an action word. The action we take, through our intention, process, and practice to love, and be loved, will manifest not only our experience of love, but also our understanding and belief of love.

Most of us perceive love as physical, emotional and romantic. I will expound more on this in upcoming chapters. Human love comes with expectations and conditions, based on needs, creating disappointments and barriers, which block the energy of love. True love is neither physical nor romantic in the human sense. Divine love is the unconditional acceptance of all that is, has been, will be, and will not be. Divine love is unconditional giving and receiving. As humans with egos, we seem to struggle with the concept of unconditional giving. Our giving comes with a desire for something to be returned. Or we struggle with feelings of unworthiness, believing we do not deserve what has been offered to us. I believe when humans love, as the Divine loves, there are no strings or attachments. Nothing is needed in return. Divine love stands in its own power and worthiness. It gives and receives with openness, acceptance and appreciation.

In this unconditional giving and going beyond oneself, one also receives the gift of unconditional love. If you are naturally open to love, you experience this energy flowing back to you, with no expectations. When we love as God loves, we instinctively know that what we freely give is also freely returned to us.

> *We cannot do great things on earth, only small things with great love.* —Mother Teresa

My mystical experience with the sun, the cloud, and the energy of Jesus was one of bliss—extreme happiness/ecstasy. There was this amazing synergy between Jesus and I, a profound and unconditional energy exchange—a special giving and receiving.

As humans, we are experiencing an interplay of life and love. So, there is a constant exchange of energy, frequency and vibration. These forces are subtle and difficult to detect when our senses are untrained, yet they are always present; impacting us and our interactions more than we realize. As we experience our physicality, love asks us to live this experience not only as humans, but to be open to experiences from the soul perspective. I will offer more on the soul perspective in upcoming chapters.

Our life journey seems simple enough: *Just Be Love*. Life is to be experienced, and we are here to remember that we are love within the context of our experiences. We desire and dream about love. Yet we learn to fear and doubt it, so we reject this yearning. Our journey to love is avoided or at best, misunderstood and misguided. The energy of love calls us to our imagination, and to embrace the desire of our soul and heart, like we would embrace the Divine. We then let go of our fears, our unworthiness and just *Be* love, we allow ourselves to be loved—we are alive and free.

Just Be Love is having the intention, courage and determination to act toward this purpose. It is about understanding, accepting, working through, and releasing the limiting beliefs and barriers we've created to love. It calls us to come to terms with truly loving ourselves, our sisters and brothers, and all that is seen and unseen. Love is the totality of our being. Love calls us to come home to this totality—to our divinity. We come into this world *From* and *As Love*, and our task is to reconnect with this love through the experiences in life before we leave. This is the essence of the message of this book.

Humanity has had a long-held practice of living from our intellect; our logical thinking state. One of the highest intentions we can have in these times, is the willingness to shift and merge the intellect with our feeling, emotions and intuitive state. The ability to live more from the heart, from our intuition, and our higher self, puts us more in alignment with love and our divinity. I will expound more on this in chapters to follow.

Just Be Love means choosing to look at our life experiences from the soul's perspective. By allowing the light and love of our divine essence to punch through our clouds of darkness and illusion; to illuminate each experience and see its intended lesson for our soul's growth.

To *Just Be Love* is to recognize and accept that my life is happening for me and through me, not to me. The physical body and mind are just vehicles to experience life. They are temporary and not the real keeper of truth. It is the energy of the soul that holds our truth. Out of love, I choose to see my life experiences from the perspective that governs all souls.

Love is the innocence of being. There is sacred wisdom and strength in *Just Being.* This returns us to the love we are and our divinity. *Just Be Love* is to **Be** and **Live** with childlike innocence and wonder.

Just Be Love calls us to a greater understanding and commitment to explore these spiritual truths. It is our choice to align ourselves with these truths. At any given time, it is our choice to follow our ego or the promptings of the Divine, of our soul and of our heart. Many of the teachings from spiritual masters, such as Buddha, Jesus and Muhammad encourage us to live life as the Divine guides us. Aligning with divine truths will naturally and gracefully bring us to knowing ourselves and others as love.

3

Love and the Soul

The soul allows for contradiction and pain, it dwells in darkness and light. The soul is the seed of love—nurture it and it grows.

As I go about an ordinary day, I notice these two inner voices seeking my attention. One voice is rather loud and obnoxious, coming from what seems like my fear and doubt. The other appears soft and subtle, coming from what appears to be love and assurance. I ask myself. "Is this the dance between my ego and my soul?" As I listen intently to their exchange, it sounds like this:

My ego says, "No."
While my soul says, "Yes."
Ego: "I can't change; change is fearful."
Soul: "Trust me; change is an act of love."
Ego: "It's their fault."
Soul: "The other is a reflection of our own consciousness."
Ego: "Why me, poor me."
Soul: "We create our own reality."
Ego: "I'm not worthy or good enough."
Soul: "We are love and goodness."

Have you ever had this type of conversation with yourself? This is the great paradox: The dance of a spiritual being having a human experience—of being a soul yet living as an ego. The lower self is defined by its human physical form and by its human experiences; as if this is all there is to itself. It carries the human burdens of fear, doubt, anger, shame, striving, etc. It holds the perception of separation and low self-worth. The higher self is the soft inner voice that acts like a best friend or inner guide. It is pure love and formless energy. It's the intuitive knowing that is in communion and communication with God and the angelic realm. It's not defined by human experiences; it observes our life experiences from the higher divine perspective. The higher self is open and available to connect with the lower part self. We are encouraged to openly plug into it in surrender, trust and allowing—in order to receive its messages and guidance.

The soul is our most significant part of us, yet we have limited awareness of it. The relationship and interaction between body, mind and soul are vital to understanding our divine purpose and fulfilling our soul's mission. In mainstream systems there are limited teachings or even discussions about the soul and its purpose. We educate our children about the facts of life, yet few families talk about the soul and its journey. These conversations usually revolve around the concept that our soul passes on to an afterlife when the physical form ends. Many struggle with the concept that we are spiritual beings having a human experience, and that the soul has had many lifetimes. Fear, mistrust, avoidance, and ignorance all create barriers to understanding the soul and its purpose.

When I was in graduate school, getting my degree in social work, I took a class about coping with grief. The professor gave a one-hour talk on spirituality. There was minimal discussion on the transition process of the soul when physical life ends. We learned the stages of grief, which are real and important from the aspect of human personality and life cycle, yet little was discussed on the soul's journey and how this could assist with the grieving process for the ones left behind. Albert Einstein once said, *"It is a miracle that curiosity survives formal education."*

We have physical medicine to study and treat our physical state. We have psychology to study and care for our mental and the emotional state. There is religion to study and learn about God and our relationship to God in our world. Fair to say, there is little attention paid to the study and advancement of our soul.

It's only been in the past fifty years, that the emphasis on spirituality has, once again, come to the forefront. In the last ten years especially, we have grown in understanding the importance of inclusion, unity and soul work. I believe spiritual teachings that speak of a greater connection to the true self and the concept of unity consciousness, are love based vs. teachings that are based on fear and shame. Spirituality is the appreciation of the intangible, yet meaningful attributes of our lives. It asks us to do our inner work and be in the process of co-creation, rather than just giving it all to God and then sitting back praying; hoping and waiting for the miracle.

Divine love invites us to be who we are and more importantly, who we can be. Many people today are seeking out, and listening to the true spiritual teachers, both past and present, who offer the grander message of love and a broader understanding of who we are as souls.

More attention today is being devoted to the metaphysical aspects of life. People are inquiring beyond the physical attributes of living, and opening to their spiritual, mental and emotional bodies. Metaphysical research and numerous real-life examples show that a significant part of physical and mental illness occurs on the spiritual, mental and emotional levels of the individual, more so than the physical. Yes, illness occurs due to stress, trauma, chemical imbalances, toxins, a weakened immune system and more. However, on a deeper spiritual level, I believe much of illness is related to a neglected soul.

The soul energy emanates from the Creator of all that is—connecting to the cosmos, the spiritual, mental and emotional realms of the universe, as well residing in our physical bodies. The earthly part of the soul, the part experiencing the physical world, has been ignored. The ego has misunderstood its purpose for being and has become too controlling and reactive. The result is that the ego is in charge, while the enduring love, wisdom and light of the soul has been disregarded and blocked, creating dis-harmony and dis-ease within the energy system of the physical body.

The soul, however, may have agreed to experience the illness and lessons that it brought the individual in this lifetime. The experience of illness may also be intended to be a lesson for those close to the person having the illness, i.e. family, partner, etc.

Disease, disabilities or difficult experiences, are not punishment from God. These situations, like all of life experiences, are to be viewed from the higher perspective, as experiences and lessons for soul growth and advancement on both the individual and collective levels.

Since we are spiritual beings having a human experience, a substantial part of our life experiences, including physical and mental disease happens through soul "agreements." A soul "agreement" is a contract the soul made before we were born. This "agreement" includes all the lessons we choose to experience in this lifetime, as well as the encounters and relationships we agree to have with other souls. Soul agreements include physical and spiritual experiences that involve karma (*we reap what we sow*), our gifts, goals and life purpose.

Soul "agreements" are put in place to learn lessons such as, conditional love in order to experience and learn its opposite, i.e. unconditional love, being wronged from another soul in order to learn forgiveness. We may experience disease or disability as a way to then experience and learn the practice of acceptance and determination. On the soul level we choose our parents and they choose us. We choose our mates, work occupations, living locations, etc. Our use of free will can mitigate the impact of events and people in our lives or cause greater torment for us.

For true learning and healing to occur, all life issues, including disease, should be observed and addressed from the spiritual and soul perspective. Additionally, many of us have a limited awareness of our physical self; paying little attention to the effects of life choices until we experience discomfort or dis-ease. Many deny that thoughts, feelings and beliefs contribute to our experience, due to fear, stigma, and the belief that feelings and emotions are a sign of weakness. With this mind-set the spiritual aspect and true meaning of painful life experiences or disease are diluted. So, we deny or blame ourselves or someone else. We feel too fearful and vulnerable to look deep within for the answers that would bring healing. Complementary forms of healthcare, like Reiki, Bodywork, Eye Movement Desensitization Repressing (EMDR), Brainspotting, Cranial Sacral Therapy, Reflexology, Emotional Freedom Technique, Breath Therapy, Past-life Regression, etc., merge the components of spirituality and mindfulness and underscore the importance of treating the whole person as a soul-energy system.

Bottom line: We are not educated on ways to expand the mind to the level of understanding the soul and the divine perspective. It's a tragic fact that we put so much emphasis and attention on the physical and material world; those temporary aspects of life. Quantum physics tells us: *That which is temporary is not the true reality; it's an illusion that we choose to make real.* This would include the human body—it's temporary. Rather than embrace the eternal, the soul, we fear it. At its primal root, fear is an automatic defense mechanism toward perceived physical danger. On the spiritual level, fear is the absence of love, an illusion the mind makes real; it creates **F**alse **E**vidence **A**ppearing **R**eal. Only **Love** is real.

When we only give credence to the temporary and avoid the eternal, we limit ourselves, rejecting the opportunities to experience the higher version of ourselves and life. It's like hiking a mountain trail to see a nice view; with excitement, determination and effort, a grander experience is possible. When we are in fear, we deprive ourselves from experiencing the view from the top of the mountain; experiencing life in its fullness—from the higher perspective.

Jesus said: *"In my father's house are many mansions."* (John 14:2, KJV). When he uses the word "house," according to the Gospel of Thomas, he's referring to: *The totality of our being.* I believe Jesus is saying, in the totality of our being, there are many mansions—the totality of our being is mind, body and spirit, and the level of awareness we experience throughout our life. We perceive "mansions" to be grand structures with many rooms. Jesus is inviting us to visit and explore the many rooms or dimensions in the grand house, the totality of our soul and the universe. Yes, there are many dimensions, i.e. mansions of our being and the infinite universe. There are attributes of the soul self, beyond the temporary physical body and mind. These aspects of the soul are waiting to make their way into our consciousness while we walk the Earth. Quantum physics, research on near death experiences, post death communication, people in deep meditative, hypnotic, and dream states, all reveal that we have several energetic bodies in addition to our physical one; specifically, the mental, emotional and spiritual bodies.

Jesus and other spiritual teachers have suggested the importance of learning to **be** in this world, yet realize we are not **of** this world. I believe this phrase relates to the importance of keeping our faith and perspective about the totality of our being; not being attached to, nor defined by our human experiences. We are to view our earthly experiences, i.e. what we perceive as good or bad, painful or joyful, from a higher dimension—the soul's perspective. The ego is temporary and limited. The soul is eternal, vast and multidimensional. While an aspect of our soul is here, there's still a connection to the other side of the veil; in higher dimensions of the universe. These aspects of our soul view our life experiences from a different perspective; that is more loving, accepting and compassionate than our human egoic, wounded perspective. We are here to embrace the human journey, and to discover within it, the deeper knowing of our soul. In this knowing, we come to a deeper and richer experience with God and our true self.

The Soul Seeks Life Experiences to Expand in Love

The thirteenth century mystic and poet Jalal ad-Din Muhammad Rumi wrote a poem entitled, *Chickpea to Cook*. I offer you the first part of this poem.

> *A chickpea leaps almost over the rim of the pot where it is being boiled. "Why are you doing this to me?" The cook knocks him down with a ladle. "Don't you try to jump out. You think I'm torturing you. I'm giving you flavor, so you can mix with spices and rice and be the lovely vitality of a human being.*

The energy called "soul" comes from the infinite presence of God and incarnates into physical form. The soul chooses to be brought into contact with matter (physical form), to act as a mediator and link between the Divine and each soul that takes on human form. The soul thrives on experiences. It comes to Earth to feel, to learn, to create, to receive and give love through its human life experiences. It is offered experiences through its interactions with other souls and it offers other souls its experiences as well. Soul growth is obtained through awareness of these experiences from the higher perspective. The eternal soul doesn't need to avoid pain or suffering, because it knows it can't be harmed. What our temporary human self sees as wrong, pain and suffering, the soul sees as opportunities for its learning and growth. Rumi's poem tells us in a humorous way that the task of the soul as a human is to embrace the spices and flavor of life's experiences in order to be "the lovely vitality of a human being."

The soul, integrated as a human, is the creating agent that uses the temporary physical body and mind and its experiences in the physical realm, to reach higher states of awareness; to know itself as love and wholeness. The soul is the medium of wisdom and light between humans and their Creator. Like rays of the sun shining through the clouds, the soul illuminates itself while in physical form, to experience the presence of Divine love and the higher dimensions of itself. The more elevated the soul is while in human form, the deeper love can be experienced and lived.

As humans we are containers of both an eternal soul and a manufactured ego. Consider that the soul comes here to experience life with its many ups and downs, its accomplishments and joys, as well as its pains and sorrows. The soul comes here to learn self-love, self-worth and empowerment through our life experiences. It comes to learn how to be one with itself, with other souls and with Source, while in the temple called a body. The soul in human form is **Here** for God and God is **Always** here for us—offering love and compassion through our experiences, to fulfill our soul agreements. *The soul is the living potential of God. Love is the living expression of God.* From the divine and soul perspective, our earthly experiences seek to expand our capacity to love, for soul growth and maturity.

Soul Perspective of Jesus and Mary

The life and times of Yeshua/Jesus and Mary Magdalene were about two courageous and enlightened souls accepting their mission, which was in part, to bring in higher dimensions and perspectives of love, and to balance the masculine and feminine energies. They also taught the importance of understanding, respecting and living the divine laws and principles that govern the universe. Human laws are often not in alignment with God's laws. Jesus and Mary did not promote any religion, only the importance of living from the heart and accepting one's own divinity. Jesus can be seen as a noble rebel, as he challenges Jewish laws, interacts with all types of people and treats women as equal. Some made Mary into a prostitute to further suppress the feminine and control what church fathers feared—the energies of the Divine Mother, which Mary Magdalene and Mother Mary embodied. The true stories of Jesus included his relationship and love for Mary Magdalene, and how she was at his side during the good times and the dangerous times. She was in many ways his closest confidant, offering her own spiritual wisdom and leadership as well.

The Scribes and Pharisees (supposed holy men) condemned Jesus to death because of his teachings and their fear of him. The "holy men" of that time, created a fear of God. They were threatened by the higher dimensions of love and truth brought forth by Jesus, his parents, Mary Magdalene, and his true followers. The Scribes and Pharisees and the oppressive Roman "rulers," given their actions, could be viewed as the "enemies" of Jesus and Mary. Yet Jesus said: *"Love thy enemies"*, not only the enemies you see outside of you, but especially the ones inside of you. Today, over two thousand years later, notice humanity is still struggling toward a higher consciousness; attempting to rise as love and create a peaceful existence.

The Ego, the Shadow and Lost Parts

Throughout our life experience, our ego creates and repeats a story. Fed by fear, avoidance, guilt and self-doubt it continues repeating that story. Our soul, however, views this story as a journey, calling us to remember and reclaim our innocence and divinity.

The soul comes to the earth school to expand its awareness and experience, knowing itself as love and goodness. The soul takes on a human form, temporarily forgetting itself as love. In this *"spiritual amnesia"* the human personality forms an ego, complete with a shadow, persona and mask, doing its best to cope and navigate through the dramas and traumas of life.

The ego is part of the unconscious or (some say the subconscious) mind; its focus is survival. It serves to protect us in this world—like having an internal police officer. A healthy ego serves important functions in life, such as setting boundaries, standing up for one's self, taking healthy risks and navigating through traumas and dramas. A healthy ego is one that can tolerate difficult experiences, when working through them. The emotions and distorted beliefs won't be its demise. However, a fragile, unhealthy ego feels threatened and is fearful of losing its identity and role as protector and defender. It desires to stay in its comfort zone. If the ego perceives a situation as contrary to what it knows and believes, it will view the situation as a threat; "the enemy" causing it to react in protective and reactive ways.

True ego strength is when the ego can view a situation as a "teacher," and an opportunity for growth. When the ego can do this, it's more likely to let down its guard and entertain new perspectives, creating possibilities for higher awareness and growth to occur. Ego strength is also needed for learning how to be a witness to experiences, without expectations or attachment to a particular outcome. Learning to be the witness or observer of our experiences is part of our work to transcend the ego. The ego is necessary and valuable. However, if too protective and rigid in its interpretation of experiences, it creates distorted beliefs about itself and how to effectively cope with life. For many, their ego, unfortunately, learns to build walls instead of bridges.

The ego creates difficulty and dysfunction for its human personality, through distorted perceptions and beliefs. This leads to assumptions and misinterpretations. When wounded the ego creates fears, self-doubt, and the belief that it's defective, inferior—not good enough, or it's superior to others.

To further protect ourselves, our ego creates what Swiss psychiatrist Carl Jung coined as, "the shadow." The shadow is the traumatized parts of ourselves that we repress and disown, and at times project onto others. These disowned parts become fragmented and linger in our unconscious. They are triggered by our current experiences which can bring flashbacks and body memories causing us to act out our unconscious and unresolved wounds and beliefs, often leading to self-defeating and unproductive choices.

When our human personality experiences especially painful life events, it becomes fragmented. This fragmentation is the ego's way of protecting itself. Fragmentation causes misperception and a false identity, creating a split personality within us. Due to difficult and traumatizing life experiences, especially early in life, the child interprets events and can believe itself to be unworthy, developing an inner critic. The wounded child begins to abandon itself and create lost parts within their personality. For better understanding these parts can be named, such as the unloved one, the unworthy one, the rejected one, the betrayed one, the guilty one, the pleasing one, etc. If left unresolved, these wounded parts are carried over into adult life, and when triggered by similar experiences and are played out through perceptions, emotions, beliefs and behaviors

There are also positive aspects of the little girl or boy that remain hidden and discounted as well, such as, the loving one, the capable one, the resilient one, the creative one, the courageous one, etc. The positive aspects unfortunately, can remain denied and discounted of their helpful role in affirming and assisting the self in reaching its potential.

Another aspect of the ego and its fragmentation is the creation of masks and personas to hide the parts we are ashamed of and don't want others to know or see. We are diligent in the task of only exposing the parts we want the world to see and know. This creates the façade that helps shield us from feelings of vulnerability, inadequacy or shame. Our shadow; the masks we wear and personas we act out have unconscious power, making our dysfunctional side seem normal. This is what makes these facades so elusive and difficult for us, limiting our soul's potential and personal maturity.

> *To have a shadow is not to be flawed, but complete.*
> —Deepak Chopra

The ego with its shadow, mask and persona are part of our human condition. The above statement by Deepak Chopra reminds us that our task is to accept our shadow and lost parts. Accepting our flaws rekindles self-worth and returns us to love. Our task as spiritual beings, having this human experience, is to recognize the existence of this fragmentation at both the soul level and human level and bring this dynamic to our conscious awareness. The challenge for our human side is to come to understand, accept and work through the soul issues without allowing the lower self, to go into denial, shame or blame. It's about bringing our wounded and lost parts out of hiding and reconciling the perception that we are unworthy. We must come to the realization that the lessons of our wounds reveal wisdom and bring light for healing to occur. This is how our human experience and the soul's experience together make us complete.

Since we are created in the image of God, we are asked to accept our perfection. Because of our wounds and self-created limitations, we judge ourselves as flawed and imperfect. The word perfection, in spiritual terms means: *To have Compassion for.* Healing and growth emerge through self-love, acceptance and compassion, along with positive beliefs and behaviors.

> *As far as we can discern, the sole purpose of human existence is to kindle a light in the darkness of mere being. It may even be assumed that just as the unconscious affects us, so the increase in our consciousness affects the unconscious.* —Carl Jung

Many of us are unaware or just deny that we have a shadow; that parts of us are unconsciously acting out past wounds in the present. These lost and abandoned parts create energetic shackles and the feeling of separation from our Creator and our true self. They sabotage our yearning for loving relationships, for fulfilling our purpose and full potential. Both our positive and negative parts need to be acknowledged by our conscious self. The negative parts need to be validated, encouraged and reprogramed to reclaim their innocence and worth in order to integrate all the parts and create a more unified whole and vibrant self—what I call "coming home." This is what brings light and consciousness to our darkness—unconscious. The willingness to uncover and affirm the positive shadow parts is also vital in discovering the light of our higher self. The willingness to know and reconcile the negative parts, is a courageous endeavor. Recognizing both our positive attributes and the negative shadow self is part of the task of soul work on the path toward self-mastery and the return to love.

The journey of the soul is not always easy. In doing the work of the soul, there are many difficult and gut-wrenching times of confusion and uncertainty. The search for the meaning of our lives and our true selves does not come without struggle. The quest to find that love and worthiness within may instead be overshadowed with fear, doubt, resistance, anger, sadness and shame. The very parts of us that need love, acceptance and compassion are the very parts that will talk us out of this quest. The lower self believes in reaction and exclusion. The inner path that each of our souls undertake in the earthly journey is to transform the perception and experience of separation, reaction and exclusion into integration, inclusion and proactive being and living. Few take this path. Many do not know love because they fear the inner work of it. The ego would rather subscribe to what's called "*spiritual bypass*," taking the quick and easy way out of life experiences. "Let someone else take care of this," the voice says, "like God, our partner, anybody." "I'm not interested or willing to do the inner work toward reconciling and healing the wounded parts of me to become more whole and complete."

Life is not meant to be easy; it's meant to be meaningful.

The struggles and challenges in life can create a distorted and destructive meaning for us, leading to destructive behaviors and outcomes. The true purpose of our struggles and pain are meant to move us to a higher perspective, meaning and awareness, which advances our soul growth.

In the second Beatitude Jesus said: *"Blessed are those who mourn, for they shall be comforted."* (Matthew 5:4, NIV). I believe he was speaking of the importance and sacredness of going into the grief of the wounded and lost parts of us, embracing the emotions, feeling the feelings, creating sacred space, touching and reconciling that grief which arises from the beliefs formed because of painful life experiences. This is how we find the comfort and come to know our divinity and gain the strength to work through the feelings and false beliefs, to come to a higher perspective and the truth of our soul experience; thus, remembering we are love and innocence.

Suffering results from inner conflict and continued judgment, resistance and nonacceptance of how things are vs. how we desire them to be. Suffering arrives due to holding on to distorted beliefs about ourselves and our life. This distortion creates a deep misunderstanding about the nature of our soul in relation to the nature of our human life. When we allow our pain to persist without reconciling this inner conflict, we become defined by our pain and sorrow. Suffering also comes when we choose to prolong the need for pleasure at the expense of acknowledging and dealing with our inner pain or grief. Controlling behaviors, through obsessions and addictions, are ways of extending pleasure at the avoidance of acknowledging and working through our pain. Numbing or avoiding pain through the sense of pleasure will in the long run create more paralyzing pain and intense suffering. Pain is part of living; suffering occurs when we are in nonacceptance of what is, and resist doing what I call the "4 R's" of inner soul work to: *Recognize, Reconcile, Release* and *Reframe* our current relationship to the pain, eliminating the distorted perception, disturbing feelings and false beliefs created around a painful experience. It calls us to do the following with our pain: Name it, Claim it, Tame it and Reframe it. The denial and resistance to doing our inner work is what keeps us from self-love, worthiness and happiness. It's what keeps us in separation from life and our Source.

When we recognize and reconnect with our lost parts, we mourn for what our wounded child experienced. More importantly, we can begin to reconcile, release and reframe the created story, the emotions, the beliefs and feelings attached to the uncovered memory. To reconnect with our shadow parts is an act of loving kindness and the soul's tender expression of compassion. Pain and suffering can be reduced, perhaps eliminated, when we are willing to change and reframe our thoughts, perceptions, expectations and beliefs about ourselves related to the experience. We rewrite the story, finding the comfort, the love and serenity.

We begin this process by recognizing that parts of us have been hurting and how we've learned to neglect these parts; the same way we were neglected in the past by others, especially family. We now see and accept from this higher perspective, that those who hurt us can't love us unconditionally because they don't love themselves. The love and acceptance we long for from others, cannot be provided as we would like it to be. From this inner awareness, we now can choose to freely love ourselves, while having compassion for those whose love toward us was conditional. We can then forgive and perhaps reconcile the wrongdoing, no longer expecting, demanding or even rejecting love from others. When we recognize these self-defeating patterns, we can then reconcile, release and reframe them. We find our inner strength, wisdom and comfort. We reclaim our divinity; this is "knowing the self." We come home to the self and the Holy One—we come home to love.

Inspiring examples of the 4 R's process; Recognize, Reconcile, Release and Reframe can be seen in the lives of two noted individuals in today's world. They are courageous, enlightened souls. Lizzie Velasquez was born with a very rare disease—she cannot gain weight—resulting in permanent body disfigurement. In the depths of emotional despair, and after several years of being teased and tormented because of her appearance, she affirmed herself and made a commitment to become a motivational speaker and author. Now in her mid-twenties, Lizzie has two published books and a third is being written. She travels the world speaking about self-esteem and empowerment.

Nick Vujicic was born with no arms and legs, but despite his struggles he too made the decision to live a life of passion and vitality. He is now married and a father. He is also a popular inspiring motivational speaker on the topic of finding the courage to live life to the fullest.

Check out Lizzie and Nick's stories and inspiring messages on YouTube. I believe you will more clearly understand what love, acceptance and compassion for yourself can do. I believe part of our soul's journey is to overcome the physical and emotional hardships, the false beliefs and limitations, to reconnect with the love, goodness and perfection we are.

> *Watch your mind for the temptations of the ego, and do not be deceived by it. It offers you nothing.* —A Course in Miracles, T-4.IV.6:1-2

The ego is only a bundle of images, memories, misguided perceptions and beliefs used to protect the self from pain. The ego is an illusion that we make real, so we give it unconscious and unchallenged power over our lives. We believe that it serves a noble purpose as our protector and defender. We often allow it to become our great deceiver. The ego is not you. The reality is, you are the awareness of the self-created ego housed in a field of energy.

The shadow holds all the distortion, denial and dark memories; the feelings, beliefs and emotions that go with the lived experience. The shadow has a very tight hold on what it perceives as our painful past and fearful future, to protect us from further hurt. It defines us with a distorted and self-defeating story it created about our experiences. It simply says, "My mother-father, etc. treated me bad, therefore, I must be bad." "I feel bad; therefore, I am bad." The shadow binds us to a created story and limited perspective, creating painful feelings and a belief that this is all there is. The soul, with its higher perspective, knows there is much more to our life and our experiences than the lower self perceives.

Our shadow is avoidance, so it creates our self-defeating behavior patterns. When we avoid, we are attempting to escape the lessons of our soul agreement. This is one reason we have low self-esteem, inner and outer conflict, and ultimately, physical and mental illness. There is a paradox within this avoidance. The mind-set and behaviors of avoidance may be one of the soul agreements to experience in a lifetime. So, as you take on the experience of avoidance in life situations with its outcomes of struggle and pain, to learn (if you choose) healthier ways to engage in life struggles for improved life outcomes. The false identity created by the shadow creates a false reality; blocking the true wisdom and vision of the soul and heart. When we can allow ourselves to travel the road of our soul, it takes us to our heart and to the wisdom of our higher mind and divine perspective.

The Road to Your Soul

The road to your soul is through taming the ego mind and living from the heart. The road is found and walked when we acknowledge and work with the soul. The role of the soul is to assist the individual in coming to the awareness of the importance of opening one's heart-center, so that divine love and presence can be felt and experienced. The soul role is also to alert us to our ego's four major energy blocks, which lower our vitality and limits our potential. These four blocks are: *Limiting Beliefs, Assumptions, Interpretations* and our *Inner Critic.* Our soul task in human form, is to release our irrational fears, false assumptions, limiting beliefs, and reprogram our inner critic. The soul encourages us to expand our mind's awareness of itself as love, goodness and unlimited potential. The mind is expanded, when it can entertain new possibilities beyond what it already knows.

We also tame and master the mind, when the mind can allow self-love, acceptance and worthiness to open our heart. This is self-compassion, which allows us to connect with, reconcile and release unhealthy emotions held in the body. When we master the mind, our body is open and free. We more peacefully and gracefully walk the road to our soul and our true self. We rediscover just "being" love.

Think of your soul as a kite with a string. Your ego is the hand holding the string of the kite. Your soul, like the kite, wants to be free and soar. If I am holding the string too tightly, the kite can't fly as well, if at all. The same is true with our egos. If the ego is holding on too tightly in fear and need to protect and control, you will struggle with working through the lessons and coming to a place of higher awareness and self-actualization. The key is to ease up on your grip of the string (ego). This allows the mind to entertain a higher, more compassionate perspective of itself and its world, given what has been experienced. New possibilities are created for exploration, integration and spiritual growth. Self-actualization means to realize one's full potential by expanded awareness, greater wisdom and spiritual growth.

To identify with the way of the ego is to have a very unfulfilling relationship with ourselves and with life. A loving relationship with ourselves and with life comes through training the ego to cooperate and align with the soul. Allowing our souls to lead in the dance of our lives takes us out of the drama created from misperceptions and false beliefs.

Think of your life as a learning laboratory with all its joyful and painful experiences. In this learning lab, called "earth school," the soul's endeavors to teach the human mind the value and the sacredness of its human self. As a result, it learns ways to serve others, making the world a better place. As we return to the love that we are, we naturally extend this love to others.

The road to our soul is also part of the perspective of the soul. Our superconscious, which I believe is an aspect of our soul; wants to assist us in coming to terms with the painful and misunderstood experiences. It's that higher and wiser part of us that knows there is a better and more constructive way to resolve our problems. The superconscious is that soft and subtle voice, deep within us asking us to consider a more loving, empowering way. The superconscious is the observer and desires its higher truth to come into our consciousness.

Dreams are one way the subconscious mind communicates with us. Dreams are symbolic reflections of what's going on in our conscious waking state. They offer ways for our conscious mind to reprocess and reframe our experiences. The superconscious mind seeks to be the mediator between the subconscious and conscious mind.

Due to lack of understanding and fear, many people avoid what the subconscious and superconscious reveal. The soul knows what needs to be experienced in a lifetime and knows our purpose for being here. Soul work requires becoming aware of the information from our superconscious mind and storing it in the subconscious mind for integration with our conscious mind.

As we do this soul work of releasing the clutter and energy blocks held in our conscious mind, this frees the body and mind to recognize and honor our soul's agenda. This allows us to see the truth from the higher perspective, bringing liberation and transformation. Liberation means we are free of the pattern of identifying with the ego and the unconscious shadow part of us. We can then rise as love, expanding our consciousness and ascending to the higher realms of soul experiences. Transformation happens when we see ourselves as spiritual beings having a soul experience while in human form.

Life Experiences Are Intended to Return Us to Love

Living as humans, the soul offers us a full spectrum of life experiences. It seems that the Divine loves variety, so we are offered an array of choices. Experiencing contrast, for example being addicted or disabled, allows the opportunity to learn the importance of acceptance and healthy reliance and compassion for ourselves and others. From the higher soul perspective, our experiences are simply preparation for something else, what is yet to come. Our experiences are meant to help us progress along the path of soul growth and ascension. Individual perceptions and construct will likely be different, which is part of what produces our individual experiences and reality.

Every experience we have and every relationship we encounter is stored in parts of the body, the higher mind and the soul. The lower mind is the great denier and deceiver. The soul and body will never lie, for they hold all the information, insight, wisdom and answers about us and for us. All our experiences and relationships are meant to teach us about ourselves, about love and about being part of this divine universe. *Love is as vital to our souls, as oxygen is to our bodies.* I believe the soul comes here to experience and learn all aspects of love. We choose to resist this or embrace it. Through our experiences, we choose by our free will, to move closer to the giving and receiving of love or further from it. To return to knowing ourselves as love is to return to our divinity.

It's important to realize that when individuals are hurting in the depths of themselves, they can intentionally or unintentionally hurt others. Some struggle with unconditionally loving us because they struggle with loving themselves. More importantly, our own life experiences and beliefs about our self and our behaviors, show us how much we do or do not love ourselves. Many people have little awareness as to what's denied or repressed by their mind yet stored energetically and emotionally in their body. The mind naturally wanders, producing 40 to 60 thousand or more thoughts daily; thoughts that are mostly unconscious, with 70 percent of these being negative and self-defeating.

Often, when a person experiences an emotional trigger, they are unable to tell what has happened or what the issue is about, even if there are physical and/or emotional effects. When this happens, I tell my clients to breathe into the part of their body that is experiencing the sensation of discomfort, and ask what knowledge is needed. For example, people that experience flashbacks, anxiety or panic attacks display powerful instances of the autonomic nervous system, the survival or subcortical brain region and body connection. A term called "Neuroception" refers to the autonomic nervous system ability to detect threats and danger. It's not a cognitive ability; it's the Vagus/autonomic nervous system ability. Faulty neuroception is when a person has experienced a trauma in the past, yet is still experiencing symptoms of the trauma, i.e. danger, in the present, even though the actual trauma experience is over and no longer occurring. This faulty neuroception of fear and danger happens from a past threat. The body is reacting in present time through what appears to be alarming, even life-threatening body sensations—what's called our "flight, fight or freeze" response. The survival part of the person is bringing the past into the present and the body naturally reacts to protect itself.

The body is the great indicator and communicator of what's being experienced and why. The survival brain's perception can be a deceiver, but the body will never lie. That's why it's so important to listen to our body—it's a way of listening to our soul, creating an opening to the higher perspective to our experiences and healing. The soul never loses sight of the bodies knowing, but our ego survival instincts can become blind to it. When we observe our life and how we move through experiences with our thoughts, perceptions, beliefs, body reactions/emotions, and resulting behaviors, we realize we are often operating in the opposite direction than our soul and spirit intends; such is the nature of the lower-survival mind and free will.

Know Thy Self—Love Thy Self

The Creator wants us to know our true self and love our whole self—this is what brings us back to the Source and our "I AM" presence.

Self-mastery begins with knowing the self. It's about being a disciple—a student to new learning and a higher perspective. Many spiritual teachers allowed themselves first to be disciples to higher wisdom and spiritual maturity. In this they reconciled their wounded self and evolved toward greater self-love and love of their Source. I believe that one of the main tasks of our soul's earthly experience is to know and love the self, which has been the message of spiritual teachers past and present.

> *The soul would have no rainbows, if the eyes had no tears.* — Native American Proverb

In nature, rainbows happen when the sun's rays pierce through storm clouds and reflect off the rain. Rainbows need the sun and the rain against the backdrop of a dark sky to display their colors and glory. This is a powerful paradox and metaphor of life. Without the tears we cannot display the light from within, transforming our pain to create the rainbow—the higher meaning of our life's journey. We are here to connect, and to have awareness of our emotions and feelings.

An emotion is a reaction, and a feeling is an interpretation of the emotion. Emotions come from our body's sensation and reaction to the environment. The mind interprets the body's emotion and creates a feeling. Connecting to the emotion held in our body and being aware of our mind's interpretation of this emotion, is important to knowing and healing the self. By being in touch with our body sensations and the resulting emotions and recognizing how the mind interprets the emotion as a feeling, helps empower us to make more healthy and constructive choices.

The 4R's: To *Recognize, Reconcile, Release* and *Reframe*, assist us with knowing and healing the self. We cannot heal what we do not feel and *recognize*; then *reconcile, release* and *reframe* within ourselves. Healing and soul growth come from these actions: Name the body sensation and its emotion; feel the feelings within the mind; then reframe the conscious mind to a healthy interpretation. It is important to counter negative or disturbing feelings by viewing the experience that created them from a higher, wiser perspective. This creates empowering possibilities for transformation and well- being. By seeking to understand our life experiences from our higher, soul perspective, a renewed insight is created—the rainbow.

To know and love the self we must open our heart, connect with our soul, and allow what I call the soul-heart to release us from our fears and false beliefs, so that we may return to the rainbow of love and wholeness. To know and love the self helps invoke our "I AM" presence and return us to the abundance of ourselves and the universe.

Knowing the self is a way to lead the self. This requires knowing the whole self, especially the repressed parts of ourselves. Richard Schwartz, Ph.D. founder of the Internal Family Systems model (IFS) developed the 8 C's of self-leadership. This model is used in working with clients to help achieve a healthy dialogue with their inner critic and lost parts. Using the 8 C's during conversations with these parts help to develop connections and insights as to why these parts do what they do. Also, they can reveal what is needed from the whole to feel more included and integrated; more effectively managing and leading the self.

Dr. Schwartz has found that using these eight components assist in creating safe and constructive inner dialogue; establishing cooperation and better self-awareness and emotional self-regulation. The 8 C's are traits of love, resonating with our higher self as well as encouraging self-leadership. They invite a supportive dialogue, while seeking to include and understand.

The 8 C's of Self-leadership are:

Curiosity	Clarity
Calm	Courage
Confidence	Creativity
Compassion	Connectedness

The ego version of knowing is thinking. It's all-knowing defense makes itself the teacher. It struggles with being the student here in earth school. Knowing the self comes when we're willing to be the student again. When we can once again be humble in the role of student, as a disciple of God, we awaken to soul awareness—to the love and the wisdom within us.

A dose of humility helps take us out of self-centeredness; thinking we are the center of it all. Knowing the self and awakening to the love that we are, involves coming to the realization that we are of the One—the Creator of all. All comes from the One, and all returns to the One. This is the desire of the Creator and the desire of our soul. God awareness is the knowing and intention to give of ourselves as a student, back to the teacher—to God.

Jesus said: *"You can do these things and so much more."* In my conversations with Jesus he would often refer to me as a master and say, *"We are all masters; we just need to believe and live as such."* His energy and demeanor are one of humbleness and the desire for power-with. He desires us to learn and master the ways of the spiritual laws, which naturally dissolve the self-centeredness. To remember the love that we are, we must live more from our heart and be mindful of our feelings and emotions. This will awaken us to our soul and awaken us to *Just Be Love*. This is the destiny of the soul, the yearning of the human heart, and the quest of the higher mind. The soul and heart speak through the expression of our feelings and allows the emotions held in our bodies to be expressed and affirmed for reprocessing and healing. The following are eight other key components leading to self-mastery and soul growth.

1. **God awareness**: There is only God. Life and love start and evolve with and through Source. This realization creates a fundamental shift in our perspective and way of being.

2. **Awareness** that all is interconnected and interdependent: We affect the known and unknown around us and the unknown and known affects us.

3. **Practice the acts of**: *Focus, Introspection, Mediation* and *Realization*.

4. **Rise above** the misinterpretations and illusion of the ego and shadow parts.

5. **Learn to let go** of doubt, mistrust and striving. Face your fears and the beliefs that feed fear.

6. **Develop the ability to surrender** unhealthy attachments to others and to material possessions.

7. **Accept and live life in the moment:** Be aware that the soul is always safe. As humans we must come to a place of viewing all experiences from the higher perspective, trusting that the universe has our back.

8. **Shift your focus to your process**, your intention, attention and steps in daily life, not just the need for outcome. When we focus on our process, we can trust that the outcome is for our highest good. Choose to do your best, then *Surrender, Trust* and *Allow*, so you can *Receive*.

Letting Down the Wall to Build a Bridge

I've come to understand it is the Divine's intent that all souls in human form move from fear and ignorance to love and truth; toward an expanded version of themselves in unity with the Divine. The lower mind, with its limited perceptions and beliefs, creates a protective wall around the heart; I suggest we build a bridge instead. Through Divine love and grace, the soul invites us to open our heart and expand our mind. The heart opens when the mind gives permission and surrenders, allowing the heart and what Eckhart Tolle called the "pain body", to express our true feelings and especially emotions. This creates the bridge to the higher perspective, and the mind's expansion into higher consciousness.

Our feelings and emotions are the anchor to our human-ness and the bridge to our higher self.

The bridge is constructed by getting in touch with our deeper feelings and emotions and telling the truth **to** ourselves **about** ourselves, and then telling this truth to another. Our emotions are the language of the soul, and our thoughts and feelings are the language of the mind. Working with and through our emotions and feelings constructively, helps to heal and transform us. Our negative, victim or perpetrator thoughts and feelings keep us stuck.

I believe the Divine desires our soul and heart to be the agent (mediator) for the mind, but the mind wants to be the agent for the soul and heart. A free and willing mind and an open heart unite us more fully to our soul. The heart is the road—bridging our mind back to our soul. Yet many of us live with minds that resist the whispers of the soul-heart. The mind cannot truly know or understand the soul without the heart and without reconnecting to our body. Being in the heart and being honest about our feelings and especially our emotions is what moves us to the higher soul perspective and reality of our life experiences.

I offer a prayer of communion with Source and aid to know the self:

Divine Creator. The one Love beyond Love. Guide me in opening my heart to the majesty of your ways. To still the waters in my body and expand the pathways of my mind.

The Soul Knows

Our ego creates illusions and distortions about itself and about love, so it falls into the traps and dramas of human love. The soul, lift's the veil, breaking us free of the illusions. Our soul knows the higher perspective of Divine love. It calls us to rise as love and wants the lower self to unite with the higher self in sacred union. To me the spiritual meaning of the term "soulmate" is: *The reunion of our lower wounded self with our higher and wiser self.* Thus, you mate with your own soul. Then you bring this unity into union with Source. Humanity has created the familiar, yet incomplete theme of, "soulmate" two souls recognizing each other through like vibrations and energy attraction to each other on the spiritual and emotional levels. And yes, it can be on the physical level too. The reason society's "soulmate" version is incomplete, is because it excludes the importance of everyone merging the parts within their individual selves first, in order to unite with the Creator. In the marriage of our whole self to Source, we than can more fully discover and unite with our earthly soulmate/s.

As souls, we have unlimited potential to move our human form from a survival state to an actualized state; from a stagnant, separated and depressed state to a state of joy, appreciation and cooperation; a more unified state embodied within our individual uniqueness. We can move from fear, greed and power over to love, acceptance, gratitude, compassion and power with. What will create this more evolved state of higher being? It will be the movement from a primarily thinking state to more of a heart-centered, intuitive state; from being mostly in the head and ego, to living more from the heart and our spirit-filled essence. Throughout life, our intellect and heart are meant to be balanced in awareness and use.

The nature of the ego is to create a problem; making something out of nothing; by assuming, being critical, judgmental, having limiting beliefs, etc. Could it be that many of the problems in our world are related to catering to the ego at the expense of neglecting the soul? I believe this is part of our individual and collective journeys; learning the necessary lessons for our spiritual evolution. A new cycle and higher level of consciousness is upon us and invites us to go deeper into ourselves in search of that part of us that's connected to Source and the higher dimensions of ourselves. This connects us to the creative rhythm of life—enabling us to more deeply understand and accept our soul's purpose, its lessons and move through them with love and compassion for ourselves and our teachers.

The laws of nature allow for what seems to us as chaos to exist along with order. One leads to the other. There are two dominant themes throughout human history and evolution: *Struggle* and *Progress*. Struggle, like chaos weaves into progress as order. As humans, individually and collectively we are confronted with life struggles in various forms. Our soul calls us to confront our struggles, so we may learn and grow, because it knows struggle is part of the process toward progress. Over the span of human existence, our spirit has always risen to overcome the struggles and hardships. Because of this, we continue to make progress toward higher states of consciousness. The dynamic of struggle and progress, like chaos and order, are ways of the spirit in action.

That Which Has Energy—Has Soul

The ground we walk on the plants and creatures, the clouds above constantly dissolving into new formations - each gift of nature possessing its own radiant energy, bound together by cosmic harmony. —Ruth Bernhard

All of life is energy. If all things are created by the Divine, all of creation would have the energy of soul. So, rocks, the soil, trees, fish, and the sea are all forms of living and vibrant energy; they have souls. It can be said that what has energy has life, thus soul. Soul is not exclusive to just humans. Divine love invites us to bless and honor the soul journey of our brothers and sisters and all souls that inhabit the Earth and the Cosmos. Part of the evolution and maturity of our souls is to walk with each other as two becoming one; as being both the student and the teacher to each other. What does that tree have to say to you, that rock or the sea? Connecting to the energy of the soul is part of the remembrance that will lead us to the love that we are.

Our Remembrance

Everything we experience happens for our awakening and remembrance. Life happens for the purpose of changing and expanding our perception from self-limiting, self-defeating behavior patterns to seeing and experiencing the higher perspective and the possibilities that it brings. Our experiences, especially, the painful ones, are meant to be recognized, reconciled, released and reframed from this higher perspective for our soul's growth. It takes courage, strength and determination to do this. In the Gospel of Thomas 62: Jesus said:

> *Rather, the kingdom is inside you and outside you at the same time. When you come to know yourself, then you will be known. You will realize then that it's you who are the living sons (daughters) of the living Father (Mother). But as long as you do not know yourself, you will live in poverty, and you will be that poverty.*

Our awakening to freedom and abundance resides in knowing our self. The remembrance of love dwells there also. Given the part of our soul agreement that pertains to fragmentation and "spiritual amnesia," we take on an ego and shadow, and create a life story that causes us to go to sleep and begin a lengthy dream. Our task is to journey back to the Divine, to awaken from the dream that created the false self—the illusion. This reawakening is to remember where we have always been and will forever be. It is a journey not of distance, but of remembering. It is the longing of the soul and its calling that is never truly forgotten.

I close this chapter with the lyrics from a moving song written by Susan McCullen and sung by Shaina Noll, entitled: *You Can Relax Now*. The words speak of waking up from the dream; remembering we are loved and divine.

You can relax now
Come on and open your eyes
Breathe deeply now.
I am with you. Oh my sweet, sweet child.
Who do you think you are.
You are the child of God.
And that will never change.
You had a dream.
You misunderstood.
You thought we were separate.
But now you hear my voice and
You can relax now.
C'mon and open your eyes.
And breathe deeply now.
I am with you.
You are the love of my life.
You are my one creation.
You are eternity.
And that will never change.
You had a dream.
You misunderstood.

You thought we were separate.
But now please hear my voice and
You can relax now.
C'mon and open your eyes.
And breathe deeply now.
I am with you.
Oh my sweet sweet child.
Who do you think you are.
You are the child of God
That will never change.
You are what you are. You are eternity.
You are divinity.
That can never change.
That has never changed.
Just a dream…
open your eyes and breathe.
You are eternity.
You are divinity.
You can relax now…you can.
You are a child of God.
Open your eyes and breathe.
You can relax…

(Permission granted by Susan McCullen)

4

Love – The Heart of All that Is

Lord resides in the hearts of all beings; I am the God of Love. —
The Bhagavad Gita Ancient Hindu Bible

The Heart – Entry Way for the Soul

It is my understanding, that at conception, the fertilized egg in a mother's womb is energetically connected with a soul, from its etheric dimension, beyond the physical body. As the soul engages more with the fetus from the etheric realm, it acts like an electrical cord of a lamp that is plugged into the outlet on a wall. This lamp has a two-way light bulb. Approximately three weeks after conception, the heart begins to form, the soul enters the heart of the fetus at this time. Five weeks after conception, the heart begins to beat. The dimmer light of the lamp is turned on, life in the womb is activated. When the mother goes into labor or decides on a prearranged C-section date, this announces the soul more fully entering the infant's body. During the birthing process the soul's aspects enter more fully, through the heart. The pineal gland in the brain is also more fully activated. So, the lamp switch is turned up, illuminating the bulb even brighter, as the energetic charge is engaged into the infant's human life. The newborn's earthly journey outside the womb begins.

We used to believe that the human heart responded to the commands and impulses from the brain, that the brain was running the body. Research, however, over the last 20 years, especially by a research group at the Institute of HeartMath, has shown just how significant and powerful the heart is. The heart is the first organ formed in the fetus. In fact, the heart begins to beat in the fetus before the brain is fully formed. The heart has its own brain with its own neurons—as many, if not more, than the brain. The heart is a sensory organ and can process information like the brain. The heart's electromagnetic field is five thousand times more powerful than the electromagnetic field of the mind. The heart is the most powerful source of energy in the body.

The longest running nerve in the body is the Vagus nerve, connecting the brainstem to the body. It encompasses the major nervous system. It is through the Vagus nerve that the brain automatically receives, controls and monitors several body functions. It's like an electrical circuit linking our throat, heart, lungs and stomach to the brain. The Vagus nerve connection resembles the USB computer connection. The word Vagas in Latin means "wondering." This is why this nerve has been called the "wondering" nerve, sending signals from the brain to the throat, heart and stomach, and carrying signals from the heart and stomach to the brain as well.

Research shows that the heart sends more signals through the Vagus nerve to the brain than the brain sends to the heart. The human heart is really the "brains" of the body. If our heart stops beating, within three minutes the brain begins to die; yet we can be brain dead, and the heart will continue beating.

The heart is the meeting place of the physical and the spiritual. It is the place of divine truth and abundant life. Research shows the heart holds much of the energy and information that comprises the essence of who we are.

Love is the electromagnetic core frequency that runs throughout the entire hologram of life. Our body, especially our heart, is part of this electromagnetic hologram. Metaphorically speaking, our body is like our solar system. Our heart is the sun, pulsing and radiating electromagnetic energy and impulses, giving waves of information and messages to the brain, which is the earth. The other organs of the body represent the other planets. The trillions of cells in our body are like the trillions of stars. Some say, there are as many synapses in the brain as there are stars in our galaxy. Our body is a reflection of the infinite universe; our heart, like the sun, is the life force energy that feeds us love through its pulsing vibration. The emotions we generate in the heart also create electromagnetic waves of energy in our bodies that extend outward. These vibrate and resonate within the infinite universe.

Science tells us that we are made of what's called "star stuff." The elements of carbon, oxygen, nitrogen, hydrogen and iron are found in the stars and when a star explodes and dies it releases these elements as "star dust." We have these same fundamental elements in us by way of atoms and molecules. This means that life as we know it, including every single atom and molecule within us, came from the death of a star. They say we are part of the very make-up of the cosmos. There is no separation. We are the stars and the stars are us. We are part of the way the Divine knows itself. The consciousness of humanity is interconnected with the consciousness of the Divine, the stars and all that is. I know what this means for me. What's does it mean for you?

A Loving Heart Creates a Peaceful Mind

The human brain is an incredible thinking and processing organ and is vital to our functioning. It has a significant effect on our physiology and psychology, given that areas of the brain can be activated, and that chemical reactions released, as we perceive and interact with our environment. However, the heart signals have a greater effect on brain functions, influencing emotional processing and cognitive faculties such as perception, belief, attention, memory and problem-solving.

The biblical phase in Proverbs says, *"As a man thinketh in his heart so is he."* What we believe and hold in our heart of hearts will transfer to the brain and throughout the nervous system and cellular networks, which travels through our entire body. We become what we think and believe through the emotions of the heart. Fascinating research by the folks at HeartMath shows that different rhythmic patterns of the heart affect the brain. This in turn impacts our emotional and cognitive functioning ability. During times of high stress and negative emotions, the pattern of neural signals traveling from the heart to the brain hinders cognitive functions, which limits our ability to think clearly, have recall, retain information, learn, reason and make constructive decisions. This could be one explanation why we become more impulsive and hypersensitive, making poor choices, when under emotional distress or change. If under prolonged stress and/or trauma, the heart is emotionally wounded and closed off; we can become fearful, guarded and depressed.

In contrast, the more stable the heart pattern, the more the brain produces positive and productive states of cognitive and emotional stability. There is a concept called coherence, which in cognitive terms means one is rational in thought and in expression of thoughts. Research shows that when we are heart-centered, and we come from the thoughts of acceptance, gratitude and compassion, we create a positive emotional state of heart coherence within us; a state of mindfulness. In other words, the more we can be in heart coherence, the more we are in spiritual, mental, emotional and physical harmony. When the heart is calm, the mind becomes calm as well, thus creating heart-mind coherence—inner peace and inner confidence.

Being in a state of heart coherence can not only have a positive effect on us, but also in our interactions with others. The evidence is clear that sending the frequency of heart coherence creates an energetic field that can impact others in our families, neighborhoods and even the world. The more coherence is attained collectively, the greater the possibility of reducing the rate of violence, sickness and poverty. This research is showing that the heart impacts our spiritual, emotional, mental and physical well-being, much more than we had previously thought. It affects our social and environmental well-being as well.

The Heart, the Intelligence of the Soul and Connection to the Divine

Given these discoveries, we now see that the heart is the true center of empowerment, harmony, joy and self-actualization. The heart is also the place of understanding, acceptance, compassion and forgiveness. There are specific energy centers in the body-mind called Chakras.

Four of the seven main chakra centers are:

The Heart Charka: I love. The giving and receiving of love, desire for balance and devotion.

The Crown Chakra: I understand. Located 5 inches above the top of the head. This is our connection to the Divine mind and unity consciousness, awareness of the fullness, the everything and the emptiness, the nothing.

The Third Eye Chakra: I see. Located above and between the eyebrows. The third eye is related to our intuition and the pineal (God) gland located in the center of the brain. It also relates to the Divine mind, clear thought and knowing.

The Solar Plexus Chakra: I do. Is located four inches above the navel and relates to our inner power, sense of will and self-confidence.

I believe these four energy centers, hold inner wisdom, intuition, and the willingness to recognize the remembrance of Divine Love. They are evolved parts of us that, when open and flowing, are the source of what I call the 4 I's: *Innocence, Intuition, Imagination* and *Inspiration*. When open and flowing; these chakra's offer us the guidance, wisdom and knowing to reach our highest potential.

The three other chakras:

The Throat Chakra: I speak. Having to do with speaking our truth and desires for higher consciousness and spiritual growth.

The Sacral Chakra: I feel. Located an inch below our navel, impacting creativity, procreation, emotional joy, fantasy and sensuality.

The Root Chakra: I am. Located at the tailbone area; this is about our sense of physical security, connection to family, community/tribe and Mother Earth.

These three energy centers, when open, provide the motivation, determination and action to achieve a desire or goal.

The heart chakra is the mediator between the three heavenly and three earthly chakras. The crown chakra, third eye chakra and throat chakra are heavenly chakras. The earthly chakras are the root, sacral and solar plexus.

The heart is the source and pathway of love and healing. The road to connecting with the soul begins with an open heart. Answers and healing happen when we go into the heart. The heart holds the wounds from life and is the catalyst to understanding these wounds from the higher perspective. It reveals the wisdom toward healing. It transfers the healing impulses to the brain in the form of new possibilities for reframed beliefs and behavior patterns. Our mind chooses whether to begin to explore and integrate this new awareness into growth.

I believe all answers to healing and unlimited potential are found through these chakra energy centers, especially the heart chakra. If you desire healing and transformation, begin by going into your heart, be still and listen through the chakra energy centers listed.

The Path to Higher Awareness Is Relatively Short

The distance between the mind and the heart is approximately fourteen inches. The heart is the anchor to our humanness and the bridge to our higher self. Fourteen inches is a short distance to create a shift in perception, emotion, belief and awareness. Let me put these fourteen inches into perspective. The distance between Earth and our closest star, the Sun, is ninety-three million miles. The next closest star is Proxima Centauri in the constellation of Centaurs at 4.2 light years away or 25.2 trillion miles. Some believe these two stars, along with other stars, are feeding us with the energy of love and higher consciousness from millions of miles, even light years away. However, we only need to travel fourteen inches within ourselves to this higher awareness and peace. Our fear and doubt make this inner journey seem difficult and long. Love, willingness, fearlessness and determination are the main modes of travel needed on this voyage to higher awareness and inner peace. A loving, open heart and a receptive mind turn the journey to higher consciousness from appearing light years away to only inches.

Living as a STAR

The concept of STAR is a loving and accepting way to be and move through life experiences. The acronym for the word STAR means to:

Surrender
Trust
Allow
Receive

Surrender: To let go of our human will and align with divine will; to not give in or up to the feelings of fear, doubt or lack; to focus on what we will gain or benefit for our highest good and act accordingly. The ego views surrender as giving in or up. It believes something will have to be given up or something will be taken away. This is the main reason we won't take a positive risk and step out of our comfort zone. This is the primary barrier to healthy change. The ability to surrender from the spiritual perspective happens when we let go of the resistance and surrender to the flow of the universe and our soul's higher good. To surrender is to open to greater possibilities and opportunities; to relax in mind and body, so the spirit can flow with and through us. To surrender is to have faith that the unseen and unknown of the present will reveal itself in the future. To Surrender is to Trust.

*To **Trust*** is to believe in God's loving guidance and grace. It's grounded in faith, with the courage to align our inner desire with God's knowing. Trust that the Divine always has our back and our highest good in mind, especially in times of uncertainty. The willingness to trust creates openness and a pathway to love, intimacy and greater abundance. Trust is the foundation of relationship building. With Trust we can Allow.

*To **Allow*** is to accept and let life unfold and happen within us and for us. It says yes to love, the universe and to our higher self. It recognizes and embraces the expansiveness of life. To allow is to be open to possibilities and free of judgment and expectation. This liberates us from the need to control toward a certain outcome. To Allow is to Receive.

To **Receive** is to open ourselves to the gifts and wonders of the universe; the gift of the heart. We yearn to receive the Divine gift of unconditional love and acceptance. Yet a part of us resists this desire. Receiving is a form of perception. *Can you receive with innocence and gratitude—feeling deserving? Or do you receive with guilt—feeling undeserving?* Our task is to reconcile this inner conflict and feel worthy and deserving of receiving from the abundant universe.

The ability to: **Surrender, Trust** and **Allow** are keys to **Receiving**. For they create the willingness to open our heart to receive much more. Life calls us to be open to receiving; our higher self knows what is important for us to receive. We experience love and acceptance when we surrender, trust and allow. We receive love and abundance when we offer gratitude. Often the lower self feels disappointed, because it only sees from its needy and limited perspective. Rejecting the possibility that it received exactly what it needed.

As humans, when we *Surrender, Trust* and *Allow*, we accept and *Receive* the Divine knowing and truth of the universe and our higher self. It's yielding to a greater power, a greater love and wisdom of the universe. In this surrendering, the ego sheds its interpretation of surrender as weakness, and rediscovers the Creator's meaning of surrender as strength in the power of acceptance and letting go. In this new-found strength, we create the opportunity to be fearless and free of resistance. *Trust* requires vulnerability; its divine intent is to create a connection that opens us up to *Receive* what the Divine wants us to be and to have. Being a STAR means expressing our open and loving intent to experience life, while being mindful of the Divine process and flow.

The Heart Knows

Listen to the wind it talks. Listen to the silence it speaks. Listen to your heart it knows. —Native American Proverb

The Divine is experienced through the body's strongest and most powerful energy center... The heart. This is one reason why a true spiritual experience cannot be described with conventional logic or language. Only the heart can truly feel and comprehend the experience. Living more from our heart center is crucial to answering the most important question: *Who*

Am I? For this question can only truly be answered through the awareness and wisdom of an open and willing heart. The heart holds the wisdom, the knowing—it holds the answers to our questions.

I believe the creation process always begins in darkness and in the heart—the feminine side, and then it is transferred to the mind—the masculine side. The heart is the Divine Mother, the feminine energy, the energy of emotions and the process of manifestation. The heart is where our imagination resides, where our giftedness lies and holds our childlike innocence and wonder. Living from the heart means our mind is accepting and expanding to accommodate the energy and wisdom of the Divine. Living from the heart offers us the opportunity to overcome the perception of duality, and live life with more grace, passion and a higher perspective. *Just Be Love* is the intention and mantra of the heart.

5

Is Your Heart an Open or Closed Door to Love?

The worst prison would be a closed heart. —Pope John Paul II

The heart holds the energy and expression of love. Imagine there is a doorway within us to love and this doorway is through the heart. When the heart is emotionally closed, so is the door. I am fearful and guarded, and I refuse to look within. I am scared, and so I am not free within the chambers of my heart. My light is dim, and unknown shadows haunt me. My coping strategies are to either judge and/or blame others in order to protect myself and/or blame myself to the point of shame. I want someone to rescue me from my pain and darkness. Yet I push away the other, as I yearn for them to embrace me. I seem to do the same to the-me-inside-myself. I am closed. I am confused. I do not realize that what I do to you I do to myself as well.

Physical and especially emotional trauma can cause a person to create an emotional barrier around their heart for protection from further hurt. This creates a closed heart, and over time it can cause, what the medical community now calls, *The Broken or Sad Heart Syndrome.*

When trauma occurs, the ego struggles to allow the chambers of the wounded heart to be rinsed clean of the emotional blocks—to free itself from the prison of misconceptions and false identity to which it subscribes. Doing the inner soul-heart work, opens the door to embrace the love I have been yearning for all along. I free myself. I bring light, innocence, and awareness to what I made dark, sad and had buried. I see more clearly now how love and openness leads me to the awareness of my "I Am" presence; the soul part of me that is closest to God—my true identity.

I would rather have eyes that cannot see; ears that cannot hear; lips that cannot speak, than a heart that cannot love. —Robert Tizon

38

When the heart is open, love flows. When the heart is closed fear resides. Openness is the first step toward surrendering; it is the way of remembering and embracing love. To be closed is to reject and be separated from love. Opening up frees us, heals and transform us. Openness is truth and freedom. Staying closed and sad is denying faith, leaving us to feel unsafe. What we are closed to will continue to irritate us. What we are closed to will imprison us. To close is to exclude; to open is to include. Openness allows us to look within ourselves. Openness brings comfort as we free ourselves to shed the tears of the wounds that created our darkness, which had once made us closed. Openness allows us to see and accept our self as we are, and it frees us from pretending. In this openness we can more freely see and be with our sisters and brothers. We can do so because we know and love ourselves, and we now know and see the other as love too. A pure heart is an open heart, which creates a loving heart. A loving heart is a free heart. A free and open heart knows and expresses its wisdom, which flows from the Source of all wisdom.

> *Love is an open heart and a maturing mind. Love is absolute. But*
> *the conception of love varies with the individual consciousness.*
> —Paul Twitchell

Can I love what I have feared, open what I have closed, freely embrace and feel what I have resisted in my life? As we embrace that which we have feared, we create an opening to love and are able to transform. Choosing to be open to the feelings of the wounded heart is the way to experience love and freedom. Remaining closed is part of our humanness. What is darkness always seeks the light. It takes courage and commitment to open the heart's wounded chambers and guide it to the light of divine truth. Serenity in body, mind and soul comes when we make light of what was once dark. This is our birthright and soul's journey.

Life's light is love. When the heart is open, the light of love is lit, rising like a flame; illuminating beauty and goodness in all we encounter. We see and know through the eyes of our soul-heart. We see the essence of creation and of ourselves. When the heart is closed to love, we live in a void that is absent of the true essence of life. When love is awakened in the heart, our unique divinity and spark is experienced. The soul's journey in human form is to awaken the heart and remember love. Our body and mind are the temple housing the soul. God's infinite treasure of love is hidden in the heart.

The heart is the human symbol of love. Many cultures and faiths throughout human existence have understood that the soul desires to live from the heart. When we are living from the heart there is greater connection, trust, and willingness to be vulnerable, because we love and accept ourselves. This love and acceptance are then extended to our brothers and sisters.

In the Aramaic language of Jesus, the word for heart is, *"Lebhon,"* which means the center from which life radiates—a sense of expansion and power. In Islam the Prophet Muhammad said the word, *"Taqwaa,"* referring to God consciousness being in the heart. In the Mayan culture, people greeting each other say, *"In Lak'esh,"* meaning, "You are another me." The ancient Hindu greeting, *"Namaste"* means to bow and greet. *"The Divine in me greets and honors the Divine in you."*

The ancients and the great spiritual teachers of different cultures and times have lived from the belief, *"My heart is your heart; my soul is your soul; you are me, and I am you."* They lived and practiced All is One. In the movie Avatar the Na'vi are humanoid species from a planet light years away, displaying profound love, wisdom and reverence for all life. They greet each other saying, *"I see you."* This is a deeper way of saying, *"I love you; I see into you; I see the soul and the Divine in you. I see you as you truly are; I see you in me and me in you."* The ancients, the spiritual masters and the Na'vi are asking us, in these current turbulent and fascinating times, to be and live from the heart.

Love is Experienced with an Open Heart and Expanded Mind

As more people choose to move from their heads into their hearts; from their thinking state to their emotional state; we will transform ourselves and our planet. We will remember who we truly are and reconnect with the God consciousness. We will come out of hiding and stop pretending. We will naturally ascend to the energy of inclusion with the Divine. We will have returned to the soul-heart of the Mother-Father God. So, *In Lak'esh* my sisters and brothers... ***I see you.***

6

Love and Family

Love is saying "I feel differently" instead of you're wrong. —Unknown

It's within the framework of the family that we learn what love is or is not. Aside from nurses and doctors during our birth process; the first human experience of interaction and connection we encounter is with family. The family is where we first experience the feelings of inclusion and belonging or exclusion and isolation. Research shows that when people are in the dying process, they talk more about family than God. It's often a deceased family member that comes to greet the dying person, to help him or her with the transition from physical form to the formless. When you ask family, ministers, health-care workers or hospice volunteers what a dying person talked about during the time before his or her death, many will say: "Their family." People close to death reflect on their experiences of love. They reflect on how love was experienced, whether it was conditional or unconditional in the relationships with their parents, siblings, partners or children. They talk about what they learned about love and its joys and sorrows. They express regrets about the barriers to love within those relationships.

We leave the physical world either having experienced the fullness of giving and receiving love or we leave empty of that experience. Many seem to have a greater understanding of love as they begin their transition process. I believe the three most profound moments of understanding love are during the process of human formation in the womb, during our birth and during the process of dying/transition. These experiences are very humbling, and of divine will and mystery. Each of these transition processes are times of being a STAR: as we *Surrender, Trust* and *Allow* ourselves to go into the unknown to Receive and experience divine love and grace. I imagine our awareness of love is most profound in these life-transforming processes, because of our surrender and trust in these life-transcending experiences. For these are the times we are **not** subject to human ego consciousness, but we are energetically more fully conscious to experience, the journey of our soul, the higher parts of us and the Divine. You may question, *How is it possible to experience love when we are not conscious of our development in the womb, our birth or at our death?*

The answer for me this is: The soul is always present and aware of that which it is—**Love**.

Love is experienced at an energetic level in the unknown as well as in the known. The soul has experienced pure love with its soul family and the angelic realm where love is inclusive and expansive. It invites oneness to be viewed and experienced as a continuum. Part of our human task as a soul, is to remember that kind of love and to create it while living with its earthly family.

Much of the meaning of life comes from our experiences with love. Within the dynamic of family, we learn how love can be connecting, joyful and life affirming. We also learn how love can be hurtful, confusing and sometimes cruel. Yet, on the soul level, it is all perfect and of purpose; part of our soul agreement and growth.

Family shapes our primary understanding of human life. It's the foundation where most of our beliefs about love and life are formed. Our understandings about intimate relationships are formed through family. Family is where we first learn the giving and receiving of love. It is where we are first hurt in the name of love and where our first opportunity for learning to forgive occurs. Some of us enter life without the connection and support of family. For many, life is lonely and painful, and just doesn't seem fair. We develop beliefs that we are not enough, not wanted or loved.

Whether we grow up in a family environment that is healthy or not, we can learn to devalue ourselves and separate from love and the Divine. A vital component toward healing our pain from family wounds comes when we remember ourselves as love.

Reflecting on family experiences we can come to a crossroad, a place of a conscious and heart-centered decision to do the work of introspection and reconciliation of pain and hurt by family. We can choose to arrive at a place of acceptance deep within us, which allows us to freely forgive ourselves and others to free ourselves from a self-imposed prison.

On the soul's journey to remembering, there are no short cuts, bypasses, easy fast-track ways or pills. It is only through acknowledging and meeting our pain and fear, with an open and trusting heart and a willing mind, that the meanings and beliefs we've created about our self can be transformed.

This inner process and the work of telling ourselves the truth, will allow us to discover once again the love that we are.

Family of Origin: Choice or Punishment

The famous Psychic Edgar Cayce was once asked, *"How do I know I'm growing spiritually?"* Cayce's reply was, *"Ask your family."* Love within the family must be renewed again and again. For love asks us to see ourselves and each other repeatedly with fresh eyes and an open, accepting heart.

Given the struggles and wounds created through family experiences, it is important to ask ourselves a soul-full question – *"Why did I choose my parents/ family?"* Asking this question is huge; going after the honest answer, is healing and transforming to the soul's growth. It also is a way of creating understanding, resolution and closure with greater acceptance, compassion and forgiveness of our self and those family members who wounded us or whom we wounded. Asking this question and coming to its answer helps us take responsibility for how we've learned to be in the world; a profound and liberating step for our happiness. It helps create greater understanding and clarity on a soul level about the choices we are making and why.

It is also important to recognize that even with our struggles and wounds from family, we are always loved and supported by the higher energies of the universe. The Divine is not punishing us, rather, the Divine desires that we look within and work through the lessons our soul is here to learn while attending this earth school. Through this chosen experience with our soul brothers and sisters, we come to recognize the higher perspective about experiences happening for us and through us as a means of learning and growth.

Extended Family

We have a nuclear family, an extended family, and a religious or spiritual family. Also, our educational systems, places of work and civic organizations can be viewed as aspects of family. Our community, our state and country, are a family, as well as all that inhabits the Earth, make up our collective family unit. On the soul level, we even have a soul family. The cosmos is the totality of all family systems, and we are part of the cosmic family. Since love is of all things seen and unseen, love is experienced and known in the micro of earthly family units as well as in the macro of cosmic family system. The Father-Mother God is the loving parent, who only knows us through the eyes and heart of unconditional love, acceptance and compassion. Our Divine Mother-Father holds us intimately in the energy of love and care. This parent never abandons or forsakes us and is the home of Divine Love and appreciation for us. This divine parent is the great teacher, the true expression of love and family.

As individuals, we become more conscious, our perceptions change, and we act in more healthy and loving ways, when we do the inner soul work necessary to heal our family experiences. Humanity is impacted as we grow in acceptance of oneness. We then foster greater cooperation and collaboration between us and our family of origin, as well as our extended family.

7
Love and Self-Worth

I myself am the enemy who must be loved. —Carl Jung

Often, when we think of love, we think of how it relates to loving someone else, rather than considering how we love ourselves. Love can be confusing and painful. The term *"crime of passion"* is a crime thought about and/or committed in the name of love—love that's been rejected or lost; forgetting the love for ourselves and focusing instead on the pain of someone not loving us. I believe the real issue is our struggle with loving and accepting ourselves; with knowing ourselves as love.

The mystic Rumi wrote, *"Our task is not to seek love but to find the barriers we've built against love."* One of the biggest barriers we build against love is the belief that we are not lovable and that we are not enough. Our wounded self creates this barrier to protect itself from hurt. In doing this it also prevents us from experiencing love more deeply, especially God's love.

As humans, we are born with the understandable need for nurturing and safety. We are also born with the need for love and acceptance. If we don't feel a sense of safety and security, our sense of feeling loved, nurtured and accepted is compromised. When these basic developmental needs are unmet, due to unloving and painful experiences, we forget that we are love and goodness. We begin to create defenses to protect our fragile self. Our ego develops, and we begin to create barriers by thinking, feeling and believing we are small and separated; that we are not loved, which is a way of perceiving our self as not good enough.

From an early age, many of us fail to learn how to love ourselves and begin to view ourselves as unworthy. This happens through life experiences of abuse, neglect, abandonment, betrayal, a death of a loved one, parents' divorce, put-downs, physical and/or emotional disability, stifled imagination and creativity, the list goes on. We get wounded by our parents, our relatives, and friends, at schools and even at religious intuitions. These childhood experiences, and our resulting thoughts, emotions, feelings and beliefs create the nature of trauma and wounding. If unresolved, these wounds are buried in parts of our body and mind. They are carried into our adolescent and adult years as unconscious memories and programs, which are triggered and reinforced by partners, friends, our own children, our coworkers, etc.

Our wounds create negative and distorted perceptions and beliefs about ourselves and our world, reinforcing low self-esteem and creating more emotional pain. I've heard many of my clients over the years, describe low self-esteem and self-worth as the loss of the spirit or passion within them. Our wounds and low self-worth cause us to compare ourselves to others, *"seeing ourselves as less than."* On the flip side some people overvalue and inflate themselves, becoming grandiose and entitled at the expense of others. Both sides of this human defensive strategy are developed to protect the wounded and fragile self. Feelings of inferiority or superiority lead to disharmony with the way of spirit. They lead us to think, feel and behave in a vacuum of fear and insecurity, leading us to believe we are unworthy and inferior—incapable, and unlovable. This dynamic creates the central core spiritual wound, the belief of separation from Source. This is the core spiritual wound all humans experience. At birth, we come into the world as innocence, love, light and joy. We separate from our mother's womb and we begin to experience ourselves as a soul having a human experience. As we begin to interact in the world, we have needs and desires that are not met in timely and/or healthy ways. We begin to sense that we are not loved, significant or worthy, so we begin to feel and believe we are not enough—the wound of separation begins to emerge.

Lise Bourbeau is an expert in human development and decoding the physical, mental, emotional, and spiritual connection of symptoms and illness on a metaphysical level. Through her research she has discovered five core wounds of the human personality. They are: *Rejection, Abandonment, Betrayal Injustice and Humiliation.* Through the human experience we usually are subject to one of the first three human wounds, rejection, betrayal or abandonment. From this wound comes one of the last two, injustice or humiliation. These core human wounds reinforce the core spiritual wound of separation, leading to guilt or shame and self-doubt, blocking our bond with our Source and our ability to feel safe, confident and connected with ourselves, others and the Earth.

In coping with our core wounds it's important to recognize and examine our core negative beliefs; the identity we've created about ourselves within the context of our experiences. These beliefs lead us to deem ourselves worthy or unworthy, loveable or unlovable. We create a story that we tell to ourselves about ourselves, and then we tell it to others as well. This becomes the truth of who we believe ourselves to be. The words we use and the story we tell, reflects our self-worth and the quality of our life. In many areas of our life, we settle for what we believe we deserve. Ask yourself these questions: *Do the negative beliefs I hold, create confidence, growth and happiness for me? Who would I be if I didn't define myself through this negative belief, with its created story and meanings? Who would I be if I didn't compare myself to others? Who would I be if I didn't define myself by the wounds of life and by what I don't have? Who would I be if I had greater self-confidence to be more my true self? Who would I be if I allowed the wisdom of my soul's truth to define and guide me?*

Why do we buy into the beliefs of the lower self and reject the soul's truth? There is no need to hold back on giving or receiving love in the present. It is only our perception and faulty belief that prevents this. If we are refusing to give or receive love in the present because of our past, we are still living in the past. We are denying our own love and happiness today because of yesterday.

Love, self-worth, and happiness are experienced in the present, not by our story of the past or future. The gift of experiencing and knowing ourselves as worthy is already in our energy field. Our task is to surrender and allow ourselves to create new possibilities, to receive enriched results. Allowing ourselves to emotionally and energetically change our perception and belief about ourselves creates the higher perspective and possibilities, which offer us the actual truth of who we are. To accept this moves us to embrace and experience the deeper, more loving part of ourselves.

Shame and Guilt

What is the difference between shame and guilt? Guilt refers to what I have done or haven't done. Shame is who I believe I am. Shame speaks of the very essence of who I believe I am. Shame is much deeper and more paralyzing than guilt. Many mistake shame as guilt. In human terms the ego (lower self) will make what I have done or haven't done more important than who I am. In spiritual terms, the who I am, is of greater importance. This is the soul and heart of me—who I am. The ego wants us to focus on what I've done or haven't done. Our soul asks us to focus on who I am. Some people are consumed with the belief that God is punishing them. This guilt can turn to shame, believing they are unworthy of God's grace and favor. To shame someone, especially children, is a form of spiritual attack, manipulation and emotional abuse.

In the energy of shame or guilt we allow our ego to attack the self and we are unwilling to hear the soft still voice within that seeks to support and comfort us. We devalue our God-given gifts and talents; our true purpose of being here. We struggle to freely love and accept ourselves, as a result, we cling to or withdraw from others. We compensate by focusing on our external world—its demands, details, and the collection of stuff that we believe will make us look good and feel happy.

Guilt causes us to be consumed by feelings of self-doubt, worry and unworthiness. Shame causes us to doubt ourselves and feel unworthy as well. More tragically, shame causes us to fear our feelings, so we avoid, deny them. When we become emotionally overwhelmed and consumed by the belief that we are unworthy, we emotionally dissociate to protect ourselves. We mentally and emotionally leave ourselves for a period. It's like emotionally going asleep, while still being physically awake. We lose the cognitive ability to regulate ourselves in healthy ways, struggling to effectively cope with life situations. Shame causes us to lie about ourselves and deny our needs or be too demanding with our needs. Mental illness to some degree can be a by-product of shame, especially depression, anxiety, obsessions, self-harm and addictions. Much of mental illness comes from suppressing feelings of the mind and especially the emotions held in the body. Shame creates a spiritual crisis, because in the energy of shame we disconnect from Source, ourselves and others. We become small, unworthy and separated from life with feelings of being powerless and helpless. With the belief that love, and worthiness cannot exist within the shackles of shame, only inner torment and loneliness is felt. Shame keeps us from feeling safe, from trusting ourselves and others; it prevents us from being authentic and vulnerable. When experiencing shame, we see little hope and feel little or no purpose for being in this world.

There is such a thing as natural conscience or self-imposed guilt. You do something, and you instinctively know that it's wrong, so you naturally have a sense of guilt. An example: You cut in front of someone in a grocery store checkout line. Conscious guilt is recognizing it was impolite to cut in line. This form of guilt is good and has value in making moral choices. Learned guilt on the other hand, is guilt we feel when we've been told our behavior is wrong or bad. Family and society systems create learned guilt. Examples: You are 5 years old and you accidently spill your cup of milk and get scolded by a parent. Or in third grade you got in trouble by the teacher for not paying attention. Or an adult involves you in inappropriate touching and you are told not to tell or else you will get in trouble. These experiences can cause us to take on guilt, as we learn we are bad or not good enough by the verbal and non-verbal messages of others, especially adult authority figures. Guilt if not resolved often leads to feelings of shame.

The way to overcome shame is through the process of being the STAR. To *Surrender, Trust and Allow*. By identifying, working with and expressing our feelings we understand that feeling bad doesn't mean that we are bad. Trusting ourselves to feel our feelings, emotions and honestly express them, allows us to be more authentic and *Receive* the gift of experiencing the essence of our true self. This is no easy task. Our feelings and especially emotions are buried deep inside, because we learned to fear them. Since it often wasn't safe to show them, so we learned to hide them. There is discomfort feeling our feelings and expressing them. As we grow in love and confidence, we learn to be comfortable with our feelings again, recognizing that feeling is healthy and empowering. It was in the unsupportive and non-accepting environment that we learned our feelings were not okay. The task is to create our own supportive environment for getting in touch with our feelings and expression of them.

Overcoming shame is to go to the very core of our being. To embrace our shame is to journey on the path of discovering our true self. It's like learning to walk. We take small steps to build confidence. As we practice, we fall, yet with support and the determination to change, we can empower ourselves to get back up and work it again. This is our birthright and soul's journey. Be loving and patience to the parts of yourself that struggle with letting go of the shameful pattern. This is part of the healing path to overcoming the grip of shame.

Self-Worth and Intimacy

S elf-worth is intimacy with the self. To be intimate means, to be close to the one I cherish and to see into them with acceptance and non-judgment. To be worthy, is to allow for closeness with the self and grow. To attain true intimacy, we need to feel cherished and have closeness with the self and our Source before we can do so with another. Guilt and shame, along with fear and self-doubt deter us from intimacy with our Source, with ourselves and with others. Intimacy, especially with a partner, also means: *Into me you see.* It conveys that I can trust and be safe and vulnerable with you and my feelings without judgment. One reason people struggle with connection and intimacy, is due to feeling unsafe, and the fear of vulnerability. Feelings of unworthiness surface when we are judged and don't feel safe. It's important to be in touch with and comfortable with feeling our feelings, especially the painful feelings. This creates healthy vulnerability and connects us more with ourselves. We can engage in the perception of not feeling safe, rather than run from it. Self-worth and intimacy mean, not running from what we are feeling and experiencing. We won't feel safe and empowered, if we are repeatedly avoiding what doesn't feel safe within. If we avoid being intimate with ourselves, we will avoid or surely struggle with intimacy with others.

The Search: Outside and Inside the Self

The ego takes us on an endless search for love outside of ourselves; the need to compare ourselves to please others, and to do whatever it takes to gain the acceptance, approval and love of others. We are fooled into thinking that when this happens, we will know love and then feel worthy, alive and complete. Love, happiness and a sense of self-worth should be experienced first from within. Coming to this realization is part of self-mastery. Self-mastery is self-discipline; a "can do" attitude, and awareness and regulation of our emotions. Self-mastery develops from self-love, a sense of self-worth, and taking responsibility for our own happiness.

Recall from chapter 3 on the soul, the metaphor of the kite being the soul and our hand being the ego holding the string. The way the mind expands in awareness is when it can ease up its hold of the string, allowing for some slack for the soul to move and guide the ego through life experiences that expand the lower mind to obtain a higher perspective and increased self-worth. This shift happens from the inside out. No one outside of us has the power to do this for us, nor keep us held back. Allowing this shift to take place within us is one of the main reasons for being here and experiencing life in earth school.

Emotional pain comes from resistance and/or avoidance to feeling. The negative and self-defeating thoughts about ourselves lead us down a path of resistance and non-acceptance of the *"what is"* in our life. Eckhart Tolle said in *The Power of Now* that the two keys to unhappiness are *"resistance and non-acceptance."* The Universal Law of Non-Resistance teaches that whenever we resist some situation, we will give more power to it. Jesus said in the Gospel of Thomas, 70: *"If you bring forth what is within you, what is within you will save you. If you do not bring forth what is within you, what is within you will destroy you."* Jesus and Eckhart are encouraging us to bring forth and reconcile our fears, shame and vulnerability so that they no longer limit our sense of worth, connection and potential. What we resist or deny will persist and weaken us. What we confront and resolve within us will strengthen and empower us. This is a spiritual truth and an important soul lesson.

The Art of Projection

Projection in psychological terms is a defense mechanism by the ego that creates the shadow. It involves taking our own unacceptable qualities or feelings and ascribing them to other people. For example, I am upset by others being rude, yet I am often rude to others. Projection creates a false truth, only to reinforce a false belief about ourselves and/or others. It distorts a person's perception away from love and the actual truth. Our shadow projects to feel protected and safe. The interesting thing about projection is that whatever irritates us about someone else, is usually something within us that is not resolved or healed. That's why we are bothered by the other person's behavior—it is reflecting to us what we have repressed or denied within us.

The Act of Acceptance

Acceptance is loving someone as they are and as they are not. This includes ourselves.

Acceptance creates space in the present for something new and more beneficial to replace what's holding us back and no longer benefits us. Acceptance opens the door for other possibilities, allowing a different reality to be considered. With acceptance, comes gratitude, because you realize and sense that a greater and wiser intelligence is working in your life. Once we accept our limitations, we can begin to move beyond them. What we accept we begin to conquer and move forward from. Acceptance is a *moving forward* energy, bringing love and light to what was fearful and resisted.

When we don't accept the *"what is,"* we build a wall around our hearts and create a self-imposed prison in our mind. Lack of acceptance takes us down the road of denial that the ego sees as safe and secure, yet creates greater insecurity, and turns our pain into suffering.

We don't have to like the experience. When we won't accept it, we remain stuck in the wound and its self-defeating energy. We want to judge and blame others for this struggle. Then our lower self turns on us, so we judge and condemn ourselves, reinforcing the false belief and story of not being lovable or worthy. Judgment is simply the *withholding of love*. We create victim or conflict energy within us, and this thinking adds toxins and dis-ease to the mind and body.

Acceptance is an act of love and compassion, reconnecting us to the spirit and passion of our true self and to life. Acceptance is telling the truth about ourselves, to ourselves, without shame or guilt. It brings a sense of inner power and confidence back into our life, allowing us to open and receive. Healing and transformation begin when we accept what our lower self deems unacceptable. This allows us to freely move beyond what is blocking us. We can't let go or release something unless we name it and claim it—take ownership of it and responsibility for it; without being defined or consumed by it. When we acknowledge and accept that something is impacting our lives in unhealthy and unproductive ways, we create the desire to change and be the best version of ourselves. To heal is to accept the whole self in this moment with unconditional love. To love and accept the self is to liberate the self from false identity and allow us to reclaim our self-worth, self-empowerment and inner peace. It moves us to harmony and begins to return us to our divinity.

Acceptance puts us in the energy of truth and authenticity. It offers us greater clarity about our fears and struggles, allowing us to see what's been missing with fresh eyes and deeper knowing. It moves us into the heart and allows us to see more clearly and to create possibilities that we didn't think were there. Acceptance gives us inner strength and confidence to move through and beyond what we fear and resist. It leads to greater understanding and reconciliation within us and with others. Acceptance creates a bridge to love and self-worth. When we love and accept ourselves, we honor ourselves and acknowledge that we are part of a loving universe.

Healing, in part, begins through the process of accepting our shame or guilt, our fears and doubts, and reconciling them through the heart and the higher self. The process of healing involves the mind allowing a new belief to form within. Healing is the shift in perception and results in the belief of knowing *"who I am."*

Let Your Heart and Higher Mind Be the Master and Your Lower Mind Be the Servant

The ego often misinterprets the lesson that the soul agreed upon. Lessons are reexperienced because the universe wants us to understand the higher perspective. When we experience painful experiences, like a love relationship ending, or the loss of a job, our pain and heartache may turn into despair. We allow the person, experience and painful emotions to define us. The lower mind is now the master and uses attacking thoughts and behaviors, especially toward itself, as coping strategies. It seeks relief by escaping from intense spiritual, emotional and physical pain. We lose awareness of who we really are. We may consider suicide, hurt others or turn to other self-destructive behaviors such as, addictions, impulsive eating or shopping, etc.

The key is to not lose ourselves in the thoughts, emotions, feelings and beliefs that arise when we experience pain and heartache from our experiences. We must learn to allow our heart and higher mind to be the master and our lower mind to be the servant. This is the way to the higher perspective. A boat sinks when it fills with water. Likewise, we sink when we have difficult experiences, and we allow our negative thoughts, feelings and beliefs to prevail and wall off the chambers of our heart and cloud the pathways in our mind. Negative thoughts are attacking thoughts, so they are an attack on the self. It is important to be mindful of our thoughts, recognizing whether they are attacking us or empowering us. Our thoughts and feelings are just that— thoughts and feelings. They come and go like clouds come and go in the sky, or waves come and go in an ocean. Thoughts and feelings are not us. Like the clouds or waves, they are temporary, while the sky/ocean, the soul, is eternal. I composed these words below to convey this concept with more clarity.

Thoughts as Clouds or Waves

Clouds and waves are always moving through the experience of itself. Clouds and waves come, and they go. Waves and clouds offer us wonder, temporary beauty and joy in appearance, color and design; or create darkness, turbulence and storm. Thoughts of the mind are like the clouds in the sky, or waves in the ocean, always moving, some with beauty, some with turbulence. Our thoughts like the clouds or waves are temporary and so they appear real only in this moment. Yet in the next moment the cloud or wave will pass or subside to become unreal alongside the backdrop of the eternal sky or ocean. A great error in life is the judgment and attachment to thoughts, believing I am that thought; I am that feeling in each experience. This is the created story we make of our life. Can I let my thoughts come and go like the clouds, or like the waves? Or do I allow myself to attach to the thoughts, be attacked and consumed by the thoughts; or be defined by the experience that arises as thought? Within the fact that thoughts come and go, the question arises: Who do I want to be in the coming and going of my thoughts?

Given the latest research on the heart and mind connection, perhaps the main cause for a person's heart to be out of divine rhythm is the stress and pain of hanging on to thoughts, especially negative thoughts. Irregular rhythmic patterns go from the heart to the brain, creating chemical reactions in the different brain centers, causing cognitive distortions, limiting the ability to think clearly and to make healthy choices. Stress, trauma and pain can cause us to be out of heart coherence, and so the brain is vulnerable to making impulsive, even dangerous choices. Many of us make subtle, less dangerous decisions, yet they too can have painful consequences and may limit our potential, as well as personal and spiritual growth. Pain that we allow to become our suffering, causes us to turn to self-destructive choices as a means of coping. This is an indication that we struggle with loving ourselves and have allowed ourselves to be attached to and defined by our thoughts around our experiences.

When we are rejected and hurt by someone or something, we have a choice. We can reject and hurt ourselves, or we can allow our soul and mind to expand to a higher perspective, seeing the truth in the difficult experience and remembering ourselves as love and goodness. The willingness to seek a higher perspective and the soul lesson from the experience will bring us to inner peace and greater self-worth.

> *You yourself, as much as anybody in the universe deserve your love and attention.* —the Buddha

Forms of human love, like physical or romantic love, can be seen as object-referral, i.e. person is defined by an object, person, situation, possession, etc. If I seek love and validation outside of myself, I create expectations, disappointment and instability for myself. Divine love is self-referral; the self knows and seeks love and validation from Source and within its soulful self. The ego will create evidence to show how unloved and unworthy I am. This is my self-created barrier to self-love. If we had a friend who thought, believed, and said half the things we think, believe, and say to ourselves, would we still want them to be our friend? When Jesus said, *"Love thy enemy,"* I believe he was referring more to the enemy within us, not just those outside us. As Carl Jung said, *"I am the enemy that must be loved."* If we don't love the enemy inside of us, we are rejecting and neglecting ourselves just as our parents did, just as our third-grade teacher did, or just as our best friend did in high school. The so-called enemy inside us is really the scared, rejected, wounded and lost part of us that has lost its sense of self-worth. That part needs to be heard, understood, accepted, and loved. We all have wounded parts that seek to remember and be reconnected back to love, acceptance and worthiness. They seek to find their way back home to the childlike innocence. No one can return them home to the state of remembrance and love except the person who in the end really pronounced them guilty, unloved and unworthy; "the me—inside of me". It is through our difficult and dark times that we are meant to realize where love and light are needed within us.

Who Are You Really?

Two of the most powerful words are *I AM*, because of the words you put behind them. I AM is what you believe about yourself and who you become. Take a moment to read the following statements below, slowly and intently. Pause for five seconds between each statement and notice the thoughts, feelings and beliefs that arise within you. Do so without judgment; just observe whatever arises.

- I am a human being.

- I am a lovable human being.

- I am a lovable and worthy human being.

- I am a capable, lovable and worthy human being.

- I am a perfect, capable, lovable, worthy and radiant spiritual being, having a human experience.

What did you notice, hear and feel as you said each statement to yourself? Did your feelings change in some way as each was read? Did it get more difficult to hear and affirm? Did you notice any inner resistance to the words? Were the statements more difficult to believe as you progressed? Each statement is true, yet as you progress, each holds a deeper truth of who you really are. There can be a tendency for the lower self to kick in and say, *"You know we are not lovable or capable."* The essence of our pain is the internal denial and rejection of these affirmations and spiritual truth. Acceptance is self-love and a way of transforming the negative belief that we are unworthy. The daily practice of saying these affirmations to yourself with one hand over your heart, in a quiet place or in front of a mirror, is one way to help reclaim your sense of worth and wholeness. This exercise is especially helpful during times of conflict, change and increased stress.

What self-imposed barriers to love have I created? Answering this question is an act of self-love. It begins to move me out of the false self; the story I created to protect myself from pain. To move beyond this created illusion and remember who I am, I must do the inner work. I must descend to the valley of my wounded, shamed self. In going down into this personal valley of pain and grief; I must name it—name my struggle and pain—and claim it—take responsibility for how it's impacting me and my choices. I then can understand the how and why I learned to show up the way I have. Then I can tame it—I see and accept it for what it is, the beliefs, the story I created. Then I can choose to reframe it—for personal and spiritual growth—to rewrite and live the actual truth of who I am.

The Earth is comprised of valleys and peaks; ebbs and flows. Our life also involves valleys and peaks. Our dark valleys are the teacher and an opportunity, not an enemy or a threat, as the lower, fearful self wants us to believe. As we begin to reprocess and reclaim our innocence, integrity and sense of true self, we come to a peak—the *"ah ha"* moment, where the lesson is more fully understood and learned—remembering what was forgotten and what the soul came to experience and work through. We can begin to rewrite the story and live the other side of our soul agreement. Our life experiences are meant to teach us to remember self-love and self-empowerment.

Some say, *"I've lived this way for fifty years; it's all I know." "It's too hard, too painful, and I can't get beyond this unhappiness."* This is our wounded self, convincing us to maintain the status quo. This is the little girl or boy in us who only knows the main spiritual wound of separation, and the other core human wounds mentioned earlier. These are wounds from our past, which part of us believes can't be resolved in the present. To buy into this false evidence in the now is to reinforce the core wound of the past and keep reliving it. This is a part of you creating the self-imposed barrier to love, self-worth and healing. It's only a part of us. The wounded parts are encouraged through Divine love to reconnect with the part that knows the self as love. This is what brings us back to love, self-worth and wholeness.

Ask yourself:

Do I allow others to define me, my love of self, and my worth?

Do I allow others to determine my authentic self?

What happens to my sense of personal power and confidence when I allow others to define my love of self and sense of worth?

Are many of the choices I make self-supporting and empowering, or are they self-defeating and destructive?

If I had greater self-love and worth, how would my thoughts, perceptions, beliefs and actions toward myself and others change?

What would I suggest to a friend or relative to reconcile their inner struggle with self-love and sense of worth?

The way you answer these questions is an indication of how much you love yourself and a measure of your self-worth. Consider this statement from scripture, *"Love your neighbor as yourself."* One of the main principles in life is to love, value, and respect ourselves. You and your neighbor are the same. When we love ourselves, then and only then, can we truly love our neighbor.

Let's go back to the last question above about the suggestion to a friend or relative. If you took your own advice, would it not assist you with your own struggle? You know how to help and heal yourself, otherwise, you wouldn't have given your friend or relative that helpful suggestion. We are grander and wiser than we allow ourselves to be. The answers are always within. To love is to go within and uncover the buried treasure of our true worth and potential.

8

Love Me; Hold Me, Father-Mother

Your children need your presence more than your presents.
—Jesse Jackson

Thoughts came to me late one night about the love many people yearn for from their earthly mother-father. In this yearning, if rejection is often experienced, we then look for love outside of the family, only to perhaps experience greater emptiness.

Lost and alone, I long to be loved and held by my mother, by my father. Instead I look for many other ways to feel their love and their presence, only to experience deeper emptiness and stronger yearning. My wounded, lonely self keeps searching and reaching out for my father's and mother's love; the experience of being accepted and held in esteem, only to feel more rejection and more hurt. I pause in my yearning to ask, *"Why do I no longer feel safe with mother and/or father?"*

I ask, *"Where is this father-mother love to be found?"*

The soft voice of Jesus within me says,

> *I will love you and hold you, if you'd like. I have always loved you. Yet you couldn't know since you were asleep and believed yourself to be unloved and unworthy. You have felt alone, afraid and have forgotten about me.*

I notice for the first time that this voice comes from deep within and not from without. I turn and face myself in a mirror in total surrender and openness. I realize I have found my soul; that part of me that can love me and hold me as I desire and deserve. I wrap my arms around me, and I cuddle up with me, like a soft fuzzy bear. The voice through me acknowledges my fears and tears for how unloved and alone I'm feeling. I let the wounded me inside me know of our innocence, that we have been doing our best and that we are deeply loved and appreciated.

I hear the soft voice of Jesus say to me,

> *I created you and you left home for a while to find someone else to love you and hold you. It's not your fault or the fault of the ones who rejected or betrayed you. You left home; that's what souls agree to do to know love and be valued by another soul.*
>
> *Your earthly life at times is difficult. You deem yourself unworthy and unloved. You say, "Others gave up on me, so I may as well give up on me too." You wander aimlessly, becoming further away from home. Then one dark night you realize, if you truly desire to be loved, you need to return home to the arms and the bosom of yourself.*
>
> *Allow these words, which come from your Creator to affirm you. 'You are my beloved child, forever innocent, forever loving, and forever loved. You are limitless and pure just as the Creator from which you came. Therefore, awaken and return to me. I am your true father-mother and you are my beloved child.'*

My soul smiles and I feel a glow I've always known was there. I was too attached to the belief that love was somewhere out there. The energy of my soul opens wide as I realize it's been waiting to say, *"Welcome home, my beloved...Welcome home."*

I embrace my soul, connect with my soul, and I experience my soul as never before. I am loved and held by the Source of all that is. I am loved and held like I've always wanted to be. I am at peace now, tears cascading from the well I have for years made dry. I have found and connected once again with my real father – mother. I smile and realize how far I have traveled to be loved and held. The journey seemed so far and so hard, because I was searching and yearning from outside of me. I found parental love through Divine Love; by looking and embracing the I AM within me. Such is the journey of the soul. Such is the love of the Divine. I realize now that the journey is rather short, once we go within. The Mother-Father God is already there; we only need to have the awareness of this and say, "Love me; hold me, Father-Mother." Then listen for, *"Welcome home, my beloved...Welcome home."*

9
Love and the Mirror

One does not meet oneself until one catches the reflection from an eye other than human. — Loren Eiseley

Remember the Walt Disney movie *The Lion King*? There's a battle between the lions, Scar and Simba. Scar portrays the dark, shadow type of energy who tricks Simba into believing he's killed his own father. Holding this belief, Simba is consumed with understandable grief, guilt and shame. Thinking he killed his father, Simba feels defeated, hopeless and empty of purpose. With his sense of self-worth shattered, he is banished from his kingdom and goes off to hide. He meets a wise, light-hearted baboon named Rafiki. Rafiki takes Simba into the dark forest. There, Simba finds out who he really is by confronting his fears and shame. Rafiki guides Simba to reclaim the light within himself, his true identity and true path. They end up at a pond, where Simba looks down at the water and sees a reflection of a face he doesn't recognize. In his loving way, Rafiki pushes Simba's face closer down near the water and challenges him to look deeper, look harder into the reflection he sees. Suddenly Simba recognizes his father in the reflection and realizes he didn't kill his father. He was tricked by Scar. He realizes in that moment it was Scar who had killed his father.

Simba then sets off to confront Scar (who symbolizes Simba's dark side) and banish him from the kingdom. Simba confronts his darkness, reconciling his shame and self-hate. He rekindles his inner light by transforming his false beliefs. His fear and shame are dissolved by the light of truth and remembrance. He releases his grief to gain conscious awareness and acceptance of who he truly is. He can now return to his homeland with dignity to become the rightful king that he knows himself to be. His love, acceptance and compassion guide the kingdom to flourish once again.

The Lion King is the story and journey to *Just Be Love*. This movie reflects the human condition and the inner battle of the Scar and Simba within us. It also reflects the importance of seeking out the Rafiki, the higher and wiser self within, as well as the guide who comes from the outside to teach, challenge and support us in finding our truth and rightful purpose.

> *Life is a mirror and it will reflect back to the thinker what he thinks into it.* — Ernest Holmes

Like Simba, we may struggle with looking at our reflection in the pond or mirror, especially during our dark times of confusion and anguish. We struggle with looking deeper and harder to find who we truly are. We often don't see the image reflecting at us. We may choose to only see the sad, disappointing self; the one who is standing in front of the mirror, not the one who is standing in the mirror reflecting back at us. Our inner critic with its limiting beliefs, assumptions, self-doubts, etc., creates self-talk that mirrors what's held deep in our unconscious/shadow mind, which causes us to avoid taking positive and tangible action toward change and growth.

The mirror can be seen as the reflection of unconditional love that wants us to see who's really there, rather than the one we project there. The reflection never rejects or condemns us. It just lets us be. The reflection is always accepting and nonjudgmental. When we look in the mirror our eyes meet the true image of the real self. We may struggle with accepting this meeting, allowing our wounded and shameful self to project the false and distorted image onto the one who holds our innocence and divinity. We often stand in front of the mirror yielding to the Scar within us; to the viewpoint and voice of a critic and deceiver. We only notice what's at our surface. We may only see the judgment and the disappointment, as we look halfheartedly in the mirror. We see the pimples, the big nose, the bad hair day, the doubting one, the undeserving one and the shameful one. We feel the judgment from others who we let define us. We see what disgusts us, not what makes us unique and divine. We sense what drains our energy, not what inspires us. The more we allow ourselves to see only the image at the surface of the mirror, we will only see the imperfection and judge ourselves unworthy. This makes our false beliefs the false God, creating a hell on earth.

The mirror is not foggy or dirty, it's only our perceptions and beliefs about who we see standing before us. Our belief about ourselves is reflected by our relationship with ourselves and others. What we energetically project to the outside is who and what we will attract (reflect) back to us. The loving universe always mirrors back to us who we think we are, for awareness and growth. The image in the mirror is patiently waiting for us to more clearly recognize the true depth of the reflection, the eyes and heart of innocence, pure love and grace.

Can you look deeper into your reflection? The depth of the reflection will reveal the truth of who you are.

The inner critic's self-judgment and deception contribute to our criticism of God's perfection. In other words, the lower self does a con job, distorting our divine image—like looking into that distorted mirror at a circus. This distortion prevents us from seeing ourselves in our divine image. The true reflection is the vision of perfection created by God. It invites us to love and nurture this image so that we can transcend the self-judging patterns that block acceptance of self and self-love.

Sadly, we give power to the "Scar" inside us and in people around us to define who we are. We often don't seek help from the Rafiki's of the world or the Rafiki within. When we turn away from ourselves or the teachers we meet, we turn away from our divinity and from love.

Look Through the Eyes of Innocence

The person, who is the reflection in the mirror, can take away the shame and pain; they won't trick us or betray us. Look deeply into your mirror. Look with eyes of unconditional love and acceptance, at that little one, like Simba, that once was carefree, spontaneous and joyful. Look into your mirror with self-understanding, acceptance, compassion and forgiveness. Let go of the story that led to expectations, comparison, self-judgment and resentment. Just look deeper into the loving self, that's reflecting to the self that feels unworthy. See the resilience and strength within you that you have perceived as your flaws and weaknesses.

What You've Been Denying—Yet Yearning For

With the perception and thought of *Just Be Love*, look deeper and harder into the mirror. Be fearless, and maybe for the very first time see with conscious awareness and acknowledgement the love and perfection that you are. Allow unity with all that is to be with you and your reflection. With appreciation, gratitude and care, be that STAR: *Surrender, Trust, Allow* and *Receive* the unity with the two images in your mirror. Can you love yourself enough to *Just Be Love*, to be at peace with your divinity? For this will be your inclusion to the fullness of yourself and your life. Your mirror is waiting to bring you home to yourself and to love.

Be with your reflection in the mirror. Open your heart and merge with the one in the mirror. See with the 4 I's of your *Innocence, Intuition, Imagination* and *Inspiration*. Listen to the soft voice of your loving, accepting self, reflecting from the mirror; echoing…"*Just Be Love.*"Take a deep cleansing breath and ask: *What do I feel in this moment? What do I sense in my heart? What does my body want me to know in this moment?* I surrender to the truth in my mirror—the love that I AM.

My Mirror

My mirror recognizes and reflects the truth
that I struggle to notice and affirm.
My mirror only sees and knows me as love,
love I struggle to accept and embrace.
My mirror supports and nurtures,
what I choose to judge and reject.
My mirror quietly asks that I Just Be Love,
with the one who truly sees and knows me.

I look deeply now in my mirror.
I see my innocence, perfection and radiance,
I would before hide and condemn.
As I let go of what I thought I was.
I see more clearly now who I am.
What a gift I give to myself this day.

Thank you mirror, thank you,
I finally recognize and have found the one,
I've been looking for all along.

10

Love and Fear

Fear is only the absence of love; where there is Divine Love there is no fear.

I awoke one morning, fearful and anxious. I lay still and quiet, using my breath to slow my overwhelmed, fearful mind. Jesus enters my presence and he begins a conversation with me. He offered his insights and guidance to better understand my struggle with fear. His message is all of us struggling with fear. Please be advised, I am offering my interpretation of his message, as I experienced his energy and presence.

Jesus begins the conversation regarding emotional fear saying: *"Fear not."* David: Okay but I'm doing the best I can right now.

Jesus: *Physical fear is your natural and automatic physical reaction to a perceived physical danger. This physical reaction is your divine given alarm system to protect and assist you on the physical level. Physical fear creates both emotional and mental reactions. Your emotion is the body's reaction to your conscious or unconscious perception and thoughts or the environment. Mental fear and the feelings that come from it are the mind's understanding of the body's reaction. Mental fear is learned and comes with worry and doubt. Mental fear blocks the ability to trust and have faith in Source and then trusting yourself to follow this guidance. Mental fear is the greatest barrier to loving the self and realizing your highest potential. It is the mind's imagination going in a disempowering direction. Your task is not to avoid fear, but to learn to honor it, listen to your body where the fear resides, and let it teach you. The emotional experience of fear and its resulting mental feeling of anxiety are meant to be freed and transformed through the practice of love and self-assurance. Your fearful experiences are opportunities to practice transforming fear and anxiety into love, trust and self-assurance. The soul is here to experience life;*

however, you are not here to be consumed and defined by the fear of life experiences. Your health, happiness and potential are compromised by your resistance and struggle to reconcile your fear. Your fear is the result of trusting your ego self, at the exclusion of trusting the Divine first and foremost. To trust in the Divine is to resolve your fear.

David: Do you really understand what I'm going through here, the worries and struggles in my life?

Jesus: *Could it be that your worries and struggles are teaching you to trust your higher self and your Creator? Fear is your mind needing to protect itself from a perceived threat. Consider the example I spoke many years ago of how birds and other creatures don't fret and worry. They trust and stay open to being cared for in divine ways. Fear is being caught up in a mind-set that dwells in your painful past and predicts the 'what if's' of your future. Fear comes when you worry today about what you feel you won't get and can't control in the future. How can you be free and at peace with this sort of thinking? You have made it this far, so why create a problem?*

David: Yeah, but we are different than the birds.

Jesus: *Your 'yeah but's,' and 'would-a,' 'could-a,' 'should-a' are ways your doubtful self pulls the plug on your life force energy and your divinity. Your thought, your belief that you are different and separate from the rest of creation is perhaps your biggest hindrance. Different doesn't mean you are better, nor have it figured out any more than anyone else. Do you realize that much of nature is wiser and more trusting than you? Your lack of trust, along with your distortion and pre-occupations with comparing and competing with others is what's getting the best of you.*

David: But my situation isn't turning out the way I wanted it to, and I fear it will happen again.

Jesus: *It **will** happen again, for your thoughts and beliefs make it so. It turned out just as it was to be. You just can't accept this and so you condemn yourself, me and others. Your mental fear causes you to run or hide from yourself and life. Do you see how you create your own struggle and unhappiness by falling into ego's trap?*

David (with frustration): Why do you make life so complicated and difficult for me?

> Jesus: *Why do you believe it's me making it this way? You oversee your perception, thoughts, emotions, feelings and choices—you have free will and are an active participant in the creation process. You developed an ego to protect and manage yourself. You have judged yourself guilty, when in truth you are innocent, always have been, and always will be. You even judge me guilty and a part of your problem. You have made us all guilty, especially yourself. Yet you alone are in the prison. You have locked yourself in there for safety and protection. This is your disconnect from love. To be consumed and defined by fear is the mind's way of perceiving you have been taken away from love. Love is never taken away. Your perceptions create your reality of love or fear. You have developed a fearful, rigid mind-set, so you could learn at some point to develop an open, accepting heart—this will free your mind.*

> *In **A Course in Miracles**, I expressed: 'A meaningless world engenders fear because I think I am in competition with God.' Your task is to "discern" what your ego mind has created, and what God has created. The ego wants to compete with God. However, what your ego creates is meaningless, because it involves the energy of distortions and fear. Only what is named as God has actual meaning, because what is created by God is what actual truth is, and so you need only give meaning to this. This understanding and discernment will release you from fear and return you to love.*

Jesus looked at me with tender and loving eyes. I take a deep breath and I see and feel the energy of the open heart of wisdom and compassion that comes forth from him. He tells me:

> *Your mental fear is the making of a limited and untrained mind; it's a learned coping strategy. Fear can be a motivator and catalyst for change and growth, or it can paralyze and hold you captive from unlimited potential and love. The only difference between being excited and ready for something and being fearful of it is the perception, feeling and belief you put to it. Do you see how fear causes you to hold back and to settle for less in your life? Your soul, your spirit wants you to question and challenge your fear with willful courage and face your fear. This is the way to truth and innocent knowing.*

Avoiding fear creates more fear and distorts divine truth. Your soul doesn't evolve, and your mind won't expand when you are consumed with fear and doubt. You choose to subscribe to the fearful and doubting part of you rather than the loving and confident higher knowing of you. You desire a life of ease without discipline and steadfast commitment. Your depression and anxiety come from listening to the voice of your lower self where fear, doubt and mistrust reside. Humanity must realize that the entry to forms of mental and physical illness is due to the discord in the mind, and the disconnection from the emotions and the heart. Your life force energy is blocked, and your lower mind is in charge at the expense of your soul. The overuse and dependence on medications and forms of addictions numb you to your feelings, and so they numb you from the experience of your soul and love. In your wounded-ness, you become fearful of loving and being loved. In your fear you decide to avoid and numb the very aspect divinity has given you to learn, heal and grow—your feelings, and especially your emotions.

You like the saying, my dear David, 'Our feelings are the anchor to our humanness and the bridge to our higher self.' When you don't live and apply this, you drown in an ocean of feelings rather than learn from them. Your feelings and beliefs are held in the mind. Your emotions are held and expressed through the body. Emotions are the pathway to finding and living your true and authentic self. Your feelings, beliefs and emotions will lead you to the meaning behind your experiences and create awareness of the answers to the questions and resolution of your struggles. Please know that to avoid your feelings and emotions is to avoid your answers, to avoid life—and to avoid love. I want you and humanity to find the answers. Why do you think you have feelings and emotions? Why do you choose to avoid and numb the very gift given to heal and liberate yourself? Where is the learning, peace and love in avoiding and running from yourself? In being so consumed and defined by your feelings and emotions? What are those other sayings you like? Oh yes, 'You cannot heal what you don't feel' and 'What you resist will persist.' You must go to this place of inner knowing. Love will take you there; fear will not.

Peace comes from the virtues of will and courage to engage with your painful emotions and distorted beliefs. Challenge your doubts and step into your fear. Divine love, truth and peace will greet you there. You avoid looking inward because you harbor fears of what you may find there. You fear your darkness and what's been called your shadow. You resist the step of taking inventory of your past within the warehouse of the mind, which has become overstocked with false beliefs, self-defeating thoughts and behaviors that only cause more headaches and heartbreaks. Please understand mental fear is only the absence of love and faith in this moment. You are trapped in your survival mind, which creates the false evidence you have gathered based on your past experience that you make very real in this moment. You are often looking for evidence of how unworthy and unloved you are, yet you discount the evidence of how worthy and loved you are. This is what causes you to feel stuck and trapped. The energy of fear is imagining what you don't want to have happen and then creating exactly that through your thoughts, emotions, feelings, beliefs and choices. This energy then becomes your created experience and repeated story. Being controlled and defined by the grip of fear eliminates possibilities.

Acknowledging and working with your fears and painful feelings will in time, set you free. This is spiritual truth in the highest degree. To bypass spiritual truth is just that, spiritual bypass. Spiritual bypass is avoiding painful feelings, emotions and not working through them. When you bypass them and 'give it to God', there is no learning and growth. Bypassing the feelings that are part of your experience and avoiding this internal soul work, creates further discomfort and disconnects you from love, from your authentic self and from me. Know in this moment you can choose differently. Fear creates foolish choices; love creates wise choices.

David: My feelings are too painful! It is too scary and difficult to expose myself to these feelings. I will not survive.

With a gentle smile, Jesus replies:

This is the grand illusion that you have convinced yourself is so real. Your feelings will not destroy you. Emotions and feelings are intended to lead you to your awakening and to your remembering. They are there to assist and guide you in realizing who you really are. They are your teacher in the classroom of your life experiences. Feeling unsafe about your feelings and emotions creates fear; and fear creates avoidance behaviors. Avoiding your feelings lowers your life force energy and inhibits truly knowing yourself. If you believe and trust in my love and in yourself, you will not allow fear to get in your way.

David: You mean I can do this? I have that power and choice?

Yes, you most certainly do, my beloved David. Yes, you must work at it and discipline your mind to work through, resolve and then release what no longer serves you. In the perception of fear and doubt there is a still point—the calm and wisdom within the storm of fear and uncertainty. Like a hurricane has the eye in the center of itself, the calm in the midst of its turbulence, so too are you to discover and use this still point within you. It is often found through trusting the Divine and such practices as attentive breathing, observing your thoughts, prayer, meditation and other mind-full endeavors. To cling to your fear and doubt diminishes your inner wisdom, strength and determination. Yes, you must trust and allow in the release of what you have made real. Remember you receive holy truth and higher awareness as the replacement when you go inward and still; when you accept — when you surrender, trust and allow. As you work through the many layers of trauma and hurt from your past, you will discover how much you don't love and trust me, and yourself. You believe that to surrender is to be self-defeated. Emotional fear blocks the heart, mental fear, impacts the heart as well, and often makes the mind irrational, which causes you to mistrust, creating the sense of unworthiness, and reinforcing your perception of separation from Source and the loving and supportive universe.

When you allow the wisdom and truth of your soul, your divinity, to expand the limiting beliefs held in your doubting mind, you release the chains of fear and your false identity. The work of the soul to expand the mind does not come without tears and wrestling with what you thought was real versus what is divine reality. This is the reconciliation of your created paradox. It requires you to be an explorer, a warrior, trusting yourself to go into the unknown within and fight the battle of darkness on the journey to light. The battle is fought with willful intent, loving kindness and innocence. It's fought with acceptance, compassion, and an open and forgiving heart. It is you, the caterpillar (false self), struggling to release yourself from the cocoon of the lower mind beliefs, to come to your true nature as the butterfly (divine self).

The ways of the ego at times, make you out to be a small and separated self or at other times an all-powerful and all-knowing self. Fear is the result of the perception of duality and fear creates a spiritual disconnection from Source and your true self. The truth is you are inclusive with all of creation. Love is inclusive. Love invites and embraces you as creation. As I've told you several times, you are a master, and you are asked to master these divine truths. This is the invitation I extend to you and to humanity. You have been invited to learn self-mastery by overcoming fear. Choose to master and cultivate the higher perspective within difficult situations. Feel the fear, move through it and forward from it. Acknowledge and celebrate your strengths, resilience and goodness; this will move you through your struggles with more grace and peace.

It won't all happen overnight. The universe wasn't created overnight; it was and is a process. Your life, like all of creation, is a process. Love is being mindful and focused more on your process, not just the outcome. Your survival instincts demand proof and certainty, so it creates fear of the unknown, and an unconscious belief that only the outcome is important. Fear stifles the process of creation and disrupts the co-creative rhythm of the dance with your Creator.

Fear is what created the distortion of my teachings and the account of my physical life and death. Most people don't realize I never used the word sin. In my native language of Aramaic, I used the word 'Satah,' which means to 'miss the mark, to turn astray.' My crucifixion was much more than the forgiveness of Satah. It was created due to human fear, caused by the lack of understanding and belief in my teachings—divine truth. My love for humanity and understanding of God's purpose allowed for my follow through of the crucifixion. The word resurrection means to 'restore.' I desire humanity to restore itself back to its divinity and the 'I AM' presence. My resurrection and ascension displayed my understanding of this divine truth. The resurrection was a miracle to you; however, it wasn't really a miracle, it simply was an expression of divine love and the Christ energy in action. It also showed you that death on the energetic and soul level does not exist. There is no reason to fear neither the Divine nor your soul essence. To have a fear of God is a man-made doctrine that only creates further separation from Source. A relationship cannot be sustained and thrive in the energy of fear. Fear is due to self-doubt and belief in your unworthiness in the heart and eyes of another. To fear God is not to trust and respect God. To fear God is to fear love and life—to live in the energy of shame, guilt. You cannot have a loving and authentic relationship if you fear God or a fellow human. Fear is not the true message and desire of the Divine; the message and desire of the Divine is Love.

Do you understand how fear keeps you from the peace and truth you seek? You choose resistance over surrender, mistrust over trust and judgment over acceptance. You seek the seen and the tangible vs. believing the unseen and your inner knowing. You choose to live life the opposite of how it's intended—you choose fear over love. I feel for you my beloved—please choose to remember what you have forgotten—please choose love in this moment, for I only know you as love and innocence. Brother David, this is why I said to you through our experience with the sun in the cloud … Just Be Love. Your fears, like all of your struggles, are your teacher and an opportunity for learning and growth. Fear is not intended to be the threat and enemy. Love your enemy, especially the enemy within. Your soul's task while in human form is to experience this truth, and how it frees and transforms you.

From a calmer place now, I ask, So, I am to love my fear and painful feelings?

Jesus with a gentle voice says:

Just Be Love, David. For love is always the answer. Love is all there is. Just "Be" (aware) mindful of your process of being, while having a fearless and lovely day! We'll talk more another time. Peace be with you, my brother.

In reflection of my conversation with Jesus, I've come to appreciate that fear results from the perception of danger. Fear, especially compulsive fear like worry, is an interpretation by the mind that opposes love. This will diminish one's sense of faith, i.e. trust, leading to distortions of the true reality and essence of life. Love and fear are nothing more than two forms of energy, each with its own vibration and frequency, which creates its own unique emotional and mental state and experience. Love calls us to overcome our fears. As fear arises from within, it's important to face and challenge the fear; to work at reconciling this in order to discover the truer self. In doing this, fear dissolves and only love and freedom remain.

I close this chapter with inspiring passages from novelist and poet James Baldwin who said:

Not everything that is faced can be changed. But nothing can be changed until it is faced. Baldwin also stated: *Love takes off the masks that we fear we cannot live without and know we cannot live within.*

Ellen Wheeler Wilcox wrote a poem called *Conversation*, her vision and idea of meeting God face to face. It expresses the dream, the illusion and how fear is part of this illusion.

> *God and I in space alone... and nobody else in view... "And where are all the people, oh lord" I said, "the earth below and the sky overhead and the dead that I once knew?" This was a dream God smiled and said: "The dream seemed to be true; there were no people living or dead; there was no earth and no sky overhead, there was only myself in you." "Why do I feel no fear?" I asked, meeting you here in this way? For I have sinned, I know full well and is there a heaven and is there hell, and is this Judgment Day?" "Nay, those were but dreams" the great God said, "dreams that have ceased to be. There are no such things as fear and sin; there is no you... you never have been. There is nothing at all but me.*

11

Loving with Freedom or with Possessiveness

Freedom is not a gift bestowed upon by other men, but a right that belongs to us by the laws of God and nature. —Benjamin Franklin

Human love is either offered with freedom or as possession. Freedom and possession come in many forms; we can be possessed by our own negative thoughts about ourselves and/or our world, or we can learn to free ourselves from thoughts. We can be possessive with material goods or have little attachment to them. We can have relationships that love with a sense of freedom and respect or we can be possessed by relationships we're in. In this chapter, I will be referring to loving with freedom or possessiveness in a relationship. I will explain some of the way's possessiveness distorts the true meaning of love and how loving with freedom is more of the Divine intent of relationship, especially with intimate ones. First, let's look at the chemistry of love; what happens in the brain when falling in love.

The Chemistry of Love

Romantic love is one of the most powerful emotions a person can have. Our brain is wired to love and be loved. It's a basic human drive. Research by Helen Fisher, Ph.D. and others have shown with MRI brain scans how certain regions in the brain are involved and activated in the process of falling in love and forming attachments with a partner or child.

Most notably, falling in love activates the caudate nucleus, an area near the center of the brain, referred to as the primitive reptilian brain or survival brain, that has been present for thousands of years. It's also the part of the brain's reward system, associated with wanting, craving and motivation; also associated with focused attention and learning. This is the same area that

73

feels the high, or the rush with addictive drugs and risky behaviors. The caudate nucleus creates cells that produce the neurotransmitter dopamine, a chemical that creates feelings of pleasure, ecstasy, jealousy or obsession. Studies on the brain indicate that romantic love produces high levels of dopamine, which influence mood, reward and motivation, throughout different brain regions. Increased levels of dopamine create euphoric feelings and the resulting behaviors for the beloved. In this "falling in love" stage, lovers become infatuated; obsessing in romantic thoughts and actions day and night. Studies also show that people in the falling in love stage display similar obsessive traits as someone with obsessive-compulsive disorder (OCD). The reason for this is due to the high level of dopamine and low levels of the neurotransmitter serotonin. Usually the romantic love stage lasts 12 to 18 months when the dopamine and serotonin are restored to normal levels. Some researchers have concluded that these studies show that love can be possessive and addictive.

Love also arouses the body's autonomic nervous system and releases a hormone called oxytocin that assists with several body functions. This hormone is found in mammals as well as humans. It facilitates bonding and is related to attachment. Oxytocin also increases trust and love for a partner and can affect parenting abilities. This hormone also has a dark side as it can produce suspicion, jealousy and envy. It acts as a neurotransmitter, reducing the stress hormone cortisol. If we feel less stressed, we are more likely to want to connect and bond with others. Higher levels of oxytocin are found primarily in women. This hormone is released during the birthing process. It initiates contractions of the uterus and stimulates the mammary glands to produce milk. Oxytocin also stimulates bonding between mother and baby. Males have a hormone called vasopressin, which is also related to bonding. Research shows that adults with high levels of oxytocin and/or vasopressin tend to have a greater ability and desire for connection and attachment. They also tend to have the willingness to keep romance and physical touch as an important part of their intimate relationship. Oxytocin has been called the "love" or "cuddle" hormone. One way it's released is through physical touch. The more touching and connecting a couple engages in the more oxytocin is produced to keep the love connection thriving. This is one way to sustain a healthy and long-lasting relationship. Research on longevity in relationships has found that couples who maintained a loving relationship over the years sustained high levels of oxytocin.

Love Connection

L ove creates a connection between people. There is a sense of a bonding between us. We can trust in each other's words and more importantly, our actions. The first stage of trust is vulnerability. Can I be myself with you, without being judged? A sense of connection and bonding cannot exist without a degree of vulnerability and trust. If trust and vulnerability are lacking, there will be difficulty for the couple to effectively navigate what I call the 4 C's of relationship. *Communication, Commitment, Common goals* and *Consensus.* Trust and connection create the sense of safety, bonding and intimacy that makes a relationship grow and thrive. It creates security for us; we feel cared about and cared for. Once trust and safety are in place, partners who desire a growing, thriving relationship will strive to move beyond the need for safety and security. They will support each other's desire to be their highest self and call forth the best in each other.

We experience an array of relationships in a lifetime, those with family, friends, intimate lovers and co-workers. Some last a lifetime and are very deep and meaningful, and others are casual, superficial and short lived. The desire to experience love and connection will naturally bring us into relationships. Healthy relationships create space for personal development; they should stimulate and challenge us. They should open us up to new perspectives and experiences of life. Our spiritual journey is greatly impacted by interactions with others. If one is restricted in growing, the relationship is not free and thus the spiritual nature of this human experience is absent. The spiritual lessons in this kind of relationship may be more about loving yourself enough to let go and move on from what is not a loving and accepting relationship. Or the lessons may be about looking closely at the barriers created by past love experiences that were not safe and connecting.

We are all at different levels of awareness and stages of readiness to change and grow. The action that a person calls love is either conscious or unconscious. One can only give and receive love based on their current level of understanding of love. Once the perception and understanding changes, then the opportunity to express and receive love will change as well. In human form, love is the soul's adventure and experience to higher awareness, change and spiritual maturity.

As mentioned earlier, the romantic stage of love, with its physical and emotional high, will eventually subside. In romantic love our spirit is open, and we have *"hope"* that our needs *"will be"* met. As the physical, emotional, spiritual high and openness fades; the ego sees the need to override the spirit.

Our hopes turn to *"expectations"* that our needs *"be"* met. We begin to view our beloved from a different perceptive lens. We may become defensive and closed; the feelings of trust and safety start to erode. This begins the common relationship dance of conflict, power struggle for control, and need to be right. The dynamic of possessive love is now revealed, its destructive energy patterns and behaviors are triggered, and played out in the relationship.

Possessive Love

All of life is energy. Human love seems to be either in the energy form of loving freely or loving possessively. Possessive love means that I will love you my way and on my terms. It's an unhealthy attachment to the love-object, a perception of ownership based on fear. This sense of ownership is dangerous when it is driven by ego and points to a need for control and power over another. Possession is the motto of an unhealthy ego, because the ego seeks its own needs at the expense of others. It is love by control. An example of possessive love is someone who holds another physically, emotionally, financially and perhaps sexually captive for their own pleasure and benefit. Over the years, we've heard many tragic stories of people, especially females being held against their will for the sake of the possessor's pleasure and distorted need; what they deem as love. Possessive love is a jealous love and can lead to a crime of passion, should the beloved turn away from the one being possessive.

Possessive love is often driven by insecurities, a need for power and an uncaring attitude toward others. One way to deal with these insecurities is to control and manipulate others in order to feel good and powerful. This is the hallmark of a bully. Underneath it all, bullies are very insecure and wounded. Their way of building themselves up is putting others down, especially others who are emotionally fragile. Possessive love is driven by an unconscious sense of need and an internal sense of lack. Possessive love is a product of the wounded self, demanding others to meet the expectations one is unwilling to meet within themselves.

Possessive behaviors are driven by aspects of the lower self, which put the possessor in an illusion, in bondage and separated from the experience of Divine love and freely loving others. Possessiveness is their shadow; the fragmented parts overpowering and controlling the self, and projecting this toward the person they say they love.

The true purpose of relationship is to learn about ourselves within the context of being in relationship with another.

The nature and dynamics of relationship will in time always expose our lower self and wounded parts to be *Recognized, Reconciled, Released* and *Reframed*. Due to the fear of vulnerability, the possessor does everything in their power to avoid and deny this spiritual truth.

We Hurt Others Because We Are Hurting

When we go to where it hurts within us, we find what will heal us and free us. This is a spiritual truth and an act of self-love.

We have a natural desire to love and be loved. This is the Divine's desire, the heart's desire and soul's desire. When we don't feel loved and safe, we become out of balance in mind, body and spirit. We create conditions, conflict and unhappiness for ourselves. Life with others becomes conditional and full of conflict creating disharmony. This imbalance distorts our thinking and perceptions—the way we give and receive love. It can generate the desire to control and possess someone in a relationship. Both men and women can have the desire to possess; to selfishly want power over their partner. The possessor's past, and need to blame others for their repressed pain, creates an imbalance, distorted beliefs and the inability to freely love and be loved. Their need to control and dominate is stronger than the desire to let go and allow freedom in the relationship. Possessive behaviors are indicators of the fear one has of looking at themselves and the need to protect the fragile and wounded self. When there is lack of acknowledgement of their emotional hurts, their defense is to project and to hurt others. What the possessors fails to recognize is that they are really the ones emotionally and spiritually hurting. Bullying, abuse, mass murders and such, are the tragic results of not reconciling one's spiritual, mental and emotional hurts, and making others responsible, even those who have nothing to do with the aggressor's life or story. From the higher perspective, the inner pain and resulting harm to others and/or themselves is a cry for love.

Possessive people are not secure and safe within themselves, so life and relationships for them don't feel safe and secure. They are often very sensitive and fearful of rejection and abandonment. They can resort to subtle or extreme measures of control in order to prevent the love object from leaving them. Controlling the partner's finances, physical property, friendships, job and transportation, etc., are all forms of possessive love. If you need to possess someone, your heart is closed; you are living in fear and denial of your own pain. Intentionally or not, you cause pain to others. Possessive love is selfish; a form of poverty of the heart. Relationships, like life, consist of cycles and patterns. Possessive love has its cycles and repeated patterns— that of arguments and/or aggression, remorse, reconciling (sex) and broken promises. It's a pattern of codependency for both people in the relationship. True reconciliation and healing occur when we acknowledge the pattern and are willing, and more importantly able to change. This creates a shift in our energy; a healthier pattern begins and life changes.

Who Are You When Treated like a Possession?

For those of you being controlled in relationship, it's fair to say your days are full of stress, fear and worry. There is no safety, security or sense of being protected by your partner; rather, you need to protect yourself from your partner. You are in a loveless relationship with little trust or belief in yourself. You have sold your soul out of a need to please or to receive love in return. Consider, if you are "loved" as a possession, ask yourself: *Do I struggle with loving myself? Do I value myself as worthy of respect?* Perhaps you've been hoping your partner will love you and treat you without expectations or demands. *Have you learned growing up that you can only be loved and accepted by pleasing others at your own expense? Have you been conditioned to believe that it's more important to meet someone's unhealthy demands and expectations than your own? Are you often told and shown that you don't do things the way your "partner" wants things done? Are you often told, and/or have you convinced yourself that you aren't good enough in your relationships?* These are some signs that you are being loved as a possession. You are in a trap; you believe that this is what love is for you, so you attract this type of person to love and be loved by. Your version of love is also distorted by your need to please and be accepted, and by the painful and unresolved wounds of your past that you live out in the present.

Being the one seen as a possession, your heart is closed off; you are on guard; you become defensive and react either aggressively or passively, or the combination of passive-aggressive behavior. You may withdraw and go into your shell, losing yourself in what once seemed like love, now turned loveless. You are fearful and worry being in this loveless situation, and of moving out of it as well, because of the possible aggressive reaction of your partner. Perhaps you fear being alone or don't think you have the strength, confidence and resources to make it on your own. Fear makes us cling to what we know— what is familiar, despite how bad it may feel. You say to yourself, "Being in a loveless relationship is better and safer than being alone," and so you stay. You feel trapped and unloved. Perhaps this reinforces the type of love experienced growing up, so it is love that is familiar.

If you are being loved as a possession, you have sold yourself on the illusion of what you believe love to be. A part of you does know what true love is, yet you are too afraid and feel you aren't worthy of it. So, you stay in what is not real love and remain powerless in order to continue believing this created truth. You refuse to explore what your soul knows to be true. You allow your ego and your fear to keep you stuck. The need to stay with what's known stifles healthy risk-taking, leading to continued disempowerment and unhappiness. There is an even deeper and more tragic side to possessive love. Some cultures believe that women and sometimes children are to be servants to men/husbands. The woman should just allow herself to be controlled and abused in whatever way the man sees fit. The woman should yield to his wishes and degrading behaviors for the sake of his needs and pleasure. I've counseled too many women over the years with this situation. Some beliefs could lead people to affiliate with a controlling philosophy of a group, which is unhealthy, perhaps even dangerous to the victim.

I ask Jesus for his message about love and relationship:

> *I say to you, love each other as I love you. The way to love is not through selfish pleasure and control. The core of love involves unconditional acceptance, compassion and forgiveness. It is to go beyond oneself with genuine respect, kindness and validation of yourself and one another. I invite you to align with this so that you may experience the divinity of another as yourself.*

A Way Out of the Possessive Love Trap

A danger in possessive love is that it can appear to satisfy the perceived needs and desires of each person in the dynamic. The person being possessed is being stifled and paralyzed in their growth and self-actualization. He or she believes that's how they should experience love and relationship, because that's been their past relationship experiences. The possessor will say: "It's for "my partners own good, and "they could not make it without me." Yet the reality is that the possessor is controlling their partner so that they will continue to need them. It's the person doing the possessing that is needy and can't make it without the one they say they "love". This gives the possessor a sense of power and being needed. It's not love, only a twisted concept of love. It's a way of avoiding the realization that neither party in this dynamic loves or values themselves. So, they struggle with freely and deeply loving each other.

With possessive love, it seems one person is the warden and the other is the prisoner. The reality is they are both in their own prison and powerless, each in their own way. Possessive love can happen in very subtle ways over time, as well as in very extreme forms. Possessive love creates a toxic pool of drama and gross misunderstanding of what love truly is.

Possessive love creates a fearful and out-of-control energy. This is a tragic and unfortunately, all too common form of human love. It has done much damage and created many a closed heart and thus, distorted mind. It has destroyed countless marriages and partnerships, as well as parent-child relationships. It has eroded societies and caused a few wars. Possessive love is a great deceiver—the great betrayer, and a great destroyer of the true essence of love and its divine intent. It's based on learned behaviors and repeated misunderstanding of love and relationship, which is passed on through generations. It's the refusal to look in the mirror and take responsibility for one's wounds and the feelings and beliefs around the experiences that caused the wounds.

There is much opportunity for those with possessive desires—to learn that the most significant form of love is love that brings freedom. Change and growth begins when we can recognize possessive love as dysfunction and open to the possibility that there could be another way to love. Just because this is what one experienced and learned growing up doesn't mean it is the absolute truth and the way to love. What has seemed true will not pass the test of the eternal. The human mind manufactures or creates a truth based on what it perceives through its life experiences. Many of the beliefs and behaviors we learned and made true, we often later discover were not the actual truth, i.e. the higher perspective. Humanity individually and collectively has created something they believed to be the truth. Yet, through curiosity and exploration, we challenged this to discover a higher truth. A classic example: People made a truth of the idea the world was flat. The explorer Christopher Columbus questioned and explored this and discovered a higher truth.

To test what we believe to be true we must create different perceptions and possibilities to get different outcomes. We cannot create possibilities— higher and more loving experiences for ourselves, if we choose to keep believing and acting with the same mind-set and in the same patterns of our past. Change and letting go means, to challenge our irrational, unproductive thoughts and beliefs in order to rescript those beliefs and change our behavior. Rather than being defined by our past, it's vital to begin creating a better vision, opening to possibilities in the present which offer hope for the future. Hope begins to manifest in the present, when we begin to change something in the now. More on this in the chapter on love and hope.

Our ruling mind is ever moving, either with positive or negative thoughts. Positive thoughts are inspiring and harmonious. This directs the mind in constructive pathways of choices and behaviors. Negative thoughts create distortion and irrational thinking, so the mind will be misdirected, leading to destructive channels of choices and behaviors. When we take notice of and responsibility for our perceptions and thoughts, we create the opportunity to direct these in the positive direction. We begin to open to new possibilities for growth, especially spiritually, which happens through higher thinking, as we become more authentic. The higher mind focuses more on growth and developing goals and means (will and way) to meet those goals. This change in thought pattern happens from the inside-out. This shifts our energy, our vibration and changes the pattern, resulting in a different outcome for ourselves. Like love, true empowerment and sustainable change happens from within, not by forces outside of us.

The energy of love is giving and receiving. There have been times intentionally or unintentionally that we have orchestrated the distorted version of love, i.e. being the warden or the prisoner in giving or receiving love. It's an act of self-love and true love for the partner and ourselves, to recognize and name when we are in a possessive dynamic. When we avoid taking healthy action with either side of the possessive relationship, we reinforce how much we don't love and care for ourselves.

On the spiritual level we recognize we are in an unhealthy situation and seek an opening to learn authentic self-love; and the ability to share this love in a healthy and vibrant relationship. The opportunity is always present to move from possessive love to authentic love as freedom. If you are the warden, needing control and power over another, understand that to have *power-with* another is pure love. Learning to be receptive and responsive in proactive ways, rather than being defensive and reactive, is a key to loving more deeply and intimately, cultivating a sense of freedom in your relationship.

If you are the prisoner, experiencing powerlessness and feeling trapped, rather than being passive, learn to value yourself and set healthy boundaries. Worry, insecurity and fear of the unknown keep you in unloving and unhealthy relationships. Self-love, self-worth and personal empowerment frees you. First and foremost, have a loving and accepting relationship with yourself. This is freedom. What does the higher part of you truly desire in your life?

The Empty Nest: A Form of Possessive Love

Parents have an innate, loving desire to care for and protect their children. Women especially have a natural nurturing quality and assume the role of caretaker in most families. Children have many needs, creating the energy of attachment, which is healthy and part of the chemistry of love and bonding. Attachment becomes unhealthy and possessive when we need to control, in this case the child. An unhealthy attachment is the fear of loss. A parent may struggle with various levels of letting go during the child's development. It's healthy and important to allow our children to venture into life's journey to discover their own strengths and abilities. If this development and exploration is stifled, the child matures into adolescent and adulthood carrying guilty feelings of abandoning their mother. They may struggle being their own person and making their own choices. Often the mother has a need to be needed to sustain her perceived life purpose as caretaker, so this can create the dynamic of a needy child turned needy adult. The pattern can continue for generations.

Parents are definitely needed as a child matures and steps out into the world. In this role, parents are needed in different ways over the child's lifespan. This means, as life changes and it does, parents are faced with adjusting and changing their relationship they have with their child, who is now becoming his or her own person. Resistance to accepting and making the required healthy adjustments to this change will only lead to greater struggle and heartbreak. A parent's task is to accept this natural life course for both their role as parent and for the maturing child. The ability to discern the child's natural developmental need for autonomy vs. one's own parental need to control and overly protect is important for healthy development from childhood to adulthood.

On the flip side, parents, especially fathers, can struggle with knowing how to relate and/or communicate with their children. When there's discomfort in being physically and/or emotionally present to the child, the child may feel unloved and neglected by the father. This can be especially difficult for boys maturing into manhood. They may struggle with the wound of the neglecting or absent father and feeling controlled by an overcompensating mother. So, in adulthood, the son may partner with a person who will take care of him, while being ill equipped to be loving and present to his partner and a loving and present father to his children. Again, the pattern can continue for generations.

As parents, yes, today more than ever, there are many challenges and painful situations children can and unfortunately will experience growing up. Yes, it is important and a natural expression of love to protect them and alert them to healthy ways to safeguard themselves and navigate in the world. It's also important as the child matures, to allow them to be responsible for their choices and mistakes. If the parent keeps enabling the maturing child, he or she will struggle with responsibility and confidence in how to cope and work through life challenges as an adult. Like the toddler learning to walk, if the parent keeps picking them up when they fall, the child won't learn how to pick themselves up and walk on their own. The importance of balance in terms of when to and how to intervene is more difficult than ever, given what they are exposed to today. The ability to discern, what will keep them safe vs. what do they need to learn and be responsible and accountable for can be difficult to navigate. One way to discern as a parent is to ask yourself, *"Am I intervening based on my own fear and neediness or through love, to assist in developing responsible autonomy, resilience and growth in them?"*

The parent's role is to *Just Be Love*, to be a guide, a teacher and to provide the child learning opportunities, while adjusting and maturing to your own feelings and behaviors of your empty nest experience. Parenting from neediness and enabling indicates we're functioning from the lower self. This is possessive love. To *Just Be Love* is to offer love and acceptance to your child, especially as they mature as adults, bringing peace to all involved.

The Relationship Dynamic of Love and Freedom

In understanding opposites, it's important to acknowledge everything has a feminine (yin) and a masculine (yang) principle. This is part of the basis of creation. Masculine and feminine are forms of energy like a battery that has a positive (masculine) and negative (feminine) charge. We experience the sun (masculine) during the day and the moon (feminine) at night. Neither is superior or inferior, they are meant to be complementary to create balance, live in harmony and complete the whole.

In my interactions and reflections with nature here on Earth, I've come to appreciate how mountains represent strength, the masculine, and water, i.e. rivers, lakes, oceans, etc., represent flexibility, the feminine. The masculine and feminine energies with their strength and flexibility are visible throughout the natural environment. The masculine stands as a mountain and the feminine flows like water. In nature water flows to help create mountains and is flexible as it flows to create. Mountains stand strong and tall because they embrace the waters flow. Neither the mountain nor the water resists the other, they are harmonious, each doing their part with no need to control or harm the other. They accept each other's purpose for being and allow it to be. Nature is the great teacher and example of relationships working together with love and freedom—strength, flexibility and flow, sustaining itself and living in harmony with all that is.

An important yet overlooked aspect of this dynamic is that the masculine energy seeks freedom from restraints. Men, and an increasing number of women, seek autonomy, and because they primarily use the logical side of their brain, they focus on what appears "right" and "just" to them. The feminine yearns for love, i.e. a sense of connection and intimacy. Typically, women, and a growing number of men, are using more of the creative side of their brain. When it comes to relationships, they have a greater sense of nurturing, responsibility and accountability. For relationships to be dynamic and thriving there needs to be a balance of love, flexibility, flow, strength and a level of freedom. If these qualities are out of balance between the couple, the relationship can turn possessive and in time, dysfunctional.

Humanity is beginning to understand that masculine and feminine energies are not just about gender. A woman has masculine qualities, and a man has feminine qualities. Many women today have taken on traditional male's roles and thrived, especially as mangers or CEO's, also excelling in sports and even as police and in military combat. Men have taken on more nurturing roles as Mr. Mom, healthcare nurses and flight attendants. This balance is healthy. This helps us understand why "God" is described by some as "Mother-Father God" or "Father-Mother God", either way, the term more fully acknowledges and embraces both the masculine and feminine aspects of God. God is contained in all life, so aspects of God would naturally include both feminine and masculine qualities.

The dynamic of love and freedom applies to gay and lesbian relationships as well as heterosexual relationships. I trust that gay, lesbian and transgender individuals understand my use of men and women in the description to follow and take this information in the spirit intended.

Both masculine and feminine energies desire love and freedom. It's a natural, spiritual dynamic that plays out throughout the cosmos. It is important to identify and understand the nature of these two energies and how they affect human relationships. The more we understand and accept these energies, the better our ability and willingness to interact with each other's energy. Generally, I believe, the female heart desires and moves toward love, while the male heart desires and moves more toward freedom. Obviously, there are exceptions to which partner may desire more love or freedom. The man's role is not so much to understand a woman rather to learn how to love her and to call forth her feminine essence and potential, allowing her to be the best version of herself. The women's role is not about teaching men how to love, but rather to offer men the freedom to love, and to call forth his masculine essence and potential to be the best version of himself.

Typically, if you are a woman and have a stronger feminine side, your heart's desire is for deep, trusting love. There's an openness and freedom to love and being loved. When this happens, the woman can surrender and relax into a trusting and loving heart, allowing her true essence to become alive and vibrant. She longs to be filled and nurtured with unconditional love and admiration. The feminine has a deep yearning to feel and experience love; to connect on a deep and personal level.

When a woman is denied love and nurturing, her heart can become guarded and then closed. Possessive love will surely shut down the female heart, causing her to become protective and defensive. The same goes for those feeling neglected. A wounded, closed heart can become frustrated, angry, fearful and insecure. At a deeper level, this unmet desire can create sadness and a depression within the emotional chambers of her heart that ripple through her being. For centuries the feminine has been suppressed, abused and denied equality and *power-with*. In her wounded heart there is much grief and she's learned to devalue herself, to please others at her own expense. The self has been depleted and avoided. Women must come to realize that underneath the desire to be loved by another is the basic desire to love and nurture herself. This creates true freedom and peace in her heart.

Generally, for men with a stronger masculine side, the heart and mind yearn for freedom. The true freedom men desire is to know their soul, support the good of family and community, and to fulfill their life purpose. Men, however, are often more consumed with the desire to experience release from perceived restraints of commitments and demands of work, relationship and family. A man often views love, its connection and depth, as part of a flood of obligations placed on him. With this perception, the man can feel overwhelmed and restricted by a women's desire for love and connection. For the male, it's about breaking free from the perceived pressure to perform and please his partner on many fronts. This desire for freedom is often more about needing space and time to process his feelings about the struggle and frustrations of relationship. Part of the desire for freedom and space is how a man figures out what he's feeling and how best to cope and handle the situation. To protect his heart a man will often escape and seek freedom, by going into his physical and emotional cave. In his desire for freedom he can at times become confused, distant and angered. At a deeper level, the emotional chambers of his heart can become blocked by fear, sadness and a sense of defeat. Underneath the desire for freedom is the yearning for a deeper understanding of love—it's giving and receiving.

In general, men can be consumed with the need to release, not just from the burdens of life, but also the biological need for sexual release. Moving into teenage years, both girls and boys, more commonly boys, learn that sexual release is a way of coping with tension and anxiety—a way to experience a sense of pleasure and freedom. A man learns to express love and have connection through his masculine sexual energy and desire. The man must realize that, if this sexual desire is not balanced with heart (emotional) desire, his interactions with his partner's feminine essence will become misguided. In time, his partner may begin to feel a loss of emotional connection, feeling sexually used for his own pleasure and desire for release.

When it comes to connecting, many men are isolated and struggle with knowing how to connect with other men on a deep and soulful level. They struggle connecting with women as well, especially as a partner who's loving, open and capable of ever deepening intimacy. The man's journey calls for him to see himself as worthy; to discover and become comfortable with intimacy. To live with increased self-love and comfort with deeper intimacy sets the man's soul and heart free.

Women desire emotional and spiritual connections with men as much and perhaps even more than physical connections. Generally, when this desire is misunderstood or neglected, it can leave the woman feeling sad, empty and disconnected. In the presence of the woman's desire for deeper love and connection, the man at times, feels a sense of inadequacy, failure, shame; so, he seeks escape (freedom).

A need of the female heart is the desire to know "I am loved, I am safe and free to walk through life without oppression or suppression and feel encouraged to fulfill my purpose." Consciously or unconsciously, she may feel she lacks love, especially self-love. In her desire for love she may create an unconscious barrier to truly loving herself. In this dynamic the woman can unconsciously put pressure on her beloved to shower her with the love she seeks. The more self-love she has, the better she can accept and balance the dynamic of love and freedom.

The man's desire for freedom can cause him to disregard and/or misunderstand her thoughts, feelings and especially her emotions and desire for deeper love. Women have a strong desire for their feelings to be respected. The man's struggle with recognizing and expressing his own feelings and love causes him to negate her feelings. This often is perceived by the woman as: "He doesn't love me." "He doesn't care about me." She feels rejection and sees herself as undesirable and unworthy of love. She will test her partner's love; she may close the door to his love, or she will fight for his love and attention. The man becomes confused and fearful by her fight or flight reactions. He either aggressively attacks, or he avoids, going deeper into his cave. Men, you must realize she desires connection with you, despite her behaviors. She yearns for you to break free of her barrier and not leave the door closed, but to open it and embrace her with your unconditional love. The man is asked to support and encourage the woman's love, wisdom and essence, by offering her safety, assurance, connection and support.

Ladies, realize men are fearful and insecure about love. The struggle for many men is they have been conditioned, beginning in childhood, not to feel their emotions. "Boys don't cry," "Suck it up," "Don't be a sissy." Boys to men learn that feelings and emotions aren't manly and so they avoid them, hide them. They've learned, for example, through competitive sports, their occupation and going to war, that there's no strength in feelings and being in touch with emotions—this will not give them the competitive edge and it will surely get them killed on the battlefield. Their true strength is walled off in order to win and for survival. We're asking them to be in touch with something they've learned to be afraid of and isn't acceptable in society. For many men feelings and emotions often create intense fear, discomfort and insecurity. They struggle with mixed messages and meanings of what it means to be a true warrior; a warrior that is also the lover, and a gentle giant with his partner, family and society.

The male in his quest for freedom, often feels safe and comfortable engaging the outer world of work, socialization and recreation. He wants his thoughts to be respected and struggles with being in touch with his feelings and expressing them in ways she can understand. If he is uncomfortable with feelings, emotions, and fearful of love and intimacy, he will have a difficult time spiritually and emotionally engaging with his beloved. If his energy is too fixed on freedom, he will struggle with recognizing and engaging in the passionate love the women desires. In his fear and frustration of an intimate engagement, he resorts to self-protective forms of passive or aggressive behaviors. The woman is encouraged to draw forth his positive strength, confidence and desire to know and give love. To offer him safety, assurance and freedom to be himself in his exploration and expression of intimate love to her.

The woman's desire for love can be perceived by the man as possessive love; feeling her desire for love as too intense and demanding. This can lead him to act, seeking control to gain freedom from the demands. He avoids his partner through increased involvement in his job, sports, quick sex or other created distractions. The time spent with his partner becomes minimal and superficial at best.

If the man doesn't balance the need for freedom with love, it will prevent him from experiencing self-love and the confidence of giving and accepting love. The freedom many men say they want is often fear and insecurity disguised as freedom. The fear of love and emotional connection is not really freedom but separation and a barrier to intimate love. Men are called to acknowledge this and work to reconcile this struggle, to heal and to *Just Be Love*.

From the Divine realm, the Sacred Masculine in us is being called now by the Divine Feminine in us to go deeper into our healing journey, to develop more emotional strength, which can embrace and engage the feminine mood. The sacred masculine is being asked to develop the deeper understanding and more intimate expression of love—the Christ consciousness.

The Dance of Love and Freedom

It has been said that love is just a word until someone comes along and gives it meaning. As we experience life, we have perceptions and thoughts around these experiences. Our thoughts and perceptions create emotions and feelings, which lead to our created beliefs. We then form a meaning about the experience. This meaning creates our experience and story in life. How we experience life becomes our created truth. We also create perceptions, thoughts, emotions, feelings and beliefs about love, which creates our experience and story with love. This meaning and story will either create a barrier to love or openness to it. Awareness of who we are in the exchange of these dynamic energies of our beliefs raises the frequency and elevates the soul's journey in learning to *Just Be Love*. Much of the soul's ability to mature and evolve stems from our willingness to look deeper at ourselves and how we've learned to be in relationships—the dynamic dance of love and freedom.

If both partners in an intimate relationship have a wounded self, their concept of love and freedom carries an unconscious energy, a dynamic that leads each to see the other as the threat—the enemy. Each creates a conflicting dynamic and opposing action and reaction to each other, i.e. *"if you do that, I'll do this."* For example, each person in the relationship believes they are right, and the other is wrong. One thinks and may say to the other, *"You should do it this way, because this is what I learned, and I know how this relationship/situation should work."* Often, both are right from their perspective and belief; however, somewhere in the middle is the common ground. The question is, can the couple compromise and see benefit toward obtaining the common or middle ground, between each other's perspective and truth? As each person adds his or her own life experiences, emotions and beliefs that make up their story, you can begin to see how they become emotionally triggered and guarded. Therefore, conflict and power struggles between the two will unfold.

The key is to have conscious awareness, of our need for love or freedom, and which energy reflects our heart's essence. It's important to identify and understand how the inner drive of love or freedom, could cause you to seek control or to emotionally/physically want to run from a relationship. For example, typically, women tend to the physical health and emotional well-being of their family more so than men. This is one-way women express love. When a woman suggests to her partner to have better self-care, he may see her as being overbearing. Some men would say, "She's controlling me", "nagging me." One sees it as being caring and concerned, while the other perceives it as being bossy and controlling. It is healthy and important to learn to hold (be with) the *dynamic and tension of the opposites.*

I've helped couples learn how unsafe they feel as they desire love or freedom from their partner, when we can work through that unsafe emotion to discover the experience and deeper belief around it, we create the opportunity to transform the perception of not being safe and loved; discovering the higher purpose and meaning for the experience. Recall that the true purpose of relationship is to learn about ourselves and heal our wounds within the context of being with this person. On the soul level, we are offering each other the gift of love by, speaking our truth, setting boundaries, patience, acceptance, forgiveness, etc. through our struggles with the other.

For example, the man wants more freedom, yet the woman is seeking more love and intimacy. The man feels uncomfortable and unsafe and wants to run by avoiding and being absent, especially emotionally. When he learns to be with this unsafe feeling and engage himself in his feelings and body sensations (emotions), he gains the opportunity to learn more deeply why he feels unsafe and what he is fearful of. He learns to connect with himself, thus connecting with her. Through this engagement with himself, he becomes more aware and comfortable with himself, with love and her. She then feels and experiences his love. He then is free to be with love and freely express it with more confidence.

The same is true for the woman struggling with feeling uncomfortable and unsafe with the man's freedom. As she engages in her feelings, beliefs and body emotions around freedom, she creates the opportunity to more deeply explore the fear of losing love and connection. As she heals this, she learns to be more comfortable with freedom and creates healthy space for freedom and love to coexist in her life. He feels freer to then love her, and she feels freer to experience his love. It can serve couples well to understand the energy of love and freedom within them individually and how it will unconsciously be triggered, then acted out, ultimately leading to misunderstanding, conflict and dissatisfaction in the relationship. There is no right or wrong, good or bad. It is simply just another part of the energy, truth, and dynamic of our individual essence interacting with each other. More importantly, it's about lessons being worked through and learned by individual souls through human relationships.

Life and love call us to the understanding and balance of love and freedom, both within ourselves and in relationship. Both have merit and are part of the universal pattern and dynamic that drives the cosmos. Both are healthy and of value, one dancing with the other, learning how to balance and flow with both, in a complementary and constructive practice. This is the Divine's intent. Love is freedom and freedom is love.

Superficial Love—Obsession about Possessions

It should be noted that one can have an obsessive mind-set and relationship regarding material possessions and financial gain, like they would with a partner. These individuals may head companies, communities or nations and can be consumed with selfishness, greed and entitlement, holding fear of lack and driven to have more, to be more. They are often never satisfied and become enslaved by their ego's drive and self-interest. The love of power, money and material goods is superficial love. There is no true freedom or inner happiness in the obsession for power and possessions.

A Deeper Understanding of Divine Love

Love invites us to experience God as love, the lover and beloved. The ancient Greeks had four words for love; *Agape*: which means spiritual, *Eros*: physical, *Philia*: mental and *Storge*: affection. In this section I will focus on two of these words, *Eros* love and *Agape* love.

Eros love is physical, passionate, sensual; a desire and longing for another, but in an egocentric and objectified way. With Eros love, one has the desire to be loved but with expectations attached to the one they "love." Eros love is a common way we humans love. This is the kind of love our wounded self is attracted to. I make another person my "love object" and their role is to make me happy and whole. Eros is a love of need. We yearn for love and acceptance of our parents, siblings, partner, children, etc. However, since Eros love is objectified, this creates possessive love. Eros love wants intimacy with its lover, yet neglects closeness with self and Source, so the intimacy is never authentic or deep enough to be sustainable with the partner.

Eros love is always comparing and seeking what appears to be more satisfying. It is ego-centered love since its underlying belief is that it "lacks" and "needs." Those loving in this way, truly struggle with surrendering to the Divine or another person for fear they will lose themselves, and their needs will not be met. If I am loving with Eros energy I, (unconsciously) see the Divine and others as a threat; even as the enemy—someone who will reject me, hurt me, betray me or perhaps even destroy me. This type of love is selfish, seeks instant gratification and often neglects the self. Self-love is the foundation of all relationships. With Eros love, the defense is so strong that the fear of losing love makes love conditional. It's part of the lower self's belief system of needing you to love me first, then I will believe I'm loveable, then I will love myself.

Agape love is spiritual, divine-centered love. It knows we are created in the image of God and this knowing, dissolves any concept of separation into oneness. Agape love is often misunderstood, therefore, neglected in practice. This love does not compare one to another; it simply has the awareness of God's unconditional love and acceptance. In human terms, it is God's love, living and acting through the human heart. Agape love is Omnibenevolent (*God is all loving*) and Omnipresent (*God is always present*). Agape love has no needs and makes no demands; its intent is offering understanding, acceptance and good will.

Agape love offers the truest form of intimacy. Recall that intimacy can be understood as in-to-me-see; we see each other without judgment or the need to change or control our beloved. Intimacy is acceptance and love without measure. Divine Love is true intimacy, liberating us through the energy of unconditional love and acceptance. With Agape love there is also openness to sensual experiences, yet beyond the physical. It calls to be touched spiritually, experiencing the higher mind, the light body—the soul energy of us.

With Agape love, we see others as a reflection of ourselves. Prior perceptions of an enemy dissolve. We understand that all of life is a reflection and manifestation of God. The genesis of Agape love is from the heart of the Divine and how relationships are intended to be—a reflection of the Divine love. When we open our hearts, trusting in our relationship with God, we can then love our neighbor as we love our self.

In the Gospel of Mark, Jesus offered God's greatest commandments, *"Love the Lord your God with all your heart and with all your soul and with all your mind and with all your strength. The second is this: Love your neighbor as yourself. There is no commandment greater than these."* (Mark 12:30-31, NIV). Jesus stresses in this passage the importance of loving God AND loving yourself—then you have the capacity to love your neighbor. He encourages us to love first through the heart, then the soul and then the mind, and with all of our strength. Jesus mentions the heart in this passage about love, reinforcing the importance of being heart-centered. This gives us the strength, courage and discipline needed to overcome the traps and distortions of the ego mind's version of love. Mind, body and spirit researchers have confirmed the truth of this passage, regarding this sequence of love—God, Self and Neighbor. To love the self unconditionally (free of judgment) is critical; for this is what allows us to feel worthy of God's love. When we love ourselves unconditionally, we allow ourselves to have a loving relationship with God and can then love our neighbors unconditionally as well. Whatever we do to our self, we do to our relationship with God and our relationship with others.

In Eros love; we are back in resistance and non-acceptance of "what is;" back to wanting to control and possess. This separates us from Agape love and reinforces our core spiritual wound of separation. It takes courage to be in and stay in Agape love. It takes strength to know we are love despite the struggle, injustice and heartache of life. This is what Jesus was teaching and modeling to us, especially during the last three years of his ministry here on Earth.

> *Love is not something you're in, it is something you are.*
> —David Icke

With Eros love we fall in love, believing this will create our happiness and self-worth. As humans, falling in love is akin to a quest, and when achieved, we have expectations and attachments to living "happily ever after," thus setting ourselves up for disappointment.

The Divine teaches us through our experiences that to know one aspect of life, we must experience its opposite. So, we experience Eros love, (*falling in love*) in order to experience Agape love (*rising as love*). Agape love calls us to aspire, to ascend as love, because love is who we are. This is the love call of God to the yearning soul and human heart. With Agape love we surrender our human will and ascend in the energy of Divine love, seeking higher consciousness and truth. We are invited to surrender and rise-up by easing our grip on the string (ego), so our soul (the kite) can rise to higher dimensions of love and wisdom—creating spiritual freedom. This is part of the accession process humanity is waking up to, creating a more loving and peaceful existence—heaven on Earth.

The Sufi leader and teacher Hazrat Inayat Khan said, *"When the flame of love rises, the knowledge of God unfolds of itself."* Rising as love means to go within the Divine chambers of our heart to open it to the flame of love. We connect to the love our Father-Mother God has for us and all of creation. The experience of meeting the Divine in our hearts is an act of sacred unity. When we do this, we also co-create with our Creator; joining our soul's desire to express this expanded concept of love in our physical world. To *rise as love* is to experience love through the higher self, while still living in our earthy realm. Loving with Agape love demonstrates the highest form of love that is humanly possible. Through Agape love we gain the courage to change what we can and love as God loves.

Divine Love a Model of Loving with Freedom

The measure of love is love without measure.
—St. Francis de Sales

The Divine's loving energy is like no other. Love is much more than a word or emotion; love is our very essence. The search for love ends when I have the awareness I Am love; I remember who I Am—I Am now free. Living in alignment of the Divine is to live in love and serenity; this is our greatest freedom and our soul's birthright. Out of Divine love we have this gift called free will. The Divine loves us so much that we can live our lives as we choose, while loving us in all ways and always. Wow, that's love without measure! We struggle with this free will and the call to love as God loves. Ascended Master St. Germain said, *"In order to love as God loves, we must give freedom to all parts of life, including yourself; and then we must trust as does a nesting bird in the heart of God, in the heart of goodness and mercy."* Loving with freedom requires trusting one's self and, most importantly, trusting and uniting our will with the will of God.

Many of us have a distorted view of our Creator, which means, we also have a distorted view of love. Many have learned to fear God and feel unworthy of God's favor. Because of the conditioning and beliefs instilled in us by controlling systems, (parents, government, schools, religious institutions, etc.), many believe that difficult, painful experiences are punishment by God—that God must not care about them. If we believe we are not in God's favor, we can be controlled and manipulated to do things out of fear, guilt or shame. Is this really the energy and intent of our Creator? Or is this a way of using God and religion as a means of power and control over others? To me, this is, again, another form of possessiveness, cloaked as love.

Not only do people and institutions do this, we do it to ourselves as well. We can project our own belief of being unloved and unworthy, creating evidence and truth of God not loving and caring about us. This is evidence based on our false belief about ourselves, which we make very real. We judge and/or blame God or others to justify our wounded self. This creates victim energy and experiences. I don't believe God punishes us; we do this to ourselves. We believe that God is creating our painful experience, leaving us to feel hurt and despondent. Our wounded self says: "God is punishing me." "God doesn't love me or care about me." So, I punish myself through self-defeating talk and behaviors.

Again, I ask you, is this really the energy of a loving Creator? Or is this me, making God the punishing parent? This is my ego, my shadow side distorting the energy and love of the Divine. Many who feel they are not worthy of God's love are really projecting their own negative, distorted belief about themselves. This is the art of projection, and it serves the ego well. It keeps us separated from love and from the belief of our own worthiness. There is no freedom in this, only self-imprisonment.

Our spiritual journey, as souls in human form, is to experience and learn the giving and receiving of love. We yearn to experience the freedom to be our authentic selves. Can I love and be loved, for who I am without judgment or prejudice? The ego, the human side of us, seems all too often to have opinions and expectations. With opinions and expectations comes judgment and criticism, especially with those we love and care about most. All of us desire a sense of freedom, safety and security. It's our birthright and a basic human need. We want to be accepted, appreciated and loved. When we have love and freedom, we experience joy. In the realm of the Divine we are these qualities. Love is soul-ly who we are.

An example of love as freedom is the blessed Mother Mary. As the mother of the child Yeshua/Jesus, she was confronted with the mothering instincts of protecting her child from the dangers of the world, yet deep down knowing he was not an average child. Scripture says when he was only 12, she does not know where he was, she was worried, and became frantic looking for him. She tracks him down, only to discover he was preaching in the temple. She realized in that moment who he really was and the mission he was to fulfill. Out of love, she knew she had to let him go. Mother Mary knew that for him to live his purpose, she would experience much worry and grief, including witnessing his eventual torment and death.

Pure Love Is Free of Conditions

You must love in such a way that the person you love feels free.
—Thich Nhat Hanh

The essence of love does not hurt. "What, love does not hurt?", I hear you loudly ask. Let me explain. Yes, human love can push every button, test every faith, challenge every strength, and trigger every wound and weakness. It will test every value and try every ounce of patience. However, it's not love that hurts. What hurts is our perceptions, thoughts and beliefs, which create the expectations and behaviors we choose, in the name of love. This is what causes us to feel hurt and so we are not free or at peace within. We are trapped in ego needs.

To illustrate this, a woman I worked with was understandably heartbroken as her husband of 30 years wanted a divorce. As she was expressing her pain and heartache during several sessions. One session I asked her, "You had an expectation that your marriage was to last 'till death do us part?'" She said, "yes, that was part of our vow." I suggested that when her husband asked for a divorce, her marriage expectation was now shattered. She said, "yes, that's true." I suggested; it was her expectation that was causing her pain. Yes, he's changed his mind about the marriage, and your lack of acceptance of his decision, is what's got the best of you. If you accepted the fact that he's changed his mind about being married to you, and let go of the expectation, "till death do us part" how would your life be? She thought for a moment and said, "I want to understand my pain and not be so overwhelmed by the sorrow." In time, her willingness to accept her husband's decision to end the marriage, was an act of love. More importantly, this was the loving way to set herself free.

Expectations create a closed heart and disappointed mind.
Acceptance creates an open heart and peaceful mind.

In many of our life circumstances, we don't have to like and/or agree with another's decision. But if we can't let go of our expectation— "the conditions" that life be a certain way and accept their decision; we will be controlled and defined by the other's choice and remain unhappy. Do you want others to have this power over you?

Agape love is an invitation to freedom and inner peace. Freedom and inner peace come through an open heart and a mind that is quiet; free of expectations, unhealthy attachments and misidentifications. This way of love is the intent of God. Loving with freedom means letting go, surrendering to the higher divine will. Like when we drive our car, take a flight on an airplane, or getting married, we may feel some fear, uncertainty or anxiety. Yet we let go and trust that we will have a pleasant ride or fulfilling marriage. There is nothing to give in to or to give up; there is nothing to lose. When we love as God loves—with freedom, we have no sense of lack, for we recognize we have all we need. Surrendering in total love and trust, the Divine's love and guidance paves our path to liberation—the release of our worry or pain makes room for the experience of true freedom and peace, knowing we are already whole and complete.

We are on a journey to higher consciousness. Higher awareness arrives by creating space within. Space is created by releasing our misperceptions and false identity, so awareness can arise. This creates openness and allows for loving and worthy possibilities to unfold.

Loving without conditions allows space—space to experience, to create, expand and renew as a spiritual being in human form. The act of non-attachment allows room for experiencing the fullness and freedom of God's love. Love is authentic when it offers freedom. Let go of expectations about others. Love them and love yourself enough to be your authentic self. Loving without conditions is giving and receiving in sacredness. We then become fearless, seeing only opportunity and possibilities. There is no need for paybacks or the game of "you owe me." Loving without conditions means no strings. If I attach conditions to love, it is not pure and authentic love. An unhealthy attachment to someone is based on fear of loss. Divine love is infinite—so nothing is lost. Personal freedom is the precursor to loving with freedom. When we have self-love, we can remain authentic in how we express ourselves, speaking and living our truth without self-judgment or judgment, restriction or oppression from others.

Personal freedom allows us to pursue our passions and purpose; to be the best version of our self. We have greater ability to create and co-create with

Source. Personal freedom offers a kind of love that confronts and challenges us, calling us to awareness and growth, without condemning or shaming us. Loving with freedom, whether for self or others always has our highest good in mind. It propels the heart and mind to higher consciousness. This love is grounded in truth, acceptance and compassion. When we love this way, we are willing to look at our self, admit our short comings, and work to correct our limitations. We do not project or reject. We do no harm to our self or others. We understand and live in the oneness of love as you are me and I am you.

In one of the oldest of Chinese texts, The I-Ching, the book of changes, it says, *"One must know when to separate and when to unite."* A part of love in relationships knows when to work at keeping the love alive and when it's time to let go. I love myself and you enough, to set us both free. Many people don't put much effort into helping a relationship thrive, while others stay in relationship when damage is done, and love is gone. Many stay in relationship more for a false sense of security and comfort. Much grief and pain are created by unhealthy attachments to relationships.

One of life's greatest challenges involves a crisis in intimate relationships and understanding when it's time to stay in or leave the relationship. From the higher perspective, stepping away from an unhealthy, unloving relationship is a step forward. Inner peace comes from living our higher truth, doing what is best for us—what will make us happy.

When relationships and/or situations change, and they do, we are confronted with resisting or accepting the change. The relationship or situation now isn't what it was yesterday, due to death, affair, abuse, etc. When we resist the inner knowing that the relationship has changed, we are not accepting the "what is"; therefore, there will be increased grief and pain. The longer we attach to "what was," rather than "what is," the more likely we turn pain into suffering. There can be no freedom under these circumstances.

Adapting to change requires the process of *reorienting* one's perception, belief and attitude to the relationship as it was, as it can be now and into the future. The process of reorientation is like rebooting a computer to start fresh and renewed. In rebooting there is no resistance, no hanging on to what was. It's about starting fresh. True acceptance of "what is" is free of resistance and holding on to what was. It frees us from prolonged pain and suffering. To let go is to free oneself of the attachment, the energy and dynamic of fear of loss. For many, the fear of loss means the fear of losing control, the loss of certainty and security. Acceptance opens the inner door to create a healthy way to adapt to a change in relationship.

Our struggle toward personal freedom and spiritual growth has to do with the resistance to change. Our resistance to change is a form of possessive love. We want the person and/or situation back on our terms. Moving through physical, emotional or spiritual pain is a process. The degree and time I choose to resist, hanging onto what no longer is and what no longer serves me, is part of the grief process, yet this resistance and non-acceptance only prolongs the reorientation process and healing. When we resist the reality of a change, we are resisting what life has handed us in that moment. When we resist life, pain will surely be at our doorstep. Some life experiences will create joy and abundance; some will create pain and sorrow. Resisting the pain and hurt, wanting to take the quick and easy way out, wanting life to go back to the way it was before the painful event, is not realistic. Inner peace arrives, when we embrace our feelings and the emotions deep within; working through our pain to come to the place of acceptance and reorientation.

Humans struggle with the concept of impermanence; the fact that nothing stays the same. Life is all about change; the Creator's infinite universe is always changing; i.e. it's always creating, expanding and renewing. When we resist, refusing to accept change, we are resisting life, saying no to life, and the Divine process. We can become increasingly unhappy, and out of touch with our feelings and behaviors and to the process of change. The willingness to engage in the process of reorientation (rebooting), along with use of the four R's, *Recognize, Reconcile, Release* and *Reframe*, is saying "Yes" to life, and embracing change and the full range of the human experience toward spiritual growth.

All human relationships will change, even the relationship with our self, ultimately by physical transition. When I change the way, I see and feel about the relationship I had with a person, I begin to heal my pain and ease my struggle. We each choose to do this in our own way, on our own time frame, according to our own free will.

One of the most significant and life altering changes we experience is the physical death of a loved one. Death is nothing more than passing on from the physical energy of form; back to pure formless energy. Our 3rd dimensional senses have a hard time with this concept of energy transformation. We believe the person is permanently gone from our world. Our grief and loss are about wanting to again experience the person in physical form, because that's what our perception and reality have known them to be. Life, however, continues as it changes to a different form. Yes, life in the physical body is now gone, however, the energy of the soul is not gone; it has just changed, "passing on" from the energy of the temporary physical form to the eternal; the soul, formless self. The term "passing on" reinforces the concept that life as we know it is impermanent. What we call death is really transition, a moving forward—a progression to an energy state of being that is beyond our lower mind's limited perception.

In my own journey with death of loved ones, I've experienced their formless energy and communication in captivating ways. I have this photo of a wooded area that was a favorite spot of a former girlfriend, Deb, who died suddenly. A few weeks after her death, I looked at the photo and there was a faint image of a face that wasn't there prior to her death. That image remains in that photo over 10 years later and is a reminder to me and those I share it with that the soul is real and formless eternal energy.

During a time in my life, I was deciding to make a major career change. I heard the voice of my father, as if he was right next to me, say, like he would have said it, "Go for it." Immediately after hearing his voice, I felt much calm and confidence come over me and the career decision was easily and effectively made. I have learned the importance and value of changing my perception of death. Death is not to be feared; it is an illusory concept of our ego. Yes, it is natural to experience grief and the pain of loss and is not to be denied or quickly smoothed over. Our task to is feel the feelings, relish in the memories, and most importantly, come to a place of acceptance and adapt to the soul's journey of transition to a higher state of being. Our pain and sorrow become less; we can then experience the energy of the person as they truly are, a formless being who is still loving and connecting with us from the other side. Now that's love, and that's freedom.

This newfound awareness offers us the opportunity for greater peace throughout the grieving process. I have heard numerous accounts from others who have lost a loved one, how they have come to accept the loss of their physical presence and experienced encounters with their loved ones through the formless realm. This is a form of divine love, based on the person's willingness to view the experience from a higher perspective and reorient the human relationship they once had to the relationship their souls have now. This is love and renewed freedom as the Divine intends.

If we are willing and trusting, we can begin to experience those who have transitioned, as energetic beings beyond time and space, experiencing their presence in an energetic way through our true essence as energetic beings. Death is the great teacher of understanding our true essence. It's all about energy. Einstein said, *"All that really matters is energy."* The process of birth and death are identical. They are just a change in energy states. Conception and birth are the transition of soul energy to physical form, which now temporarily houses aspects of the soul. Physical death is the transition back to formless soul energy (i.e. our true, multidimensional self). When we can accept this, we then realize the deceased ones haven't left; they have just taken on a different form of being, a different expression of energy as formless, higher vibration and light.

Research with people who have had a near death experiences (NDE) show that afterwards they begin to live life more devoted to love and selflessness. They experience a spiritual transformation demonstrated by the insights gained through the NDE and experience of the multidimensional self (aspects of the self that dwell beyond the physical world). This teaches us much more about the eternal, energetic parts of us that are always present both in the form and formless states. When we acknowledge and accept this, we begin to change our relationship with those who passed on, with this world and the universe.

The above concept of change to the relationship can be applied to any type of change we may be experiencing. We have many types of relationships in our seen and unseen worlds. Viewing change through the eternal lens will naturally impact all our relationships. Our life becomes a spiritual experience, not just a human one. True freedom and wisdom are found by loving, accepting and moving through change, from the higher perspective toward learning the intended lesson for the soul. *Are you in resistance and non-acceptance to the changes in your life? Who do you become when you resist and don't accept the change? What would happen if you were to be more open and accepting of changes? Who would you be if you realized that the change happens to create greater possibilities and awareness for you?*

I had a client a few years back who had lost her husband to natural causes and two years later she lost her son to a tragic car accident. Her grief work was quite profound, and it was a gift to assist her and witness her journey. One particular session, after several months of intense work, she said to me with much awareness and confidence. *"You know David, I lost my husband and then I lost my son, but now I've found myself."* I smiled, went over to where she was sitting and gave her a hug and said, *"You are such a blessing and loving soul, you have come home. Your husband, son, I, and the universe celebrate your growth and homecoming."*

Love allows openness. It transforms us with greater awareness of the cycles and the rhythms of the universe. It offers us greater insight into God's love.

Faith, like freedom, is about trusting and surrendering without expectations to the greater knowing and wisdom within ourselves and with the universe. We create a more open alignment with the Divine mystery and intelligence. Soulful and spiritual surrender means trusting and letting go without an attachment to an outcome. We become a conduit for the ways of the higher realm to flow through us. We are then in the energy of allowing—allowing the universe to provide for our highest and greatest good.

What the ego thinks we need, and what our soul and the Divine know we need are not the same. Ego needs are often based in fear, protection and survival, while the soul desires are based in love, vitality and growth. By being a STAR: *Surrendering, Trusting,* and *Allowing*, we then open up to *Receiving* what the Divine and our soul truly intends for us to experience and know.

Loving with freedom means I see you as equal; I seek to have power-with you. I desire to assist you in being the best possible version of yourself. I choose to walk with you in mutual and cooperative ways. We have the freedom of non-judgment and non-attachment; in that I do not lose my sense of me or my wholeness in your presence. Whatever I surrender to or set free in life will bring me greater awareness and meaning for my soul's journey. Loving with freedom allows for differences, is tolerant and patience, making space for creativity and growth. There is no need for judgment or comparison for I see you in me and me in you.

When we love with freedom, we view mistakes as opportunities to learn and grow. There is freedom in true understanding and entering the beloved's world as best as one can, with acceptance, without needing to fix it—knowing I can never truly understand another's experience, feelings and struggles. I can only witness their life course while they're in my presence. I choose only to be responsible for my own thoughts, perceptions, feelings, beliefs and behaviors. I accept the other for who they are, offering loving kindness, seeing them as one who is walking this life's journey as best, they know. I have no need to alter their path for my benefit alone. I offer them the freedom, through acceptance and compassion. Loving with freedom comes from the soul-heart which seeks to know and be present to the beloved's soul and heart, valuing their wisdom and honoring their spirit.

Self-Love creates freedom. When we love ourselves, we see our value and worth. Freedom is our birthright and a law of nature. We can choose to step away from relationships and/or interactions that are not healthy for us. There are times when saying "no" to someone is saying "yes" to our self and our soul growth. We can be grateful to the other person for providing us the experience and opportunity to give ourselves the "gift" of loving ourselves enough to step away from what no longer serves us. We see the lesson and take steps to empower our self and grow from the experience. This is love from the other person's soul to ours. *Do you see how this perspective offers empowerment and freedom? Do you see the love and opportunity for growth in this? Do you also notice the challenge in getting to the place of making this decision for ourselves?* It is the desire of the universe, that we remember who we really are as we progress on our soul journey. For us to know love and light, we must experience darkness and struggle. They are opposites on the continuum of life. One is a part of the other; both are lessons on love and freedom.

Divine laws are formed by the energy and intention of love and freedom. To live with this sense of personal freedom within, and express it outwardly, is part of our purpose for being here and part of our soul's journey. If you desire freedom, resolve your belief in separation and unworthiness. Reconcile your unhealthy attachments and fears of loss. Release your false belief and misidentifications and learn to understand and reconcile the dualities of life. Allow yourself to be the observer as you participate in your experiences. Cultivate the qualities of understanding, acceptance, gratitude, compassion and forgiveness. Live more from your heart—that's where you find your truth.

I close this section with a poem I wrote titled, *Can You.*

Can You

Can you love instead of fear?
Can you love midst life's uncertainty?
Can you love what is your unknown?
Can you love when it hurts?
Can you love through your tears, when others don't seem to care?
Can you love when it seems unfair?
Can you love in your despair?
Can you love when it's not fun and want to run?
Can you love the parts you've hidden;
the ones you think aren't there with you?
Can you love the one who you see in the mirror?
Can you love others when they don't love you back?
Can you love those who don't love themselves?
Can you Just Be Love?

12

Love and Loneliness

The most terrible poverty is loneliness, and the feeling of being unloved. —Mother Teresa

There is a contributing factor to many illnesses today, and this factor is one you would likely overlook. It gets little attention, yet it is impacting our lives in very subtle, yet tragic ways. I believe a major contributing factor to illness is loneliness—social isolation. A disconnect with ourselves and each other creates quiet, yet dangerous traits of social divide and discontent. It appears that many people today avoid connecting with themselves, each other and their Source at a deeper level. The consequences are becoming more apparent and critical for not only ourselves but our planet as well.

In my own contemplation, I've concluded that the main reason for one's feelings of loneliness is spiritual disconnect, the loss of faith and belief in a power greater than one's self. This disconnection manifests itself in the unwillingness and/or distraction to connect with Source and others to co-create, to self-actualize and make the world a better place. This results in seeing the world and life with the perception of fear and separation. I believe spiritual disconnection and loneliness are also the result of being defined by the self-created story we tell ourselves and to others.

Spiritual disconnect also creates a lack of awareness and the willingness to explore and ultimately answer these fundamental spiritual questions: *Who Am I? — Why am I here?* When we feel no relationship with Source, these two questions seem to have little meaning. Without the recognition that we come from love and the infinite Source of the universe, we can neglect a meaningful sense of purpose or direction in life, and the awareness of the spirit within us; which is due to a low self-esteem. The sacredness of the person and their life purpose is unclaimed. There are numerous factors that contribute to a person's spiritual disconnect and resulting loss of purpose and life direction.

Loneliness and Our Well-Being

On physical, mental, emotional, social and spiritual levels we are designed to connect with each other. Relating is part of our essence as a human system. Research indicates that loneliness has become a social epidemic. It's affecting our health and sense of well-being, leaving many to feel alone, deprived and powerless.

A study by Julianne Holt-Lunstad, PhD, and Timothy Smith, PhD, of Brigham Young University, examining the relationship between health and human interaction, brought startling results. People with non-active social lives were fifty percent more likely to die sooner than their socially active counterparts. Holt-Lunstad and Smith concluded that reduced levels of social interaction have the same adverse health effects as smoking fifteen cigarettes per day. The effects of social isolation are worse than non-activity or obesity. Research by doctoral student Sarah Perssman, and Health Psychologist Sheldon Cohen, PhD, of Carnegie Mellon University of Pittsburgh, points out that the more social connections we have, the stronger our immune system and the greater the ability to fight infection. Researchers are finding that the stress linked to social isolation and low social support creates a host of damaging reactions within the body and weakens the immune system, making people more susceptible to disease. The loneliness factor creates a potential link to diseases such as depression, cancer and heart disease. Researchers say that being alone and feeling lonely increases your chances of an early death by nearly 30 percent. We know an infant can die from lack of physical and emotional contact. Having a face-to-face social support network is an important coping skill to combat life stressors, as well as providing a feeling of connection and belonging in the world.

Results Speak for Themselves

Research by the United Nations and other group's shows that the happiest and healthiest people on the planet are those living in areas where there is a strong sense of community, cooperation and fellowship. The Scandinavian countries of Denmark, Finland, Iceland, Norway and Sweden consistently are in the top fifteen countries in terms of happiness (life satisfaction), human development and prosperity. Iceland, with short summers and darkness nearly half the year, has among the highest divorce rates and highest birth rates in the world. Yet Icelanders have strong family, social and community support systems. Thus, there is rarely a perceived crisis, even if a family is going through a divorce, death or job loss. The people of Iceland and the other Scandinavian countries know they will be there for each other, even with the possible panic or emotional melt down of the stressful situation. These support systems help reduce the emotional severity of the difficult experience. The results of the 2018 Legatum Prosperity Index study of 149 nations comprising 96 percent of the world's population, based on nine categories of prosperity: Economic Quality, Business Environment, Governance, Personal Freedom, Social Capital, Safety and Security, Education, Health and Natural Environment. The study found that the Scandinavian countries were in the top fifteen. Norway, Finland, Denmark and Sweden were, one, three, five and six respectively.

With the world population currently seven billion and rising, how can it be that we have a problem with loneliness and social isolation? We can connect with others faster and easier than ever before, thanks to technology and social media. If you wanted to meet up with someone on the other side of your world, you could connect with them in person within twenty-four hours or less, and you could connect with them instantly by the Internet or iPhone.

I heard it said years ago that in this modern era, a major contributor to loneliness in the United States was the attached garage. With this feature, we can go right from our car and into our home without seeing or conversing with our neighbor. We can, and literally do, shut the door on our neighbor and the rest of the world. Another home modification that created further isolation was the development of the back deck. We went from the front porch, which involved seeing and conversing with people, to moving to the back deck of the house, again turning our back on our neighbor and the world. For many their homes have become a barrier to interacting with others, like having a moat around them for privacy, safety and unfortunately further isolation.

We may be connected to the electronic social media networks, the mechanical and technological world, but we seem to be more disconnected on a personal and collective level. Humans are, after all, a living energy system, not a machine. We have computers with Skype, iPhones with text and face time. We can see each other on a screen and hear our voices on the phone, letting a machine do the interacting between us. Yes, it's an incredible advancement in communication technology; yet, can you see how, over time, this can make us impersonal socially and disconnected? Communication becomes more difficult, and misunderstandings occur more frequently. Why? Because over 50 percent of communication is through body language. When we don't interact face to face, real communication is diminished and can lose depth and meaning; we have a decreased sense of understanding and connection. With email, text or social media, mistakes are made by typos, sending messages before edited or fully completed. Messages mistakenly sent to wrong people, or you message something impulsively that blows up in your face, causing a loss of job or relationship, etc.

All this creates increased misunderstanding, frustration and isolation. This may be a downside to technology and social media. However, the upside of this miscommunication is that it offers us the opportunity to be more understanding, patient and forgiving in our correspondence, while using these technological pathways. As the need for speed and instant gratification increases, patience and understanding are more tested and more important. Technology and social media forms can cause frustration and irritation to mount, resulting in greater acting out, which contributes to isolation not just in the United States, but in societies around the world. Yes, loneliness and social isolation contribute to many problems on the physical, emotional, social, mental and spiritual levels. What makes this so? Could it be related to our fear and the lack of trust in our fellow humans?

Could it be that our unresolved traumas, grief and shame cause us to be more fearful, protective and reactive? Could it be related to the fast pace which we subject ourselves to? Could it be the repeated media projection of negativity and violence making us anxious, fearful and wanting to hide? Could it be that the economic disparity and the stress to obtain financial security is creating greater discord and disconnect between us? Bullying can now be done over the phone, by text, or the Internet; this keeps many on guard and fearful of others. Now we can be hurt by others, and our identity can be taken in cyber space, as it can happen in physical space. Perhaps we are experiencing the effects of unease, fear and mistrust more than we realize. These emotions, and the experiences that create them, cause us to feel rejected, abandoned or betrayed—so we withdraw and isolate.

Here Comes the Judge

M any of us have become so emotionally and spiritually beat down and depleted by expectations, demands and judgments from outside of us and from our inner critic/judge that we just want to be left alone. Recall, judgment is withholding love. When we judge others or ourselves, we are blocking the energy of unconditional love and acceptance, so we don't feel safe and free in the interaction. To protect ourselves, we connect in superficial ways. Because I am fearful that you won't accept or appreciate me for who I really am, I prevent you from seeing the real me. On a deeper level I believe you won't love me. Since I don't feel loved and valued, I might begin to believe I'm not loved or valued by God either. Spiritual disconnection becomes my created reality.

Perhaps our expectations of each other are too high or too rigid. Expectations can lead to disappointment. When we need each other to be a certain way, we are judging. If we believe we are being judged, we can take this as, "we don't measure up," which can lead to insecurity and avoidance. Who wants to interact and socialize in an arena of high expectations and judgment?

Many television shows depict situations where a person looks good at the expense of others—causing humiliation. This can be perceived as a form of bullying. The agenda of a bully is to physically and/or emotionally intimidate others, so the bully looks good. Frequent exposure to these types of shows could give the viewer a perception that the world is unfriendly. It could cause some to become the bully in order to feel powerful, or cause isolation in order to feel protected.

Spending several hours, a day watching television or surfing the internet creates sensory overload to the neuropathways of the brain. This barrage of stimulation and information affects our mind and thus, overwhelms the body. This leads to increased mental and physical stress, anxiety, exhaustion, depression, unhappiness and social isolation. We become overwhelmed by the flood of information. To protect ourselves from drowning in a sea of information and negativity, we become mentally, emotionally cold, and physically, socially and spiritually numb.

More people are becoming consumers of information; contributing to a pattern of passivity and detachment, and a belief that they are insignificant and unable to make a difference. This type of attitude and behavior does impact the world, by creating a negative and disempowering difference.

Love and connection are transforming. The Divine desires us to be transformers rather than just consumers. A transformer is a person who is mindful, accepting, caring, connected, vibrant and involved. One who realizes they can and do make a positive difference through their higher awareness, clear direction and life affirming connection with Source and others.

The Lost Art of Listening

Deep listening is miraculous for both listener and speaker. When someone receives us with an open heart, is non-judging, intensely interested listening, our spirits expand. —Sue Patton Thoele

We live in a world of instant communication and instant service, which creates our need for instant gratification. Patience and waiting are considered unacceptable and have become lost arts. The result of this is less tolerance for others, even ourselves. To be seen and heard is to feel significant. To be seen and heard without judgment is love without measure. In general, we seem pre-occupied with a stronger need to express ourselves—to be heard more than to listen. The act of listening is an art and is a powerful expression of love and affirmation for the person to whom we listen. When someone truly and deeply listens, it says I care about you and want to understand you. When listened to, we feel valued, worthy of attention and connected. When we aren't heard, we feel judged, rejected, unimportant and disconnected, causing us to become more protective and defensive of our fragile inner self. We feel a need to insulate and isolate—creating loneliness.

Introvert and Extrovert

In the context of the soul and its human personality there is a law of polarity, a law of opposites, to which a human adheres. These are core aspects of our personalities, two of which are introvert and extrovert. These personality types display different energies. Extroverted people are energized by social interactions. They are outgoing, outspoken and concerned with what's going on in the outer world. They have a strong need to be seen and heard. Introverts, by contrast, are quiet, reflective and focused more on the inner world. For the introvert, the need to be seen and heard is less critical than with an extrovert. Extroverts are energized by social interactions and attention, whereas introverts are often taxed by the same social engagement. They need alone time to recharge. In this continuum, there are people who exhibit a mix of both extrovert and introvert traits called *"ambiverts."* These individuals can mingle in introverted and extroverted ways; they are flexible and comfortable floating in the middle range of the continuum.

Technology and social networking create a helpful vehicle for introverts to communicate with greater ease and more comfort. However, on the downside, it can create a buffer for introverts, causing them to become more introverted, thus connected in passive and superficial ways. They can interact with others without leaving their home or needing to be seen. The internet's social networking does create opportunities to develop genuine friends in ways that feel safe, and help the introvert feel secure and good about themselves. On the other end of the continuum, extroverts are energized by the increased ease of access to interactions through social networking. They can get more attention, even if it's superficial attention; developing an abundance of "friends" on sites like Facebook, Twitter or Instagram. Even if most of these "friends" aren't really friends, it makes the extrovert feel good, because they call them "my friend." This superficial access to "friends" can be an obsession for someone seeking attention.

With mindful and loving intent, social networking does offer the opportunity for our conversations to be personal, with depth and more purposeful, offering a sense of connection, being heard and valued. The question is: Through these forms of social networking to which we give meaning and importance to, are we really listening to each other and connecting? Or are these forms of social interaction creating superficial ways of truly connecting, being heard and appreciated?

Driven to Distraction

There is another dynamic happening that contributes to loneliness—the explosion and abundance of technology—the way we connect, communicate and entertain ourselves. Advances in technology, have in one sense been very helpful, but the more we're driven to connect through computers and iPhones, we lose a sense of personal understanding, of our need for each other and for real, genuine human connection. These distractions have increasingly created superficial connections with each other and ultimately with the Divine.

Many of us have become obsessed with different media forms. We say we are only going to watch thirty minutes of TV or be on the Internet for fifteen minutes, and the next thing we know, two hours have passed. I can remember thirty years ago hearing that because of technology we would experience more productive use of our time, and actually have an abundance of free time. The opposite seems true now. People are working harder, for longer hours and spending more time commuting, with little time or energy to relax and enjoy. Our work standards are geared to getting ahead professionally and keeping our employer and the stockholders happy. This creates greater employee dissatisfaction and burnout, causing people to have less time, energy and motivation to interact with each other. Sadly, and unfortunately, technology and the need for speedy customer service etc., has put some out of business, especially those with a small family business.

Recent studies tell us that our iPhones, computers and video games are subtle yet dangerous obsessions, leading to addictions for some adults and especially for our youth. Studies show that when person's iPhone or laptop is taken away for three or four days, the subject had withdrawal symptoms similar to someone who has a gambling or drug addiction. Without the use of the phone or the Internet, the subject became anxious, easily agitated and depressed. Many people obsessed with cell phone or Internet use are trying to escape loneliness and boredom. Yet, it's making them more isolated and spiritually empty. The rate of auto accidents due to cell phone use while driving has increased to such an alarming rate, that most states have made it illegal to text or talk while driving. We are becoming slaves to our created technology and social media. Some experts on technology and intelligence are warning us now on the dangers of artificial intelligence. If we are not mindful, some of our man-made technologies could end up controlling—even destroying humanity.

Our minds naturally wander. We experience many distractions as part of being human. However, with the over stimulation brought on by technology, our minds are drifting more frequently, so we become even more distracted. The mind directs the body to go and go, so we do and do, to have more and more. In this accelerated pace of going, doing and having, are we happy and fulfilled? We tend to be more worn out, distracted, impatient and unhappy. All this seems to be causing us to be more driven, overloaded and overwhelmed, taking us out of the natural rhythm of a loving and peaceful heart and a relaxed and conscious mind.

Our children's exposure to and use of technology at an earlier age creates an opportunity for them to learn much more at a faster pace. They are also more potentially driven to distraction in ways that impact their social interaction and ability to effectively cope with stress. The teaching of mindfulness meditation and living, especially in elementary and Junior high schools, is increasing throughout the United States and worldwide. Mindfulness is one way to help bring awareness and curb the wandering, distracted mind, bringing our mind back to the present. It also teaches students more peaceful interactions, through acceptance and loving kindness to others and themselves. Because of the pace of advancing technology and information overload, children especially need to learn how to calm the mind to prevent over stimulation and undue stress to their system.

Technology and social media can cause us to be physically passive, occupying our minds and our time in such a way that our bodies move less. This more passive lifestyle can isolate us as well. If we are glued to Facebook, Xbox or PlayStation, we're not in a fitness gym or on walking paths, which would increase the opportunity and likelihood of active social interaction. Unfortunately, the trend seen now in the gym or at a park is to put the headphones on, avoiding the opportunity for genuine social contact. As we are more driven to distraction, we trade connection and oneness for the security of isolation.

We trade love for fear, empowerment and community for powerlessness and dependency, hope for despair. We trade understanding, acceptance, compassion and forgiveness for greed, resentment, anger and violence. We trade a quiet mind, a peaceful and giving heart, for a racing, distracted mind, a wounded, closed heart, an anxious body and a neglected soul. Reality is, the more we strive for safety and security the more unsafe and insecure we become. Notice the state of the world today. It's a reflection of how unsafe, insecure, and how stricken with sadness and shame we feel deep in our psyche. It reflects how unloved and unaccepted we feel in many of our relationships. This creates a world, a neighborhood and even a family that feels less safe. We have become more psychologically wounded and fearful.

Technology and Oneness

Please don't get me wrong. Technology, social media and networking have done wonders for us in terms of getting things done faster and making it much easier to converse with each other. Today, we have greater access to information on many topics, from health, well-being, and finance, to science, world affairs, spiritually, and more. We have web conferencing and an array of webinars to participate in through the internet. There are eBooks to read, and many high schools and colleges offer classes through eLearning. We can even find a dating partner, join a chat room, or meetup group though the web. The World Wide Web offers information, perspectives and inspiration from around the world and beyond. As mentioned earlier, it also provides opportunities to be more patient, flexible, accepting and forgiving as we navigate technology. It offers opportunities to express our creativity, triumphs and celebrate our joyous and humorous moments. Because of technology, jobs are created. We can save natural resources by *"going green"*, paying our bills online, using less paper, or shopping online, using less fuel. Even this book can be a paperless read as an eBook on your laptop or iPad. Technology, social media and networking provide numerous opportunities and benefits for sure.

Advances in technology are paralleling the evolutionary development of humanity, meaning our technological advances are increasing as our level of consciousness and spiritual maturity increases. It is critical that we be mindful of our intent when using technology, not to let power, greed and reckless behavior undermine its benefits. As we become more spiritually aware of being connected with all of life, technology and social media provide greater opportunities for broader connections to all that impacts our life. I believe the World Wide Web was divinely inspired, providing an endless web of support, and a sense of connectedness and community. All strands of the web are connected and reflect infinite intelligence.

Sadly, but important to note, is the reality that some choose to use this technology for negative purposes; to hack others, send a virus, create a scam, or to cyber-bully. Those who choose to use their creativity and intelligence to attack people through cyberspace are exposing the "invisible perpetrator." It indicates how much they are hurting and struggling with loving themselves and shows their lack of spiritual connection. Their lack of spiritual connection leads to their struggle with positive human connection. Remember, we hurt others because we are hurting. They offer the rest of us the opportunity to express compassion for their struggles. Perhaps by offering them loving and forgiving thoughts, we will reach them through the divine highway even as they disrupt the cyber highways.

Everything invented has energy and the potential for constructive or destructive use, depending on the user's intention. All that makes up our information age is no different. When we use technology to enrich our lives socially, mentally, emotionally, physically and spiritually, we energetically connect with all that is good and possible. We are then in alignment with kindred souls, the energy of Mother Earth and the Universal Source. We experience oneness—a web of connectivity. Using the technological web as a loving information tool, we more fully connect to the sacred web of oneness— providing opportunities for us to *Just Be Love.*

In the Moment

L ife truly happens in the moment. Joy and relating to others happen in this moment. We seem preoccupied with capturing moments on our phones, cameras and videos in order to savor this moment in the future. We post it on Facebook and other sites for family and friends to get a sense of our experience in that moment. It is an effective and powerful way of connecting and sharing with others our experiences and memories. I enjoy taking photos of my travels, experiences in nature, of sunsets, animals, mountains, streams and interesting looking trees. Through these moments, and the beautiful experiences they create for me, I've come to realize how the use of a camera can easily take me out of the moment. In my "wanting" to take the photo in order to have a picture for the future, I deprive myself of truly experiencing the present. I lose the essence of what is unfolding in the moment. I disrupt my present experience for the future. Can you relate? How innocent it is, yet how it can take us out of the joy and sacredness of the moment. This common distraction contributes to our spiritual disconnection. Ponder the beauty, joy and sacredness that are missed. Is it worth sacrificing "being in" the present in order to "have it" for the future? In this moment, consider how many obligations and things distract you from being in the moment—distract you from love and living a more sacred life.

There Is a Time and a Season for All Things

The above title paraphrases a Bible passage. It seems that there is a time and season (a purpose) for all things in this infinite universe we are part of. Loneliness would be no exception. A funny thing about loneliness—it can be paradoxical. Many people are lonely, yet they struggle with being alone in reflective and meaningful spiritual solitude. They struggle with understanding and accepting others; perhaps because they have avoided the opportunity to be with themselves, allowing for more personal reflection and acceptance. If I have lost the desire to love and accept myself, I will struggle with loving and accepting you as well. I will distract myself in many superficial ways, eliminating the opportunity for personal time.

In our hectic and fast paced world, there is value in slowing down and making time for solitude. This is an act of self-love and self-care. Solitude quiets and refreshes the body, mind and soul. It energizes the body and can clarify our mind in purpose and commitment to ourselves and our world. The key is *to learn to be alone, yet not be lonely*; to balance alone time with fellowship time. This is a noble and beneficial endeavor. Many spiritual teachers stress the importance of this balance. When we can be alone and not be lonely, we anchor to self-love and the ability to have a meaningful relationship with our self. We have learned to be our own best friend; to be with our feelings and discover what they're telling us. We've made peace with our ego and our shadow. We no longer need to hide with the mask of pretending. We have become comfortable and alive again in our own skin. Our so-called imperfections melt away into compassion for the all of us. We have a sense of wholeness and completion that we've come full circle, as our awareness of the love that we come from allows us to claim the love that we are.

The paradox of human relationships is this: *In relationship we learn to be alone. In our aloneness, we learn to be in relationship.*

All our relationships, as we know them on the human level, will eventually end by physical transition. It is in our aloneness that we learn to have a relationship with the person we spend our entire life with—our self. When we are comfortable being with ourselves, we can be more present and open with others and set healthy boundaries. In the spiritual dimensions, loneliness does not exist. Remember, love includes—fear excludes.

Do You Need to Be Needed?

The needier we are, the more we may struggle with loneliness. To be needy is to rely on others to fill an inner void. We end up helping others not just to help them but, more importantly, to fulfill our need to be needed and feel significant. If I am offering loving kindness and assisting others in the hope, they'll treat me the same, I am creating conditions on my love and my giving. When I focus on others, I can be doing so to avoid looking within, seeing the empty place I hoped others would fill; that part of me that says, "I'm not lovable" and "I'm not enough." When I do this, I do not love my neighbor as myself. I'm avoiding myself by focusing on my neighbor. This only perpetuates the cycle of dependency and loneliness. My happiness and needs are rarely satisfied, since I've made others responsible for them. There is no contentment and inner peace in this. There is no genuine connection with my neighbor or myself.

Loving myself in healthy ways opens me up to connect with others. When I let go of some of the distractions and take time to go within and connect to the love I am, I return to the one inside who truly needs me. In connecting with and knowing the deeper self, we will naturally desire to connect with and know our neighbors.

Loneliness Looks Down. To Love: Look Within, Up and Around

The universe exists through inner connectedness and community. Most of creation is made up of the same stuff; just a few molecules different. It all began with love—the Creator replicating love in a magnificent array of diverse forms we call the universe. We yearn to experience a deeper connection and intimacy with Source, ourselves and others—it's what we came from—our human nature within our divine nature.

Research shows the average person looks down at their phone 150 times per day. This amounts to nearly 4 years of their life. The struggle with fear, shame and feelings of not being enough lead to the perception of separation and spiritual disconnection. This also causes us to look down and shut out life around us. When we do so, we also shut out our awareness of and deeper connection with each other and our soul-full selves. We also close off our connection with our Creator. Reality is, we are never truly alone, for the connection and communication with the Divine, the ascended masters, the angels and our soul is always available. Loneliness results from the increasing disconnect from our soul, from love, from Mother Earth and the wonders of the universe.

To feel safe and secure in society today, especially at night, our cities and towns are lit up by streetlights and neon signs; most building are illuminated. Because of this, we are unable to get a clear view of the stars in the night sky and the moon. With our need for man-made lights, many of us have become oblivious to the mystery and beauty of the universal lights that we ride with on this galactic merry-go-round. We lose the communion and communication with the higher realms of the universe. In looking up at a star-filled night sky, we can't help but realize we are not alone. We are part of a great wondrous expansiveness, surrounded by love and grace. Look up and around and know that we are that star and that star is us. Many of us fail to notice the blue sky of day, the beauty of the rising sun, the majesty of a sunset, or the wonders of cloud formations. With awareness of the natural environment, we come to appreciate that we are a part of something vast, beautiful and sacred. We are that tree we see in the woods, and that tree is us. I am that individual on the other side of the globe, and he/she is me. We all come from the same creative Source of loving energy.

Looking within ourselves, we discover that loneliness cannot exist when we experience the oneness of ourselves in relation to all that is. This dynamic, this relationship, is always and, in all ways, interconnected and interdependent. If, while in this physical body, we accept and embrace the deeper connection and eternal relationship with our soul and of all creation that surrounds us, we will naturally connect with our brothers and sisters in more open and loving ways.

Our man-made distractions are diversions from the infinite love and connection available to us. These distractions and diversions can cause us to have a sad, lonely heart, and may lead us into states of anxiety and depression. Our distractions are superficial ways of finding meaning and purpose in our life. We can reduce these negative effects by being in balance. Be aware. Discipline yourself to strike a healthy balance between the use of technology, your interpersonal relationships and work commitments. Integral to maintaining this balance is the commitment to periods of quiet reflection and spiritual retreat, either alone, in groups or both. Look up at your neighbor, your world and the universe. All this offers us a sense of connection and support. We are first and foremost spiritual beings. We are here to live by the universal laws and to live more from the heart; to connect with and learn from our feelings and emotions; to love and support ourselves, each other and our planet. We are designed to create soul-full communion and meaning in our lives.

Our current times call us to a deeper more accepting and compassionate connection with our self, our neighbors, our planet and our Creator. This is part of the awakening of the new Earth. Life and its experiences invite us to come together in love, acceptance and unity. Loneliness is the result of judgment, fear and exclusion, while connection is grounded in love, fearlessness, acceptance and inclusion.

13

Love and Forgiveness

To forgive is the highest, most beautiful form of love. In return, you receive untold peace and happiness. —Robert Muller

I asked Jesus about forgiveness, this is what I heard.

> *Forgiveness is a loving and compassionate "effect" to what seems like an unjust "cause." My teachings and actions were intended to offer you a guidepost to reconcile your inner confusion and torment, with what you believe was done to you. The perception that experiences are done "to" you makes them difficult "for" you to understand and accept. The act of an unjust experience is offered for you. Your misfortunes are opportunities to evolve and enrich yourself and your world. All experiences are meant to be learned from the perspective of divine wisdom, which is unconditional love and acceptance. While you mourn understandable feelings of sadness and injustice, in time, the bud of divine wisdom will blossom into newfound inner peace through forgiveness and non-judgment. Remember, I said forgive them for they are not aware of what they're doing. When you resist the act of forgiveness you also are unaware of what you do, especially to yourself. The perceived tragedies of the world are opportunities to Just Be Love, through the practice of forgiveness and reconciliation.*

What is Forgiveness?

Forgiveness is one of the most powerful healing tools we have for reconciling and moving on from the wounds and hurts of life. It is also one of the most profound acts of unconditional love and acceptance a person can offer themselves and others. However, for many, the act of forgiveness is one of the most difficult and avoided human endeavors. Our resistance and struggle with offering or accepting forgiveness creates much pain and inner torment.

Forgiveness, like grief, is a process. It's not so much something we get over, it's something we move through, in our own time and at our own pace. The act of forgiveness, like understanding, acceptance and compassion, can be applied to every hurtful or difficult experience we encounter in life.

Forgiveness, like love, takes on different meanings for different people, depending on our experiences. This meaning is what becomes significant to us and creates sorrow or joy, resentment or acceptance, depending on what really matters in our lives. The more something matters, the more intense our emotions will be around it. If we make a situation matter too much, we can easily begin to lose our self and our spiritual essence by becoming too emotionally attached, even obsessed, and defined by the situation and those that hurt us. The act of forgiveness and potential reconciliation lowers the emotional intensity of what we've made matter, thus allowing peace to fill the space that once held resentment.

If one chooses, forgiveness offers the opportunity to reconcile a damaged connection created by a wrongdoer. Forgiveness, therefore, is the doorway to reconciliation, thus reconnection with another and ourselves.

If you have been wronged by another, you may have a heavy heart, burdened with resentment and bitterness. Living in these emotions is a painful and paralyzing way to be, and over time can take a toll—emotionally, spiritually, physically and socially.

Forgiveness can be complicated. The true intent of forgiveness is to free ourselves from the belief that we've been wronged; a victim of injustice. More importantly, it's about freeing ourselves from the guilt of what we've done to others or ourselves. It's the process of reorienting of one's perception, belief and attitude around the hurtful experience. The ability to live our lives with love and generosity is impeded when we don't reconcile or forgive. Forgiveness doesn't mean that we must love and be generous to the person who was disloyal to us. It means we forgive them to liberate ourselves.

> *To forgive is to set a prisoner free and discover that the prisoner was you.* —Lewis B. Smedes

One of the reasons we have a hard time with forgiveness, is because it seems like we are doing this more for the offender rather than for ourselves. Because we want reconciliation, we may force the act of forgiveness. This can be especially true if the offender is unwilling to take responsibility for the wrongdoing. If we want them to take ownership for their actions against us, we are creating an expectation that they will fix things. The possibility that our expectation will not be met, only leads to more resentment and disappointment. When we have this expectation, we can give our inner power away to the "cause." As Jesus mentioned, forgiveness and compassion for ourselves and the offender reduces the emotional charge of the "cause." An alternative is to *accept* the fact that the offender may be unwilling, for whatever reason, to take responsibility and accountability for their actions. When we acknowledge and accept this, we become empowered and liberated, giving ourselves a fresh start regardless of whether the offender apologizes or not. We create freedom and happiness, when we take healthy action on our own behalf to heal. We can choose to work at reconciling and releasing the resentment and let go of needing anything from the offender. Our goal is to empower ourselves toward personal freedom and happiness.

Forgiveness is an act of love and love is freedom. To forgive is to be free and a way to love. It's the willingness to move beyond our suffering, to reconcile our disruptive thoughts and emotions, and to let go of that wounded part of us. The willingness and ability to go beyond the wounded self is to rise as love and to let go of what no longer serves us, so in time, we are restored to our whole self. It will help us know that we are love. Going beyond the wounded self, is the thought and energy of unconditional love and freedom. Lao-Tzu said: *"When I let go of what I am, I become what I might be."* Forgiveness is an act of courage and faith; it moves us to a higher level of awareness and truth about ourselves and our life. It's choosing to value inner peace and happiness more than resentment and pain. Forgiveness helps take us out of the self-created story of our past, so we can begin anew.

Forgiveness is often a continuous process. By this I mean that, in this moment, I can let go of the feelings about a wrongdoing and free my mind. A week later I get triggered by an unrelated event, and my mind wants to take me back to square one. This is the nature of the lower mind, always wanting to take me back to the past and to pain, which creates discontent in the present and a hopeless view of the future. In this forgiveness process, like any healing process, we are peeling away another layer of the hurt. Life is a process with many layers to be experienced, worked through, understood and peeled off.

Expectations Complicate the Forgiveness Process

Holding on to anger is like grasping a hot coal with the intent of throwing it at someone else; you are the one who gets burned.
—the Buddha

We hold on to expectations and resentments, because it gives us the perception and feeling of power and control over something, we had no control of. It becomes a lens through which we see ourselves and others; it becomes something we have to feed, keep alive and justify. We believe if we don't hold on to the expectation and resentment, the person who wronged us must have more power than we do, because we've become so powerless. We do whatever we can to make them wrong, because we feel so wronged. Truth is, hanging on to expectations and resulting resentment creates more suffering. Harboring thoughts of resentment or bitterness is bondage and imprisonment. It causes us to remain in the past, confused in the present, and uncertain of the future.

Many people unintentionally stay in the resentment and hurt, because they want the offender to right the wrong. This expectation only causes us to give away our inner power and our own ability to feel better, because we have refused to let go and move on. The longer we hang on to the resentment or grievance, the more we are drinking the poison of wanting our offender to suffer or die. Our lower self doesn't want to let go and forgive because then we are letting our offender off the hook. The higher self knows forgiveness is not about excusing the wrongdoing, it's about acknowledging it, standing up for ourselves, rising above it all and becoming the best version of ourselves so we're free of the hurt. It's learning to not lose the love that we are, even though someone has committed an unloving and unjust act against us.

The idea of forgiveness in the context of religion and mental health is seen as a critical step for one's healing— "forgive the offender and move on." Personally, and professionally I have experienced and witnessed the power and transformation that the act of forgiveness can have toward healing a wound and being a catalyst toward helping one move on with their life.

An example of this is when I went through my own divorce. My ex-wife Sue and I felt very hurt by each other, each for our own reasons. Over the course of time, by doing our own individual healing and reconciling work, we have come to a place of being friends and being present for our grown sons and grandchildren.

I've also assisted many individuals in reconciling their anger and resentment over someone who hurt them. By getting in touch with this anger at a deeper level, they then found what's often beneath their anger is sadness. By recognizing and naming the feeling of sadness, they were able to reconcile this emotion by giving themselves permission to feel the feelings and emotions. Once the feelings were recognized and acknowledged, they were more easily reconciled and released. Then the beliefs that fed the feelings and emotions could be reframed. They could then release the negative emotions and come to a place of acceptance and compassion for themselves and perhaps even the person that hurt them.

I believe a major misjudgment that "helping" professionals such as, therapists, clergy, etc., can make, regarding the act of forgiveness, is to demand that the offender be forgiven. This denies the person who has suffered injustice their free will, how they choose to handle their pain and healing process. To suggest forgiveness is one thing; to hold an expectation or to demand that one should forgive when the person is not emotionally or spiritually ready, is disrespectful. This does not offer them the time and space they need. If someone is too strongly encouraged to forgive, it can create even more guilt, anger, confusion and inner torment.

> *Most of us can forgive and forget; we just don't want the other person to forget that we forgave.* —Ivern Ball

Some people say it's important to forget what has been forgiven; *"to forgive is to forget."* Some would also say, if you can't or won't forget the wrongdoing, you haven't really forgiven. To totally forget what happened is often very difficult. Most of us struggle just getting to the place of forgiveness. Rather than forget, it's important to seek out tools and guidance to develop the ability to reduce the emotional charge and its effects from the memory. This would greatly benefit the person in resuming a happier and peaceful life as they move beyond their wounded past.

When coping with the issue of forgiveness, it's important to be aware of emotional safety. The process of any healing work can create feelings of being unsafe and powerless, of giving up control, of feeling vulnerable and defenseless. Understandably, people who have been violated and/or wronged in some way can struggle with feeling safe. They already feel a loss of control and inner power, so the last thing they want to do now is let go of control. When they've been wronged, their natural, survival instincts and defenses come up and they seek to gain a greater sense of control. They can overcompensate, especially if they've had little or no control in the past. This heightened need for protection and control can put them in a paralyzing emotional state. There is no safety or peace in this, only more inner pain.

To begin to find safety and trust others again, a person must allow themselves to be exposed to an unpleasant experience, while in a safe environment with supportive people. In my experience working with people, I have seen that when they can allow the ego defenses to ease up (which on the surface may seem unsafe and threatening to do), they're more able to experience deeper feelings and body memories and emotions. They come to a higher awareness of the painful experience and the meaning they have put to it. Their higher self will assist them to naturally reframe their experience and view of themselves. They will see their wrongdoer with greater understanding, acceptance, compassion and forgiveness. This begins to retrain the mind and call forth the healthy ego in order to tolerate and navigate through unpleasant feelings and emotions in healthy ways. Faith in divine love and its ways, along with trusting the self, calls us to ease up on our ego defenses in order to truly discover our safety and peace. The higher mind asks us to choose to do the opposite of what the lower mind wants us to do. Forgiveness cleanses the heart, reframes the mind, creating ease in the body.

The Power of Moving Beyond

Healing is accomplished the instant the sufferer no longer sees a value in the pain. —A Course in Miracles, T-5. I.1:1

The higher form of love, is to move beyond our wounded selves, doing what's right from the higher perspective, not from the perspective of the wounded self. This is what will ultimately move us from powerlessness to empowerment. The power to move beyond the wounded self requires giving the wounded self a voice; the time and space to express itself as our higher self-listens with acceptance and compassion. It also requires us to have the willingness and openness to discover new possibilities about the beliefs and truths once held and lived. By allowing these possibilities to come forth, we come to realize the value of inner peace and empowerment over inner pain and powerlessness. Consider, at some point you may want to take greater responsibility for what is happening in your emotional house by looking within at the destructive thoughts and beliefs you are harboring. Doing our inner work to reconcile the injustice and then release the burden, will rekindle a sense of inner peace and happiness.

With our lower mind's perception of being wounded, the ego gets defensive and reactive. This creates resistance and non-acceptance about the wrongdoing. These defense strategies make getting to the place of forgiveness and potential reconciliation overwhelming and difficult. To the ego, the idea of going "beyond itself" to challenge its survival thinking and its beliefs, is a very threatening idea. Forgiveness requires a shift in perception that removes the block of fear and resistance, so love, acceptance and compassion can be used to heal.

In the beginning of this chapter I shared Jesus' words to me about forgiveness, saying the unjust experience is done for you, not to you. Our misfortunes, especially painful and unjust ones, are opportunities to learn according to the perspective of divine wisdom and unconditional love and acceptance. That inner peace and freedom occurs through forgiveness or inner reconciliation. His message acknowledges that we will struggle with moving through the pain of a wrongdoing. He encourages us to liberate our self from hurt by moving to that place of reconciliation, which, if desired, can include forgiveness.

If one struggles to forgive, there is an alternative process I call *"inner reconciliation."* This is a process of shifting the energy we hold about those we believe did us wrong. More importantly, inner reconciliation is a way of reorienting the relationship with ourselves around the wrongful act. The concept of the 4 R's—*Recognize, Reconcile, Release and Reframe* can be useful in this inner reconciliation process. The 4 R's are meant to assist us in telling the story, expressing feelings and stating our beliefs around the experience. Then begin to shift our perceptions, our interpretation of the experience, clarifying the situation for ourselves and if desired, the offender, toward the act of reframing our view and meaning of the situation to a higher and healthier perspective. This process is an option to lighten the emotional burden so that we no longer hold resentment and bitterness. We choose to learn the lesson from the pain, which helps us reclaim our inner power and sense of worth.

This process also allows us to move beyond our wounded selves to a higher level of understanding. This results in freeing us from the "effects" of harboring resentment from the "cause." Part of the 4 R's requires the ability to go beyond ourselves and either directly or indirectly, tell the betrayer what needs to be said; for example, writing a "Dear John" letter. The letter can be sent directly to the offender or read in the presence of a safe, trusted and neutral person. This process allows the wounded self, to express feelings and emotions held in, so they are heard and validated. We can make a conscious choice to reframe how we perceive ourselves and the hurtful experience. What heals the wound is the shift in thought—our perception and belief to no longer allow the offender and the hurt to define us in the present. The most elevated thought would be the ability to feel love, compassion and gratitude for what the experience taught us.

What we are today comes from the thoughts of yesterday; and our present thoughts build on the thoughts of tomorrow... "He insulted me, he hurt me, he defeated me; he robbed me." Those who think not such thoughts will be free from hate. For hate is not conquered by hate. Hate is conquered by love. This is the law eternal. —the Dhammapada, sacred Buddhist scripture.

Forgiving the Self

Illusions about yourself and the world are one. That is why all forgiveness is a gift to yourself. —A Course in Miracles, WB-62.2:1-2

People can and do forgive others much sooner and more easily than they will forgive themselves. The lower mind creates inner resistance, guilt and shame. It talks us out of self-forgiveness, because the nature of the ego is the thought and created belief in our unworthiness. The ego even believes that we deserve punishment. This is the created illusion. The energy and act of forgiveness or reconciliation releases these self-defeating feelings and restores our body and mind back to unity and wholeness. The wounded part of our mind resists and distracts us from this loving endeavor with determination and force.

The key is to be aware of our thinking and how it deceives us into holding thoughts which create the energy of fear, shame and unworthiness. There is no love when we subscribe to this energy; it only keeps us in separation. Self-forgiveness is a gift. To forgive ourselves is to be in the grace and reverence of Source. This is Earth School. We're here to learn unconditional love, acceptance and forgiveness. Self-forgiveness is the fundamental path to transforming fear into love, negative self-worth to positive self-worth and separation into union. This liberates us and creates space for inner peace and happiness to be felt and lived. The act of self-forgiveness heals and transforms us. Forgiving our self also frees everyone else in our lives. Love your neighbor as yourself. What we do to ourselves we do to others as well. The loving and compassionate energy of self-forgiveness naturally returns us to love.

We Are Here as Spiritual Beings

To forgive is merely to remember only the loving thoughts you gave in the past and those that were given you. Forgiveness is the selective remembering, based not on your selection. —A Course in Miracles, T-17.III.1

Part of why we are here is to experience situations that require forgiveness and reconciliation, as both the giver and receiver of this dynamic. The "selective remembering" comes from the Holy Spirit. It is through the Holy Spirit and our higher, wiser self that we come to the place of reconciliation, the end of separation and return to unity. Forgiveness brings us back to the Holy One. It allows us to remember the oneness of all, even with those who hurt us.

Forgiveness brings us back to our spiritual essence. It brings us back to the present time—the now, in order to move beyond our past and live a brighter today. Our personal power and sense of self is restored when we remember and demonstrate acts of love, especially self-love, by speaking and living our truth in the present. The act of reconciling and/or forgiving the offense is an act of self-love. This work toward inner peace and happiness demonstrates the desire, anchored by action, to know and be the love and joy that we are.

When we can go beyond our wounded self, we enter the spiritual realm, creating a higher perspective—giving higher meaning and purpose to our life. We create possibilities to expand our minds and enhance our lives. By going beyond our wounded self, we make our own lives richer. This is a truth long understood and at the heart of all meaningful spiritual traditions and practices. It's a mystery and transformation that can only be understood by an open heart and a willing mind. When we experience this higher perspective, we are in the heart of the Divine and an active co-creator in the energy and dynamic of love. We are no longer "prisoners" of our own harmful thoughts and beliefs.

> *Do you want peace? Forgiveness offers it. Do you want happiness, a quiet mind, a certainty of purpose, and a sense of worth and beauty that transcends the world? Do you want quietness that cannot be disturbed, a gentleness that never can be hurt, a deep abiding comfort, and a rest so perfect it can never be upset? All this forgiveness offers you, and more.* —A Course in Miracles, WB-122, 1-3

Research shows a direct correlation between the ability to forgive and the degree of happiness and life satisfaction we experience. There are two paths in life—love or fear. These are the only two true human emotions. Fear is the absence of love. Fear creates conditions, leads to the perception of separation and beliefs of unworthiness. Love is the highest vibration. Love promotes joy; it offers understanding, acceptance, compassion, forgiveness and possible reconciliation. The path of love will lead to peace and joy; the pathway of fear will lead to continued pain and suffering.

14

Love and Hope

All hope is yours because God cares. —Unknown

Hope, like love and faith, is grounded in spirit. Hope creates an inner knowing that our experiences and choices have meaning and value regardless of the outcome. Hope is not only found in our desire for certain experiences, but also in the meaning and value we obtain from them. The three greatest virtues are faith, hope and love; the greatest of these being love. Where there is love, all things are possible. Love is the common theme. When we combine love with faith and hope, with power and wisdom, we have a higher vibration. Hope is the foundation of all human achievement. It is part of our essence and inspires miracles.

Faith is belief in the unseen and unknown, trusting in divine truth and possibility. Hope dwells in the future, while love dwells in the present. Hope is a state of mind; having faith through a trusting heart. Hope is reinforced and strengthened by faith. With hope we choose to be mindful and present in this moment, acknowledging the unlimited possibilities that are not only available for us today, but also guiding us into our future. Hope plants the seeds of possibilities; the planting of the co-creative process. Hope, like love and acceptance, helps to cultivate the energy and will for possibilities to bloom.

Hope is an attitude and the willingness to be patient, flexible and steady. It's found in our willingness to let the situation unfold as it needs to be, to trust ourselves and allow for the process of life to unfold. Hope is the courage to face the dark and the unknown, both inside and outside of ourselves. It is the persistence and determination to keep going despite uncertainty. Hope requires that we stay positive and optimistic through the uncertainty and adversity.

An unknown source said, *"Hope sees the invisible, feels the intangible and achieves the impossible."* Hope carries a powerful energetic force (*invisible*) that seeks to transcend the limits of the physical world. With hope, that which seems elusive *(intangible)* to our physical senses and limited thinking, becomes a *feeling* and belief to our heart and higher self. This allows us to step into the unknown (*the impossible*) where the realm of possibilities lies.

> *A pessimist sees the difficulty in every opportunity: an optimist*
> *sees the opportunity in every difficulty.* —Sir Winston Churchill

To understand hope, we must first understand hopelessness. The spiritual law of polarity says, *We cannot know the energy of one experience without knowing its opposite energy.* I believe hopelessness is due to a deep-seated perception and belief that my situation, my life will not improve. I have consciously or unconsciously created hopelessness. When people combine their feelings and beliefs of being unloved and unworthy with a perception of hopelessness, this creates an intense experience of separation from themselves, others and ultimately the Divine. This leads to the paralyzing and dangerous feeling of despair. Those with little or no hope are often very self-absorbed and have created victim energy. They see no possibilities and are empty and passive about engaging in healthy opportunities. They create *no-win* situations for themselves and cannot entertain any possibilities that life could be better. They are consumed in self-doubt and overwhelmed by fear. They cannot risk vulnerability and resist looking within themselves and doing the inner work necessary to create healthy change. People with little hope are consumed with a distorted and defeated sense of self. Their willpower is limited; they struggle to access or use helpful resources, both internally and externally, to manifest desired change.

People with little hope have mastered the way of learned helplessness. Helplessness turns to hopelessness and creates repeated patterns of self-defeating behaviors. Hurt and fear feed the ego and its distorted perception and create a strong resistance to change. An aspect of the soul has chosen to lose its sense of peace to the ways of the ego. The lower mind chooses the hopeless experience.

Our soul's journey is to learn and experience the ways to generate hopeful, constructive outcomes through self-empowerment and self-mastery. When we begin to shift our perception of ourselves in relation to our situation and our world, hope arises, and we make room for a miracle to occur.

A Deeper Understanding of Hope

To be alive is to live in the state of hope. Hope is the precondition of our mental health. Hope is the scaffolding of our existence. Hope is the reassurance of our belief in the meaning of human life and in a sense of our universe. —Henryrk Skojmowski

Hope requires determination to resolve or overcome a problem. You've heard the saying: *"Where there's a will, there is a way."* Hope develops for us to discover the will and seek a way. Think of hope as this formula: **Willpower + Way power = Hope.** The power and determination of will, along with the courage and commitment to find a way, can create a positive and productive result. Unfortunately, the power of will and way can also be used to create fearful and destructive thoughts, leading to negative, destructive consequences. Hope and faith offer us the will. Trusting, allowing and determined courage offer us the way. Love is the energy and driving force to create the will and pave the way. Like love, our will is a sustaining energy.

What I heard Jesus say when asked about will.

> *Will is the energy and power of spirit to direct creative thought into physical form in a determined way. It is the inner drive of the spirit to respond—to direct your energy where the spirit desires it to go through you and by you.*

A strong will comes from inner determination; a *"can do"* spirit to see something through, despite the uncertainty. It's the gathering of both our internal and external resources toward an action. Individuals with little hope don't believe they have the inner resources and they often disregard or reject constructive suggestions and support. All of this only reinforces their self-defeating belief system and sense of hopelessness.

Hope requires the willingness and openness to wait in the dark, in the unknown of a situation. Hope is about the future, something we desire that is yet to come. It requires waiting.

Active Waiting

All human wisdom is summed up in two words - wait and hope.
— Alexander Dumas

When it comes to hope, we can get complacent and procrastinate. I want it to happen, yet I don't do anything in the present to manifest what I hope for. Because hope is in the future, there can be the belief that there is nothing I need to do in the present other than just hope, pray and wait. If this becomes my daily norm, I will likely be passive in my action taking. The true energy and intent of hope calls us to be active in the present, creating opportunities; while waiting for what is hoped for to emerge.

Consider a concept I call *active waiting*. While waiting for my hopes to manifest, I am active in my waiting. I am doing things in the present that I believe will lead to what I desire in the future. I am developing a vision, an intention and strategies to achieve my desired goal. With active waiting I am using my desired thoughts and energy to take productive action in the present to generate that which I hope for in the future.

An example of active waiting is when parents are expecting a baby. There are nine months of waiting where the parents, especially the mother, are preparing for the upcoming birth. Another example is the concept of financial planning for retirement. I say to myself, *"I hope to have enough money for when I retire."* Even if my retirement is several years away, it's important to plan and save early on, so that when I retire, I have accumulated what I feel is adequate for my standard of living.

Hope is not about being idle in the present. It is about doing what can and should be done in the now and over time so that what is hoped for can materialize. It is also about acceptance of what is, because what manifests may not be the way we had desired. It could be much more, or it could be less. Hope asks us to be flexible and have gratitude for whatever outcome does come forth as our present unfolds into our desired future.

Another example is someone with a life-threatening illness. The medical community, family, friends, prayer chains, etc., all do their part through treatment/ technology, love, prayers, healing techniques and support. Despite these efforts, the person passes on. Hope gives way to the natural and normal emotional state of grief. Love, hope and faith ask us to reorient ourselves through acceptance and celebration of this life. It now asks us to accept this new outcome, believing that all is as the Divine and the person's soul intended. In this moment I choose, out of love from my soul perspective, to accept and set free my previous human expectations. Patience, acceptance and a dash of flexibility are part of the ingredients of love and hope.

Our lower self tends to favor tomorrow at the expense of today. For example, you go to the ice cream shop, and you see a sign that says, *Free Ice Cream Tomorrow.* Wow, you can't wait! You create an expectation of free ice cream. The next day you go for the free ice cream and say to the person dishing out the ice cream. *"I'm here for my free ice cream."* The vendor says, *"Oh no, the free ice cream is tomorrow like the sign says."* For several days you come in for your free ice cream, and each day the vendor says. *"Oh no, that's tomorrow."* Will you ever get that free ice cream? Reality is that tomorrow never comes. We can't arrive in tomorrow; we always arrive in today. Tomorrow or the future cannot be obtained or experienced today, for this moment is all we have. To only wait until tomorrow to manifest our desires, keeps us searching and idly waiting; leaving our desires unfulfilled. All that we believe will happen tomorrow actually happens in what we call today.

We can become so worried about experiencing a better, more peaceful tomorrow, that it can keep us from doing things in the present to change our current situation. It is in this moment that we are experiencing worry and unhappiness. We can choose what we experience in the next moment, by changing it **NOW**—not tomorrow or next week. This is how we move beyond the grips of ego mind. The ego needs to have us in places that don't exist—the past and future. Living and dwelling in the past or future creates hopelessness. When we are aware of this moment, the past and future collapse and merge into the moment. When we are focused in the past and/or future, we are wasting energy. It is important to be mindful about our thoughts of hope, because it can cause us to get caught up in expectations of a desired outcome. Remember, expectations can lead to disappointment, because we are trying to control something or someone outside of our self. Hope asks us to focus on, and be aware of our process moment to moment, not so much on the desired outcome.

> *As soon as we get clear about who we are and what we want, everything unlike it shows up. Sometimes things fall apart before they fall together.* —Neale Donald Walsch

Contrasts give meaning to our lives. As stated earlier, to understand one side of life we will need to experience its opposite; the other side. Universal forces seem to dictate that the stronger the light, the more intense the darkness. Life is created, transformed and created again. This is how the universe works. The dynamic of contrast is not something to judge, deny or resist. It is to be acknowledged and accepted. Hope in many ways is the experience of contrast, for within the dynamic of hope our worst nightmare could happen. Using the example of experiencing a loss, we are challenged to work through our feelings and emotions around the experience and attempt to accept the loss. Hope now comes when we begin to expand our minds, creating a willingness to change our perspective, leading to new possibilities for ourselves around the unfortunate experience. This is the energy of hope.

"A Ray of Hope"

Hope begins in the dark; the stubborn hope that if you just show up and do the right thing, the dawn will come. You wait and watch and work; you don't give up. —Annie Lomoott

Allow me to shift gears now and offer a different view of hope; from our shadow side. Remember, there are hidden parts of ourselves that we deny, repress and at times project on to others. The soul calls us to honor our darkness; the shadow of ourselves. Hope, like creation, begins in the dark. It's important to recognize and confront our shadow so that we can experience our light more fully. Hope is often symbolized through references to light in phrases such as: "A ray of hope;" "A glimmer of hope;" "Light at the end of the tunnel;" "Behind every dark cloud there is a silver lining;" "It's always darkest just before the dawn." The active energy of hope inspires our will and lights our way. It offers us inner knowing to illumine and awaken us to the opportunity before us.

Another description of hope worthy of mention. Hope can be seen as, *The push of discomfort and the pull of hope.* This means that when we push (*step*) into our discomfort (*darkness/pain*), we acknowledge and accept it. As we work through our pain, we will experience the pull (*energy*) of hope and light. Our soul does not ask us to avoid the pain; rather it asks us to engage in the pain/discomfort. Many believe that to push into (*engage in*) their pain will be too difficult. The reality is; that avoidance of our pain creates more inner pain and difficulty. We do not generate hope and happiness by avoiding our discomfort. This only creates greater unhappiness and hopelessness which in time turns into despair. Consider that when and if you conquer the great death, the other death can do you no harm. What is the great death? It is the ego-created illusion we make so real, believing we will die if we face our fear, our shadow and our pain. Can you name anyone who has generated hope and happiness by avoiding their pain?

Through our experiences, love offers us the opportunity to trust so that we can overcome our struggles and discomfort. Love, through our higher self, acknowledges the fear our low self subscribes to. Our higher self encourages us to face the discomfort anyway. This is what brings hope, light and understanding to what's misunderstood within us. Our shadow and our pain show us where love and light are needed within us, bringing hope to what we've seen as hopeless; offering awareness and peace within.

To push into our discomfort is to surrender, trust and allow. When we work these three elements, we open the inner door to receive the gift of hope, the gift of Spirit. This process is the active waiting and letting go of expectations. Yes, it takes courage, willpower, faith and resources (*way power*). In this holy moment, the power and strength of love merges hope and faith into itself, grounding us to our Source.

15

Love within the Light and the Dark

The journey that we undertake together is the exchange of dark for light, of ignorance for understanding, nothing you understand is fearful. —A Course in Miracles, T-14.VII.1:1-2

I invite you to participate in an exercise to help you understand this dynamic of light and dark and what it symbolizes for us as spiritual beings. Get a candle and put it in front of you, light it, and just notice the flame for a few moments. There are three parts of the flame. First, in the area coming up from the wick, the center of the flame has a dark space. This represents the void, the unknown. I call this space the sacred emptiness. Now look deeper into this dark area. Do you see a shade of blue surrounding the flame's dark, empty space? This is the second part. The blue represents the power, love and wisdom of the Father-Mother God, which transcends and unites the void of the darkness into the light. This blue tint is the space where divine truth lies. Now observe the space encircling the blue area; this third part is the light of the flame. The light starting at the wick is surrounding the entire dark space and blue formless space.

Notice the brightness, the fullness of the light. Both the darkness, with its emptiness, along with the light in its fullness makes up what is the flame. Consider how the dark becomes known as it is surrounded by the light. Without the light, the emptiness and darkness would remain formless and unknown. A flame is incomplete without both its light and dark parts. The blue represents the divine energy and the truth dwelling within both the dark and light of the flame. As you continue to focus on the flame, become aware of how the dark and the light merge into one making the flame complete. With a sense of surrender, allow yourself to become one with the flame. See this as connecting with your inner flame with its will and power, merging into the power and will of the Divine flame. The Divine inner flame lies in our heart, especially the back side of the heart. This connects us to the infinite Divine love within, just like the darkness of the flame is inside and surrounded by light. Our task is to not only feel the infinite light and love, but to be inside its light and love.

Genesis

I n the Bible, the book of Genesis says: "In the beginning when God created the heavens and the earth, the earth was formless void and darkness covered the face of the deep, while a wind from God swept over the face of the waters. Then God said, *"Let there be light."* (Genesis 1: 1-4, NRSV)

> *"God saw that the light was good; God separated the light from the darkness. God called the light day and the darkness he called night. There was evening and there was morning, the first day."* (Genesis 1: 4-5, NRSV)

It seems God created light and darkness to be separate and unique. Yet, they weave with each other to make our twenty-four-hour day. These passages lead me to ask some questions: Does God really separate morning and evening? Is the dark and formlessness really separate from the light? Or are they just cycles on a continuum of creation that make up the whole of the universe, the whole of the day? The universe is governed in part by cycles. In our linear and 3D perception we separate things and put things in compartments. We see order in this way of perceiving, thinking and being. The multidimensional field of the universe, however, allows for chaos and randomness. Separation is not needed to make sense and to bring order. All parts are needed and valued to create wholeness. Perhaps those who first put words to the Holy Bible needed to express *"The beginning"* in linear form, because that's what made sense to them. In writing *"The Beginning"* they separated formless and form, dark and light, evening and morning. *What if divine creation and perception actually sees these aspects as separate and unique, yet parts of the whole? What if they are a continuum of "what is?" What if the aspect of formlessness, dark and void merged with the light to create form and fullness to make up the "flame?" What if the evening merges with the morning to make up the "day?" What if the aspect we call sorrow, in time merges to become the aspect we name as joy?*

Light and dark are always present and moving in rhythm, in and out with each other. They seem separate, yet they occur at the same time; like the dark and light of a flame, they both exist simultaneously. As we look at the example of "a day," we must consider our location on Earth at this moment. We could either be in the darkness of night or the sunlight of day. We know that whatever we are experiencing at our location on Earth is exactly the opposite on the other side. The Earth and all who inhabit this planet experience either light or dark at the same time. Our location and perception determine our experience at a certain time. However, light and dark are both present, one always leads and follows the other, like the infinity circle. This is the energy, nature and movement of divine love and life.

> *What do you want? Light or darkness. Knowledge or ignorance are yours, but you can't have both. Opposites must be brought together, not kept apart. For their separation is only in your mind, and they are reconciled by union, as you are.* —A Course in Miracles, T-14.VII.1:1-3

Shadows occur when an object blocks the path of light. The shadow within us hides all that we refuse to acknowledge. Yet, deep within our being, we know that disowning or projecting our hidden self, is hiding our true self. Our lower self is fearful and denies our darkness because it believes it's bad and should not exist. So, we hide from our darkness, avoiding it or projecting it. With these actions, we assume our shadow has no power or influence over us. The reality is that what we hide, deny or project, remains as our shadow. It can pop up on its own and we have no clue that it's controlling our thoughts and actions. Our ego and its shadow are diligent in blocking the light and love of divine truth from entering our awareness.

From our higher mind's perspective, our darkness is not to be feared or ignored—it's intended to be embraced. Many of the great spiritual masters say that by acknowledging and exploring our darkness, our shadow, we realize where love and light are needed within us. Just like the flame of the candle, many of us never really notice the dark area and its emptiness, or the Divine and its truth represented in the blue tint. You can sense the power and wisdom contained within the flame when you meditate with it. There is great awareness gained by going to this sacred emptiness. Our higher self knows the answers are there. The only way to really understand and accept this is by bringing our intention and attention to the dark, empty spaces within us. Our repressed and dark parts block the light. Shadows disappear when we remove what blocks the light. When we consciously become aware, and reconcile what we've denied and made dark, we remove what blocks the light. This is awakening to love. Holding these opposites of darkness and light, in a loving and nurturing incubator and merging them together, brings insight, soul growth and maturity.

Creation Begins in the Darkness

Life forms in the darkness. The sunlight rises from the darkness. A buried seed opens in the darkness of the soil. A fetus develops in the darkness of the womb. When we step into this unknown part of ourselves, we become aware of possibilities and potential. Our darkness is the test of our faith, courage and strength to do the inner dark night of the soul work; to overcome the uncertainty; to rediscover the light, love and wisdom of ourselves and our universe.

> *Now is the time to unite the soul and the world. Now is the time to see the sunlight dancing as one with the shadows.* —Rumi

Like the flame, could it be that love, and light surround those dark and unexplored places within us? The flame invites us into its darkness, its formless void. It knows that in going into the dark we will find and experience the light of love. We fear our own darkness and pain. If we stay in the fear and ignorance, we allow our shadow aspects to block what can help make us whole and complete. The simple yet magical flame of a candle is a teacher and guide. It shows us that darkness and emptiness are always surrounded by and embraced by infinite light and love. The ego mind has a difficult time understanding this spiritual principle; to know one aspect, you must experience and know it's opposite. So, it is with light and dark. To know light, you must be willing to experience knowing darkness. To know joy, you must experience times of sorrow. To know love, you must experience fear, hate and rejection. By understanding the balance of polarity, and working toward reconciling the opposites, we merge our darkness and light as a flame of sacred unity.

There are four main qualities to our humanness: physical, emotional, mental and spiritual. Light and dark make up our physical world. We live in this and adapt to this in many ways. Since light and dark are parts of our physical world, it would make sense for light and dark to be part of our mental, emotional and spiritual worlds as well. Remember, God's love is about inclusion, not exclusion. If light and dark exist in our physical nature, they must also be included within the other three natures. Our ego's methods of fear and control cause us to exclude this divine truth of our emotional, mental and spiritual natures. This avoidance or exclusion is part of the separation from our spiritual essence and thus Divine love.

The Divine as Creator is in the dark as much as the light. If the Divine loves us in our light, then we are also loved just the same in our darkness. To have a dark side, a shadow, is not a flaw to be condemned and avoided. It is what completes us on our spiritual journey. To deny our darkness is to deny our experiences in life. If we deny something, we deny our completeness; we deny love, and the unfolding of our spiritual journey. This leads to spiritual bypass, living in fear and ignorance, pretending all is well and wanting to take the quick and easy way out. We've been known to say, "I'll just give it to God," while avoiding our part in the growing/healing process. This is being too attached to and defined by our temporary humanness at the expense and exclusion of our eternal soul. What we see as flawed and incomplete, our compassionate Creator sees as perfect. By having acceptance and compassion for our limitations we can transform our perceived flaws into loving stepping-stones on our life path.

What's Been Said About Imperfection

Our soul and ego do a dance with perceptions about imperfection and perfection. St. Augustine said, *"This is the very perfection of a man, to find out his own imperfections."* Mahatma Gandhi said, *"My imperfections and failures are as much a blessing from God as my successes and my talents and I lay them both at his feet."* Gunnar Bjornstand stated, *"If everything is imperfect in this imperfect world, love is most perfect in its imperfection."* I've come to realize that when we accept and have compassion for what we deem as our imperfection, we find our perfection.

Perfection will naturally arrive when we let go of believing we are bad and not enough. It's okay not to be perfect. That's why pencils have erasers, and why computers have backspace and delete keys. Mistakes, wrong turns and errors are opportunities for learning and growing. Author and philosopher Sam Keen wrote, *"Love isn't finding a perfect person. It's seeing an imperfect person perfectly."* This applies specially to loving ourselves and our imperfections. The more we hide parts of ourselves, the more we deny our authenticity. When we are aligned with love, we are being authentic. Having compassion (*light*) for our own or another's imperfection (*darkness*) creates perfection, because compassion is the energy of love.

Understanding Darkness

Many believe that references to the dark indicate it's wrong and evil, and that there can be no good in darkness. Yet, some souls agree to do dark and harmful actions so that others can experience and learn lessons of acceptance, compassion or forgiveness, etc. In the Gospel of Matthew, Jesus says: *"A good tree cannot bring forth evil fruit; neither can a corrupt tree bring forth good fruit"* (Matthew 7:18, NKJ). According to Neil Douglas-Klotz, a noted scholar on the Aramaic language of Jesus, the word *good* in Aramaic means *ripe,* which is another way of saying *ready.* The word *evil* in Aramaic means *unripe* or *not ready.* So, fruit is either ripe (*ready for picking*) or unripe (*not ready to pick*).

Applying the words of Jesus to my understanding of darkness and evil, I believe he is saying that; like fruit, a person is either unripe/not ready, or ripe/ ready. If you are *ripe* you are *aware* and *ready.* You are more in the light, thus doing more ripe things. If you are *unripe* you are likely *not ready,* i.e., *unaware,* more controlled by the dark aspects of your shadow, creating more unripe, i.e. evil energy and outcomes.

Yes, there are those who are unripe; those we call dark and evil in the world. People do inflict pain and suffering on others and on themselves. Like all of life, the darkness and the unripe have an intended purpose and message. It's about what can happen when people are possessed by intense emotional and/or spiritual fear, pain, and a sense of unworthiness or entitlement. When people are troubled and hurting deep inside, they can turn on others and/ or themselves. There are lessons about love to be learned from what we call darkness and evil. That's one reason why we have these experiences. To resist the lesson is to miss an opportunity to learn from the darkness and the feelings that result. This resistance only keeps us in the dark. Remember, truth and light surround what's dark. To the soul, light is our birthright and darkness is our veil. Living this truth brings courage and determination to continue moving toward the light and goodness that we are.

> *So the darkness shall be the light, and the stillness the dancing.*
> —T.S. Eliot

Many people believe that being silent and still is unproductive. Part of the way to truly find our Creator, our self, and the love that we seek is in the darkness and the stillness. Be still and know. Our Creator is asking us to be still, and to quiet our ever moving, distracting mind. Being in stillness creates powerful, active ways to listen to the gentle voice of the higher self and the Creator. Stillness takes us out of the lower mind and moves us into alignment with the Divine mind. It naturally merges our darkness into the surrounding, loving light. Meditating with a candle flame is effective and enlightening because it allows your mind to create the symbolism and meaning of the flame. When we empty to the center of ourselves, we allow the space needed to tend to our darkness. This is where the blue part of the flame resides—the Divine truth. In this space truth emerges and darkness becomes light. The stillness may communicate through words, symbols or songs, bringing us to a higher awareness of love and life. When we arrive here, we can dance like the stillness does with the light.

Bring What's Dark to Light

When we see our divine completeness in what the lower self deems to be our flaws and imperfections, we begin to come out of hiding and grow in acceptance. We begin to be more real, open and honest to and with ourselves. We experience the light that has always been surrounding us. Resisting what's held in darkness only creates more darkness, insecurity and pain. To know our shadow side and to learn to love and nurture what has been, is to offer love, acceptance and light to those parts of us that feel unloved and unworthy. When we can trust and open to the light, we are letting go of fear and embracing love.

A key: Opening the heart creates space for possibilities and the higher perspective to shine light and higher knowing on what was once dark and unknown.

Embracing Darkness Transforms to Light

One does not become enlightened by imagining figures of light, but by making the darkness conscious. —Carl Jung

Our spiritual journey as a human is about befriending our darkness, our fear, our shame and our emptiness. Doing this, we notice the light and love that come to greet us and show us the way. *I heard fear knocking at the door; when I opened the door, no one was there.* The knock creates our fear and need for certainty; yet it really is our teacher and opportunity. To open the door is faith; the willingness to accept, trust and embrace the uncertainty in our lives within the certainty of God. The door for me is the Divine. We tend to resist and feel unworthy of opening the door, like we resist touching our pain, our lost parts, and God's love. By opening our door and embracing our darkness (*pain*) we invite the light (*gain*). The purpose of the darkness is to lead us to the light. Our darkness and our feelings are the great teachers and opportunities within the paradox of darkness and light in our soul journey while in this body-mind.

If you light a match in a dark room, you instantly see how the light overcomes the darkness. Observe the power and grace of that lit match or candle flame dancing with life. Once we can light that flame within us creating acceptance and awareness, we will transform as well—I AM the light and the light is me.

Within our dark, painful and confusing experiences, a key is to know the truth that we are always surrounded by and in the light and love of divine grace. This is the remembrance of the flame in us—the journey to *Just Be Love*.

16

Love and the Paradox

I have found the paradox, if you love until it hurts; there can be no more hurt, only more love. —Mother Teresa

The above quote is a paradox. A paradox is a way of thinking that offers an idea or concept that seems contradictory, yet it expresses a truth. Human love can seem to be a contradiction. As you read the above quote, one can wonder how this can be, that to love until it hurts will diminish the hurt and only more love will remain. This is the experience and journey to Divine love. We desire love, yet we may see ourselves as unworthy of it. In the need for love, we deny it, and we are inconsistent with expressing and living it. In the need for love we have disagreement, opposition, confusion and conflict. We can become confused, angry, illogical, and even violent. When we are in the space of awareness and truth about love we become honest, accepting, confident, humble and reverent. We become authentic, caring, appreciative, compassionate and forgiving. If we truly love as God loves, the hurt will always yield to love, because love is all there is.

There is duality and contrast within the paradox. Duality is simply two states or poles split from their origin of unity. Love holds the tension of the opposites and creates space to transcend them. Divine love accepts the split of the opposites and then unites the poles as one seamless act. Like a car battery which has two opposite poles, it needs both to come together to start the car. Sunlight has its opposite in darkness to make up our twenty-four-hour day. The Holy Spirit and the spirit within us know how to hold the tension of the opposites in order to reconcile the dynamic of duality.

The universal law of polarity states: *"Everything has an opposite pole and is on a continuum of all that is."* We create a world that appears as duality, past and future, right and wrong. What if it's really not duality but rather a continuum of different perspectives and points that creates energy of varying vibrations? In reality the Sun never really sets; the Earth turns. All waves in the ocean will lead us to the shore and take us back out to the sea.

The pendulum is an example of duality, always swinging from one end to the other. As humans, we can have an image of love, that it is perfect, kind, caring, etc. This ideal that we hold about love does not include pain or suffering, only joy and good fortune. Unfortunately, this perception is misguided and leads to confusion and disappointment. The Divine invites us to embrace both ends of the pendulum because life includes movement and balance from one end to the other. Divine love is present and perfect in life's movement from sadness to joy, and joy to sadness. Love is meant to be experienced in the back and forth movement of all life situations. However, we choose which end of the pole to be on within our experiences, and for how long. The understanding and acceptance of this creates more confidence and grace as we move through the difficult and painful times. We also experience greater appreciation of the joyful times, understanding that love is still there, even when the joy is again displaced by a moment of conflict. If you desire to experience God's love, move like the pendulum with acceptance of everything that comes your way in life. God's love is in all things. The acceptance of this is to *Just Be Love.*

If we love, we will hurt, and when we learn from the hurt, we will love more deeply. If we love and accept what hurts, in time love becomes our experience. Why resist this? Why not open up and relax into its energy, like we would ride a wave? The energy of love will take us where we should go, looking deeper into the truth of the paradox of our experiences in order to discover love more fully.

Love seeks to ignite the soul, transform the heart and expand the mind. In our human form, we are wounded by love and therefore afraid to love and be loved. Yet as spiritual beings, love is all we are, so love is all there is. Such is the paradox and journey back to Divine Love.

Let me offer you another example. When we look out at the horizon, it appears to just drop off. We know that centuries ago people believed that the world was flat, and that going to the edge would mean you would drop off the earth. That belief was challenged. The explorers didn't drop off; in fact, they discovered new possibilities and opportunities in other lands that they didn't know existed. They broke free of the created illusion and discovered a whole new world. They created a paradigm shift in consciousness. This was courage and love in action, because they confronted fear and the unknown and opened the door to a greater reality and actual truth.

Yes, life is infinite and ever expanding. Its paradox and duality mixed together with uniqueness and oneness. It's different yet it's profoundly the same. Love thrives here; this is the truth and infinite energy of Divine love.

Life Isn't Good or Bad—It Just Is

I've come to realize that the soul seeks to explore the paradox concept. In doing so, we more clearly discover the illusions we made so real. Life is a continuum within what seems like a paradox. At any point in time within our life experiences, we are at a certain place on this continuum. We view a situation as good or bad, right or wrong, or somewhere in between. We determine our life to be at a certain point on the continuum based on our perceptions of the experience. When we observe a situation, it changes, because we color it with our own perceptions and knowing. This is the reason why two or more people can observe the same object or situation and have a different perception of what they observed. Understanding this concept creates awareness of how life works.

Many people who have experienced a deep meditative state or have had a near death experience, begin to see and understand more clearly the paradox effect. In these transforming states of consciousness, we are taken into the realm of unlimited possibilities, sending us beyond the horizon of what we think is reality. We are free of expectations and attachment to outcomes. We embrace the "what is" in the moment. We move to the other side of the veil. Discovering life isn't good or bad; it just is. We find that love is the source of it all.

Albert Einstein explained the paradox of life by saying, *"Life is a preparation for the future; and the best preparation for the future is to live as if there were none."* Life and love are to be experienced in the present. With innocent awareness, we experience joy and reverence at a higher, more intimate level. We see and know the perfection in it all, especially in what we once experienced as struggle and pain. We see clearly how life events all fit together. The lessons we once deemed difficult and unwelcome, now become a catalyst for growth and part of the whole of our life.

A key to moving through the paradox concept is to understand and accept the opposites. By challenging our self-created illusions, we can explore and confront our fears and misperceptions. If we move out of our comfort zone, we can go to the edge of ourselves and confront our unknown. Our shadow says, "We will die going to the edge—the unknown." We experience our edge, when it hurts so deeply that only love is left to be felt and experienced. This is the abyss, the profound, the infinite of us and our life. Love is at our edge—a love so strong that it may hurt, but then only love remains. By going to our edge, feeling the fear and hurt, we will break free, and in time all that remains is the abyss of Love.

17

Love and Freedom
Are Found in the Unknown

What's known is Knowledge. What's unknown is God.

I look at my life and ponder how much I think I know. In reality, all I know is my false sense of safety and security, for what I know is based on my past. Yet I hang on to the beliefs I formed in my past, and then wonder why my life is limited and unfulfilled. Rather than living a life of love, I am living a life of unconscious fear and illusion. *"How can this be?"*, "I" my (*lower self*) ask to my "Self" (*higher Self*)

My higher self explains to my lower self, *"The known is your false perceptions and belief that keeps you in your comfort zone, and thus your self-imposed prison. You want to build walls of protection so that you feel safe. You ramble with the same mindless thoughts and images day after day. This makes you look good and feel confident. Yet you dwell in feelings of doubt, fear and unworthiness."*

The unknown is where our freedom truly resides. I fear it because I imagine it to be unsafe. God abides in the known, yet this energy is readily discovered when we explore the unknown. The Divine, the source of all creation and the source of love, dwells in the unknown—the realm of possibilities. Yet I dare not go there, because I don't know what's there. I deceive myself, believing that my past and the known bring freedom—brings love.

Am I really living and experiencing life if I'm trapped in my world of the known? Where is the mystery, the excitement, the drive, the potential and the passion? Do I really know myself in the known? Or do I discover more of who I really am each time I step into the unknown of myself and the universe? Is there perhaps greater self-love waiting for me in that which I don't yet know about myself and about God? For it seems that the unknown is a place of clues, other perceptions and possibilities for my life—another reality I won't let in. The unknown, the path less traveled, is where the love, the answers to my life are discovered, experienced and brought into conscious awareness.

Deep within I sense my soul; I hear the Divine calling me to the unknown, which holds even deeper secrets to love. Do I dare explore what's unknown? What if I experience myself there? What if I experience the Divine there? What if I experience self-love there and answers to my struggles? What if in going there, I realize I must make changes for spiritual growth and true happiness?

My lower self perceives the unknown as a place that holds all of the traumatic memories and wounds of my life, and that's to be avoided. It says, *"The unknown is too scary and painful; I've got more important things to do today. I'll do this exploring stuff tomorrow."* Yet tomorrow is part of my unknown. You see, I tricked myself again. My Higher Self loves me so much; it will be there in what I call tomorrow. Could it be that the unknown only knows love, wisdom and freedom? I hear a soft voice deep within me say, *"There's only one way to know."*

18

Thoughts to Ponder with Just Be Love

On Earth's galactic journey and its precession through the equinoxes, December 21, 2012 marked the ending of the Piscean era and cycle and welcomed the Aquarian age and cycle. With this ending and beginning a refreshing new energy, vision and consciousness was birthed at earth's horizon. The rising of this new age offers us an awakening to higher love, wisdom, compassion and peace on Earth. We are filled with possibilities and opportunities. For there to be greater love and peace for humanity and all sentient beings that live on Mother Earth, we must start within our individual selves. Yes, let's *Just Be Love* to change the world.

The way to love and peace for humanity is through self-love and inner peace. We get there by taming the mind and tending to our soul-heart. Self-love and inner peace should be our daily practice, especially in times of struggle and pain, so that we may realize and experience ourselves in divine unity.

Life and love are meant to be simple. Yet the ego likes to make a problem of things. In our desire for power, the need to be right, love for money and material possessions, we are neglecting the inheritance entrusted to us by our Creator. It's an inheritance that deserves our reverence, and should be cherished, appreciated and cared for. Mother Earth is the creative expression of Divine love. She is an energy, and a soul, that we are connected to—it is a privilege to live here.

Like the Earth, some of us have been subject to neglect, abuse, or exploitation. Others have been the ones doing the neglecting, abusing or exploiting. Humanity has struggled with offering reverence, appreciation, gratitude, and care to each other in the name of love. We seem to struggle with accepting and appreciating our own individual divinity, as well as each other's, and that of Mother Earth.

Yogiraj Siddhanath expressed a simple, yet transforming phrase, giving us a way to look at ourselves and our world: "Our Soul Cry: If earth peace is to herald the dawn of the new age, let us all realize.

Humanity Is Our Uniting Religion
Breath Our Uniting Prayer and
Consciousness Our Uniting God."

After reading the above quote, try this simple exercise, focusing on the italicized part of the quote. Close your eyes, become aware of your breath, open your heart and your inner eye of knowing. When you feel relaxed and centered, open your eyes, and sit with this italicized phrase, softly repeating it for a few moments. When the experience seems complete, take a deep cleansing breath, and sense how you feel, how you see yourself and the world. Imagine what your life would be like if you embraced the meaning of this quote.

Imagine what our world would be like if we learned this ideal early on and practiced it throughout our lives. Imagine the exchange of energy we would experience with each other. Imagine the oneness we would experience with all beings that inhabit earth.

Humanity Is Our Uniting Religion: Humanity is the one thing we cannot deny. It connects us to each other regardless of gender, race, country, culture, upbringing, income level, religious or political beliefs. We are all part of humanity. Accepting and living this concept would make problem solving much simpler, and yield profound results. If we embraced this idea, there would be more willingness to find the common ground with each other. The common ground begins with recognizing and honoring our divinity within our humanity and our connection to all that is. At present, our individual and collective wounds, and our unconscious impulses create judgments and the need to be right— to be superior, to divide and conquer. All this creates distractions and roadblocks to the path of love, cooperation, and peace; energy that separates rather than unites us to love—to Source.

His Holiness the Dalai Lama said, *"Religion is here and now in our daily lives. If we lead that life for the benefit of the world, this is the hallmark of a religious life. This is my simple religion. No need for temples. No need for complicated philosophy. Our own mind, our own heart, is the temple; the philosophy is simple kindness."* His Holiness also expressed the opinion, *"All major religious traditions carry basically the same message that is love, compassion, and forgiveness the important thing is they should be part of our daily lives."* Along with this, we all strive to be loved, accepted and acknowledged. These are all aspects of the common ground we desire as humans. The journey of our individual and collective souls is to embrace these qualities. This would create a profound shift, a way to return to the love that we are—to serve humanity as our larger self, meditating with the intent of peace within, and radiating it out to our world. By divine design we are all spiritual beings, citizens of the infinite universe and temporary stewards of the earth. It is our soul's purpose to attain conscious awareness and strive towards common ground, creating peace with our brothers and sisters in celebration of our oneness, yet embracing our individually and our uniqueness.

Breath Our Uniting Prayer: Human life is united by the breath, which is holy and of spirit. The breath is the giver, the receiver and the sustainer of life. The breath is sacred space and fertile ground, where intention, communion and communication with Source merge. The breath anchors and activates our heart and higher soul self. Breath quiets the mind and creates conscious connection to God. We live through and by the breath; this is what unites us to ourselves, each other and our Creator. Awareness of our breathing, the gentle and rhythmic in and out, creates a meditative, prayerful state of inner dialogue with Source, where we can listen to the soft still voice within the heart.

Peace, understanding and harmony come with focusing on the breath. Prayer is talking to God. Meditation is listening to God. The most important part of communication is being fully present and listening. Breath meditation helps clear the negative emotions, quiets the mind and opens the heart, leading to clarity and inner peace. The breath is our connection to the body, mind and Spirit. When our breath comes in, the Divine communes and communicates with us; and when our breath goes out, we expand, commune and communicate with the Divine. A peaceful breath flows equally in and out, in harmony, reducing stress and inner conflict, promoting peace within, and ultimately ripples out into the world.

Consciousness Our Uniting God: The soul's main purpose for being is to achieve a higher and more loving state of consciousness. Awareness is the pathway to this purpose. Consciousness is simply awareness. Consciousness is the ground of all healing and transformation. Our task is to learn that negative and attacking thoughts create misidentifications, leading to suffering. We are not our judgmental thoughts. These do not help us realize who we are or help connect us to Source and to love. Only the conscious awareness of our thoughts that come from divine thought will assist us in uniting with Source. Our idea that "I am somebody" leads us to all sorts of strategies to reconnect, because the ego mind believes the "I" means "I'm separate," "I am special." We live as if we are separated from the Divine and all that is.

Self-inquiry is to reflect on our unique gifts and strengths. It is also the process of questioning and challenging our assumptions and what we've made true. With self-inquiry, ask the deeper question: Who am I? Exploring this question is vital. We fear change and loss (losing the false self) and we cling to our created story as if it were life itself. Life is love with purpose. Our story with its identifications, distract us from life and distorts our divine purpose for being. Attachment to our story is the root of endless searching and unhappiness. The end of confusion, unhappiness and separation comes with the awareness that these identifications are really misidentifications in disguise.

Reconciling our attachment to false identities and created burdens allows us to experience our true self as love, joy and an aspect of the Divine. Thought without awareness is the ego's work. The ego is the great deceiver; the root of continued separation from our soul and God.

The glory of love lies in the emptiness, in the openness of the mind. This will offer the emotion, the awareness to experience a higher knowing of love. This is the way to consciousness, to inner peace and to experience the joy of our soul. It is the return to love, and to remembering and celebrating the realization that we are part of the fabric of the infinite universe.

The Tao tells us:
My words are easy to know,
Easy to practice.
Yet few under heaven know or practice them.
My words reveal Eternal principals,
Enduring patterns, Pathways to harmony.
— Tao, 70

The Buddha said:
The Buddhas do not wash away ill deeds with water.
Nor remove sufferings with their hands.
Nor transfer their realizations to others.
Beings are freed through teaching the truth,
the nature of things.

The Hopi Indians hold the belief:
We are the ones we have been waiting for.

I close part one with this poem:

Love as Awareness

Love is not found in the thought of Love.
Love is found in the awareness, I Am Love.
It's through our humanity, that we remember our divinity.
It is with our holy breath that we commune and
Communicate with all that is.
It is for us to remember with higher awareness that God is Love
And all that makes up the universe is the expression of this Love.

Contents

Introduction

D ivine Love is inviting and inclusive. The energy of love is in everything, because everything is a part of the Divine and a component in the realm of possibilities. Part two comes from my deeper observations, reflections and interpretations of messages from Master Jesus about love and life.

Come journey further with me to explore the deeper meanings of what God's Love appears to be within our limited yet inquiring awareness. From our stillness, let us Just Be and observe how God's Love shows itself in the places and spaces that make up our lives, while we carry on as spiritual beings having a human experience. You may not have recognized that love was in some of these places and spaces. It is my hope that, as you read part two, you will discover a deeper appreciation of Divine love and where it can be found and felt. As you explore and contemplate this love more deeply, ponder how it can impact your concept of love and connection, and perhaps you will reconsider a held belief in separation from Source. All problems and suffering are resolved when we remember where we came from and reunite with the Source of Love.

19

The Energy of Divine Love

The energy and vibration of divine love is ever present, like Spirit,
love was the beginning with no ending.

I believe that all life within the universe is pure energy in its fullest expression. Everything emanates from this energy. All souls are conceived from the Divine womb and expand to forever exist. Divine love has the clear intent of witnessing, supporting, nurturing and celebrating all that it births. This becomes the core truth from which all other truths arise. Human consciousness is on a journey to remember and live this core truth of Divine love.

There is a field of energy that encompasses our wondrous self and beyond. Imagine how this energy can be experienced if we open-up; if we would only trust and allow ourselves to move beyond what we see with just our physical eyes—willing to step out of our comfort zone. An example is when we meditate, quieting our ever-active mind. We come to a place, an energy field within and all around us, that see's and understands more fully what we have been missing in the superficial world. We begin to move beyond the illusions of this world that we have made so real. When Jesus said let thine eye be single, I believe he was referring to knowing and trusting our inner eye, the eye of intuition and wisdom, the eye of our soul; the third eye between our eyebrows connected to our pineal gland, located between the brain's two hemispheres. This gland has been referred to as the God gland, the connection to Source, to pure energy.

The Universe Is All About Energy

The science of quantum physics tells us much about the workings of this inner field of energy and of the cosmos. Energy is vibration, which resonates as frequency throughout the universe. I like to think of this energy as the universal hum that ebbs and flows in the form of particles and waves. This invisible field is the unified field, of vibrational energy is always creating, expanding and renewing. Creation is always in the process of creating. There is both stillness and movement in creation, like the movement of our in and out breath, with its still point—the pause in between.

The energy field of Divine love also seems to be ever moving and flowing toward its beloved. Divine love is unlimited and the ultimate expression of creation that makes up this field. Einstein said, *"The field is the sole governing agency of the particle."* That means it's the invisible field that gives life and shape to our material (particle) world, the world of matter. It's been noted that ninety six percent of all existence is invisible to the human senses. Matter makes up only four percent of the known universe. It is because of this invisible and infinite energy field that we have life in all its forms and formlessness. There is an infinite number of living parts that make up the universe. Divine intelligence knows all these parts as pure energy and love.

Love As: Living One Vibrational Energy

Love is the highest expression of divine energy, creating the highest frequency. Love is the ultimate healer and restorer. Divine love is the energy that unites and ties all of life together. Love is what makes two parts into one. Examples: light and dark make up a day; we need a negative and positive charge to create electricity; or sunshine appears amidst storm clouds to make the rainbow. Marriage unites two unique individuals as one. Divine love accepts and embraces all that is, into itself, as one vibrational energy force. Consider the human body, which has trillions of individual parts, each with different functions. The intelligence of Divine love, in magical and mysterious ways, created the functioning of cells, organs and systems to live as one vibrational energy system. All functions do their part for the well-being of the whole body. Science has discovered the universal law of vibration, which states that everything in the universe vibrates and moves in a circular pattern. Our thoughts, perceptions and emotions have unique vibrations. Our life is a circle and a cycle of experiences, perceptions, emotions and beliefs that invite us to grow and thrive as a dynamic field of divine energy. Part of our task, as a soul in human form, is to align the individual vibrations of our thoughts and beliefs with Source vibration; creating and **Living One Vibrational Energy.**

> *For where two or three come together in my name, there am I with them.* — Matthew 18:20, NLV

Science is now supporting the theory that thoughts of love have positive, measurable effects on our cells, organs, and even our DNA. Thoughts and feelings of acceptance, appreciation and compassion toward ourselves and others can energetically have a positive impact on us and all that's around us, even plants and animals.

Numerous studies, such as those done through the Institute of HeartMath, show that individuals in heart coherence, when focusing on gratitude and compassion, displayed brain wave patterns and biorhythms that were affected in positive ways. Others close to them were similarity affected. Early in the twentieth century, the notable psychic Edgar Cayce assisted people in reducing the cycle of karma by suggesting they practice acceptance and forgiveness of themselves and others. This is a form of what we now call heart coherence. Karma is the cycle of cause and effect; the results of a person's prior actions in a past life, affecting their current lifetime. It is an important part of several religions, such as Hinduism and Buddhism.

In the late 1970's, Dr. Hew Len, a Hawaiian psychiatrist, was working in a psychiatric unit for criminally disturbed patients. The unit was very dangerous and staff morale and turnover were major problems. Completely isolated from the patients on the unit, Dr. Len would review a patient's chart and history, and then hold the chart in his hands. He would focus on the patient's issues, absorbing the patient's problems and pain as if they were his own. He then focused his thoughts to heal the issues, as if within himself. He would practice the "Ho'oponopono" technique, feeling with much compassion and saying, *"I love you. I am sorry. Please forgive me. Thank you."* After a few months of doing this, repeatedly, the patients on the unit became more relaxed and cooperative. Staff moral improved because there was less of tension and stress.

Numerous studies now show what the power of love and thoughts of peace can do in reducing crime, war, illness, suffering and even death. Expressing loving and compassionate thoughts during someone's illness can have positive effects on their healing.

A scientific study published in the Journal of Offender Rehabilitation noted that over a two-year period, worldwide terrorism was decreased by 72 percent because groups of seven thousand people gathered in meditation and prayer three times a day.

Another example of the power of prayer: In August 2013, Syria's internal conflict was drawing the United States to consider military intervention. People across the country, myself included, began holding "prayers for peace" vigils. James Twyman, a renowned peace troubadour, led a group of individuals to Syria and Egypt to advocate praying for peace. The result: The Soviet Union convinced its ally, Syria, to give up its chemical weapons program. The United States withdrew its military involvement, and the United Nations approved the Syrian disarmament plan, receiving the backing of both the Soviet Union and China.

Simply put, what we desire to experience in our lives, we must first feel and believe in our hearts that's it's already occurred. Creating loving thoughts expands our energy, vibration and consciousness. Having fearful, hateful or resentful thoughts blocks our energy, closes our heart and lowers our vibration and awareness. When people come together in a group and pray or meditate with the intention of love, it has a positive effect on the energy field within us and around us. In the third and seventh Beatitudes respectively, Jesus says, *"Blessed are the meek (gentle): for they shall inherit (unite with) the earth." "Blessed are the peacemakers: for they shall be called the children of God."* Despite the current unrest in different parts of the world, a planetary shift is happening today on a grass-roots level, creating an era with the consciousness of peace in many people.

Imagine a field of energy that is the basis of all life. This energy is in all things seen and unseen. It is not devoted to one particular species on Earth; no one species or person has special privilege. The unified field is shared by, for and with the entire cosmos. It is what created and sustains the cosmos as a dynamic living system. This unified field operates through the energy of infinite intelligence and love. To deny the existence of this infinite energy field and how it communicates with all that is, is to deny the essence of God, the essence of love and the essence of life.

There are many definitions of love. To simply understand love is to say love is energy. Love is, *Living One Vibrational Energy.* When we peel away all the definitions, research, dogma and drama and sit still and quiet, we can feel more deeply what our physical eyes can't see, we become aware that love is nothing more than pure Divine energy, unconditional and accepting.

> *If you want to find the secrets of the universe, think in terms of energy, frequency and vibration.* —Nikola Tesla

Love is the energy and vibration with which God created all that is. Just as each of us has a fingerprint and personality, each of our fingerprints and personalities are unique, and an individual expression of the Divine. God knows us more by our individual vibration and light than by our names. All of creation is understood and known by its distinct vibration.

Our energy pattern and rhythm put out a vibration to the universe, not just our world, and we receive vibrations from others and God's too. We detect and respond to each other's energy and to that of the environment. When we say, "I don't have a good feeling about this" or "that person makes me feel good all over," we are responding to the invisible energy field of the person/environment.

This book is the result of energy manifested through Divine guidance, insights and thoughts coming through me and expressed as words on the pages. You are taking in and responding one way or another to the energy of this book. The more positive and open we are to life's experiences, the higher our vibration will be. The more we each take responsibility for our perceptions, feelings, beliefs, emotions and choices, the higher our energy and vibration will be. When human love meets and aligns with Divine love, there is chemistry and synergy like no other. This is bliss and the true meaning of the term "soulmate" connection—the I AM inside us merging with the I AM of all that is—Beloveds in sacred unity.

Our field of energy has direct and indirect effects on the individual and the collective consciousness, behavior and even the evolution of our planet and the universe. Likewise, the energies that make up the whole of our planet and our universe have direct and indirect effects on us.

> *Every thought, every action vibrates through the infinite field of consciousness. It's important to be mindful of our thoughts and emotions for their effects are far more potent than we realize.*

Humanity is operating from outdated paradigms about energy and love. The time has come for us to learn how to be with this energy field. This is one of our soul's purposes for being here. Our indigenous sisters and brothers knew this, as do many of the spiritual teachers of the present and past. Many of us have felt a separation from divine love. We've been out of touch, experiencing disconnect with the Divine. We've gone to sleep and forgotten, even denied this energy field exists. However, it's never been out of touch with us. This energy is love. It is abundant and for the benefit of all. The more we can accept this, the more we can be in alignment and harmony with this field of energy called Source.

Individually, as we elevate our consciousness and vibration, we bring peace and healing to the planet. The more we heal ourselves and our planet, the more we create alignment with Source. This alignment returns us to the love we are. Our life is about remembering and returning to this energy field of pure love. Having conscious awareness and presence of this naturally places us in a state of heart coherence, a state of balance and peace—a state of love.

Perhaps one reason Jesus was put to death, was that he was here to offer a higher vibration and expression of unconditional love for humanity. Some struggled and were threatened by his vibration, wisdom and teaching about what Divine love truly meant. Over two thousand years later, we continue to have this struggle. We feel strings attached to this love and feel unworthy of this love. We are making progress as more and more people around the world yearn for and search for understanding, acceptance, compassion and forgiveness—the desire to remember and return to loving and being loved. Martin Luther King Jr. said it well as he struggled to bring love, righteousness, compassion and equality to the United States: *"I have decided to stick with love. Hate is too great a burden to bear."*

Like Jesus and other spiritual teachers, Martin Luther King Jr. was bringing that higher vibration and expression of Divine love to humanity. He too was shunned, condemned and killed, due to fear and ignorance of what God's love offers. Why do we deny and reject the very energy that truly ignites and sustains us? What will it take for us to more fully surrender to, trust in, and receive Divine Love?

Out beyond ideas of wrong-doing and
right-doing there is a field.
I'll meet you there.
When the soul lies down in that grass
the world is too full to talk about.
Ideas, language, even the phrase "each other"
doesn't make sense anymore. —Rumi

In this field there is no right and wrong, no up and down, no judgment or blame, no good or bad. It just is. The field is the no-thing and the everything, the stillness and the movement, the joy and the sorrow, the emptiness and the fullness of life. It's where truth and higher consciousness resides. The energy of love unites all separate things into one. This is Divine, sacred unity. This is *Living One Vibrational Energy*.

When we can put the ego aside and lay our soul down in that grass, we will again know our world as love and bliss. Our higher self's concept, belief and language of love and humanity go beyond what our lower self believed to be true. Opening ourselves up to the higher perspective of Divine love and wisdom moves us into the field of transcendence. To lie down in this field we must be willing to collapse our current version of love and align with universal love and the reality of the Creator—the nurturer of this energy field.

Don't just talk to God; don't just talk to your partner or your neighbor. Develop the practice of mindful awareness of your feelings. Practice observing, listening and touching the energy of God through others and through your world. Practice being in heart coherence, with thoughts of acceptance, appreciation, compassion and cooperation as you interact with others. Meditate with openness to have the willingness to give, to receive the energy and presence of the love and light of spirit. This can be done in solitude and in groups. Focus on awareness of your breath, the gentle rhythm of in and out—the energy and rhythm of life, and of spirit. Breath is spirit—Source energy.

Yes, out beyond our perceptions, our ideas, labels and our story of what is, there is a field of energy, vibration and frequency; there is love—always has been and always will be—I'll meet you there!

The Energy of Divine Love

Love is the energy that holds space for all that is, including you and me
It is seamless and timeless.
Its flow cannot be stopped, for it is existence.
It is made of both the formless and the formed.
Divine Love cannot be hurt;
Since it does not define itself by that which it is not.
Its patience never waivers.
When seen as the Divine sees,
We recognize its beauty is limitless and majestic, yet, simplistic.
It gives and receives without expectations or judgment.
This energy dwells both in light and darkness.
It transcends separation and duality,
Through unconditional love, acceptance and grace.
It knows itself as I AM.
As the originator of love, it holds no measure.
In its emptiness there is nothing but fullness of all that is.
This energy is the breath of awareness and acceptance,
And the heartbeat of compassion and forgiveness.
Divine energy is the beginning that has no ending,
The eternal vibrational presence of Love.

20

Love and Joy

Jesus speaks through me, saying this about love and joy:

> My dear one, love is the strongest and most powerful energy in the universe. Next to love is joy. Love is simply who you are. Joy is what blooms when you free yourself from needing to be somebody other than who you are. Where there is love, there is joy. Where there is joy, love is there too. Joy walks with love, because love includes joy. Joy is simply the reflection of love. To "Just Be Love" is to experience joy. Joy is knowing and living this Divine truth. Let yourself practice this truth daily with understanding, acceptance and compassion. Observe yourself as love walking and living with joy. Truly what more needs to be said?

Being in fear, doubt or shame separates us from Divine love, self-love and joy. Being needy creates expectations that lead to disappointments, which also separates us from love and joy. Our fear, neediness and shame create the illusion of separation. If you desire love and joy, refrain from being too needy; face the fears of your pain, reconcile your unworthiness, and come to know your true self.

We attain personal freedom when we are our true and authentic selves. This freedom also comes through unconditional love and acceptance of ourselves and others. We are free when we cease judging and pretending. Love and joy can naturally be experienced when we are free.

The nature of love and joy is seeing life with innocent, childlike eyes, an open heart and a quiet yet expanded mind. Joy amplifies the energy of love. You may say, "You make it sound so simple." Here's what I heard Jesus say in response:

> Yes, it is that simple, so why choose to make it complicated and difficult? Love and joy are your true, divine nature. Pleasure is the delight and fulfillment of the body and mind. Joy is the natural

state of the spirit and the delight and fulfillment of the soul. Joy arises when the mind can freely love and accept itself.

The paradox of joy and sorrow is that the more you discover your joy, the more you will recognize your sorrow and the parts of you that hold you back from love and freedom. Being in your heart, offers you the opportunity to more fully embrace and overcome the limiting beliefs that make up your self-created story; which limits your joy. Joy is the result of seeing ourselves and our experiences from our higher, wiser perspective. Avoiding our pain, keeps us further from love and joy—Love is reconciling our wounded self. Joy is the result of this reconciliation.

Joy arrives when we live our passion. When we appreciate how good life truly is and walk the path of acceptance, compassion, love and joy, we naturally find our true self. The soul knows the abundance of the universe. The soul invites us to rediscover this abundance by living in and through our hearts. Joy naturally arises from within us, when we offer heart-felt praise and gratitude.

Joy is the desire of the soul and our spiritual essence. Joy comes through acknowledging we are part of the very substance and nature of the Divine universe. We are the infinite universe, and the universe is us. To live this is to experience joy. It comes through co-creating with the Divine and with meaningful relationships with others.

Joy resides in the infinite and in the simplistic. There's joy in knowing that light and fullness always surround the darkness and emptiness. Joy comes by opening to the experiences and lessons of the soul. Moving through our lessons with love and grace transforms our darkness into light. Answers come from our struggle, and when we are ready and willing, joy replaces our sorrow.

I hear Jesus add:

> *So again, I simply say: To "Just Be Love" is to experience Joy. Can you just let this be, without needing anything more? Be joy... needing more only leads to struggle and disappointment. Love and joy are abundant and in the depths of your being. Go within you now my beloved, and love yourself, accept yourself. There you will experience love as joy and joy as love.*

21

Love and Grace

Everybody can be great... because anybody can serve. You don't have to have a college degree to serve. You don't have to make your subject and verb agree to serve. You only need a heart full of grace. A soul generated by love. —Martin Luther King Jr.

Like love, I believe grace is hard to define, because it's a spiritual and mystical experience. Grace is a quality we feel and experience within our hearts and souls, just like we feel the expression of love, acceptance, compassion and forgiveness. We feel grace in the depth of us much more than we see and hear it. That's why grace is so powerful and holds a higher vibration and healing effect. We don't just see elegance or beauty in form; we feel it within the core of our being. Grace is experienced in movement of a loving expression or gesture. It is felt in the accepting presence of stillness. Grace, like love, is always present and holds a steady and continuous vibration that is part of the universal hum.

Many of us have been taught that grace is the manifestation of favor and God's mercy on us. There is a commonly held belief that God doses out grace— the more we get, the greater the likelihood we will be "saved." I've come to understand that Divine grace is not something we earn. Grace is the experience of God's love, which is unconditional. Since we are love, we don't need to "earn" that which we already are. Divine grace is already given. We only need to open to it and embrace the opportunity it provides to remember our worthiness of inclusion and wholeness. I believe that salvation means, *Relinquishing our belief in separation from God and returning to oneness with our Source.*

Grace is a gift and is connected to the mystery of life. It is the unconditional love and support from God. Grace makes our surrender to the flow of life possible. Grace happens in the unplanned and unexpected. When we are struggling with money or other needs, we may unexpectedly get a check in the mail or a friend may offer us a helping hand.

Grace is the expression of God through our loving self. It is the pathway to love and the return to innocence; a form of love in action. The pathway is created through acceptance and non-judgment of others and oneself. It can also be seen and felt in the expression of appreciation, gratitude and care. To offer grace is to connect and experience one soul to another, and no words need be spoken in the experience and acceptance of grace. It is experiencing the energy of the soul that touches the heart and informs the mind. To be in grace is to *Just Be Love.*

Love in its purest divine form emits elegance and beauty. Grace is experienced through the stillness of love and the movement of life. It is the dance of tender hearts merging as one. Grace is the embrace and celebration of uniqueness within the oneness, divine love and sacred unity in action. Grace is allowing the I, the We, and the Us, to become One. To live in oneness is to move beyond ego, beyond need and lack, to a sense of being. Grace, like love, is something you move with and toward, not away from. It brings one into inclusion.

> *Spirit is a state of grace forever. Your reality is only*
> *spirit. Therefore, you are in a state of grace forever.*
> —A Course in Miracles, T-1. II:4-6

Grace returns us to the awareness of love, and to the formless spirit of our divinity. Divine grace has no rules or dogma for inclusion; the favor is granted regardless of what humanity perceives as moral or immoral. Rules and dogma stem from a need for power over. When one is in a state of grace there is no need or desire for power, for grace is truth. True grace, like true love, stands in its own power with no need to persuade. A person who experiences pure grace, like love, just has a natural knowing and feeling of inclusion with all of life. My experience with Jesus in the clouds was a powerful example of pure grace. We are already saved; our recognition of this is held in our hearts and souls. To know ourselves as love and worthy is the beginning of our return to grace. To open to grace is to accept our reality as spirit; in this we naturally experience grace for eternity. This is being and *Living One Vibrational Energy.* Unconditional acceptance of Divine grace is part of the alignment with the energy of the Spirit, which creates healing and transformation.

22
Love and Reverence

There are four questions of value in life. What is sacred? Of what is the spirit made? What is worthy of living for? What is worth dying for? The answer to each is the same. Only love.
—Don Juan deMarco

Reverence is a vital component of our spiritual essence. It is an act of love. When we are reverent, we have respect and passion for the holiness of life. Life is valued and cherished, from the smallest creature that roams the Earth to the shining stars seen at night. To be reverent is to walk through life with a sense of sacred connection to all that is. Reverence says "yes" to life and seeks to preserve and enhance life.

In reverence, one humbly accepts the experiences of life with openness and compassion for ourselves and others. It's a way of being—of coming from the heart and honoring life's lessons. Reverence comes from authentic power, which aligns our human self, more with our soul essence and with God. It brings clarity to who we are, and where we come from.

When I have reverence, I have greater respect and appreciation for myself and for my earthly brothers and sisters. I honor and respect our planet and all that inhabits it. I open and expand my heart and my consciousness to the fullness and richness of life, both the seen and the unseen. I choose to shed my ego identity, giving more credence and attention to my soul, with greater awareness of the spirit within.

Reverence means living from one's heart—touching and connecting the depths of the self with others and with Mother Earth. It also means being open to touch and connecting with God.

Reverence is being mindful of my fear, yet not letting it block my way. The quality of reverence is enhanced by doing our inner work of dismantling the misidentifications and limiting beliefs created by the false self. The ego is transcended, and reverence is manifested when we ask and answer the question: *Who Am I?* I believe reverence comes when we are willing to step into the unknown within. By exploring these unknowns, we find the clues for living our life more fully and discovering the love that we are. Reverence, like love, is found in both the unknown and the known.

23
Love and Intention

Each decision we make, each action we take, is born out of intention. —Sharon Salzberg

Intention is the energy we choose to put behind our desires and actions. Intention is the willingness to begin the creative process to manifest what is desired. Intention sets in motion an energy that impacts every aspect of our lives. Desire is longing for something to happen. It's the foundation of purpose. Desire activates intention, which in turn requires focused attention and action through concrete steps toward that desire.

Intention brings clarity to what we desire; attention brings focus to the desire. Desire and intention are creative actions that propel us to turn the present into a fulfilling future. Intention is born from imagination—a thought that holds the vibration of what we will attract. It becomes the energetic, vibrational process from which our experiences become our reality. An intention aligned with the Divine comes from the thoughts and energy of our higher self, of love and the desire to be the best version of ourselves— making the world a better place. Love and connection with Source are the true desire and intention of our soul.

I believe love is the strongest and most powerful energy in the universe. Creating an intention that is grounded in love sets this energy in motion. Our intention sends information through the body and mind, then the energy behind the intention ultimately goes out into the unified field. Out of love, the universe responds to our intentions through our experiences.

Intentions can be of good will or of disrespect toward others or ourselves. Our intention can either enhance life or in extreme cases, it can destroy life. An intention aligned with the Divine comes from our hearts and our higher mind and will support, strengthen and empower us. A misguided intention comes from the ego mind and, in time, it will create negative consequences.

We create an intention by the messages we give ourselves consciously or unconsciously. Our unconscious is the thoughts and beliefs we have that we are unaware of on the conscious level. Unconscious intentions are important to identify and reconcile, because we fail to realize what often blocks us from realizing our conscious intention. The unconscious creates what's called a *"counter intention"*, which contradicts our conscious desire. If our unconscious is consumed with fear, doubt and unworthiness, can you see how this inner voice could sabotage our conscious intention?

Both our conscious and especially our unconscious thoughts create our reality. Reframing our feelings and beliefs from negative past experiences helps to clear unconscious thoughts and manifest what we truly desire. There are often several unconscious counter intentions lingering in our shadow.

Marianne Williamson writes, *"Good intentions make the devil laugh. But what does not make him laugh are prayer, atonement, forgiveness, and love."* Good intentions come from our hearts; they're present to inspire and to spark our passion. Good intentions open the "4 I's" of the soul: *Innocence, Intuition, Imagination* and *Inspiration*. Acting to resolve our unconscious counter intentions, ultimately sets the energy in motion to create a higher vibration, which in turn attracts what we desire.

The essence of Divine love contains the energy of peace, wholeness and joy. The intention of this love will always be to seek to enhance and empower life and expand the growth of our soul. It will not contaminate, disempower or bring harm. To *Just Be Love* is to have an intention of love for life, relationships, our work and our planet.

Attention to the Intention

Tell me to what you pay attention and I will tell you who you are.
— Jose Ortega y Gasset

Regarding our intention, it is important to be mindful of where we place our attention. Attention is focus, and acts as a magnetic power source; it attracts what is focused on. Energy flows where attention goes. Energy is created by our thoughts, perceptions, beliefs and intentions. Simple fact: Where our mind goes, we go. We attract what we think. Where our attention goes, our energy goes and grows. An intention reflects our desire and the attention we give it. For example: If I say, "I don't want to be judgmental in my relationships", the attention and focus will be on "I don't want to be judgmental." As a result, I will likely be judgmental in my relationships, because my attention and thus my focus will be on being judgmental rather than being accepting or complementary. In this intention I stated what I didn't want (I don't want to be judgmental). The mind's attention and focus will go in the direction of what I don't want, not on what I do want. It's important to state only what you do desire, not it's opposite. Attention is direct focus on our intention. Being present of our attention is a form of awareness. Intention creates our future, so it needs to be clear and it requires commitment for it to manifest. Attention is specific; the greater the clarity of the intention, the more specific the focus and direction can be. Stand confident and be committed to the fact that your desire will come to be. Create passionate images about your desire, with positive, upward thoughts and feelings about it. Be open and receptive for any response from the universe. Be flexible and attentive to the response as you move forward with what comes.

Our capacity to love grows when we are conscious of our perceptions, thoughts and beliefs. It is vital to know not only our surface and conscious perceptions, thoughts and beliefs but, more importantly, be aware of our deeper, unconscious core thoughts, perceptions and beliefs. The dance between our body's emotions and the mind's perceptions, interpretations, thoughts and feelings create our expectations and beliefs. Our beliefs create our choices and behaviors. As mentioned in a previous chapter, emotions are what's felt in the body. Feelings come from the mind's interpretation of what the body is sensing and reacting too. Often the mind will misinterpret or over think the emotion and generate feelings of fear and doubt.

Observe the energy you create with your perceptions and thoughts. Notice the reason for your expectations, beliefs and actions that stem from your intention. *Are they loving, supporting and empowering you? Or are they toxic, coming from fear, resentment or greed?* Our intention creates our reality. Our attention is the focus on that reality. *What is the reality I am creating because of my past, my wounds, and the negative beliefs about myself and my world? Is this really what I want for myself?* If I desire others to be more understanding, accepting and loving, I must look first and foremost at the intention I hold day to day. Awareness of my core self-beliefs will lead me to "why" my life is the way it is.

Imagine a divine highway, and we are the driver. How we choose to drive on the Divine highway will determine the type of journey we have. There are rules of the road, true? Ask yourself: *Am I satisfied with my driving and where I'm going? If not, ask yourself, am I driving out of love or fear?* The thoughts and beliefs we choose creates an energy and frequency that will become our experience on the Divine highway that makes up our lives. We are the driver and passenger, the witness and the participant.

We are the victim and the villain, the cause and the effect, the fear or the love. Intentions are good and important. However, they become powerful and dynamic when we open and align them with the Divine's intention, attention and guidance. Being mindful of our intentions is part of the process of knowing who we are.

24

Love, the Divine Attributes and the Serenity Prayer

Let love guide my heart, wisdom guide my mind and power-with guide my soul.

A ttempting to explain the attributes of God is like trying to describe the indescribable. We can only imagine as we take in the totality of our earthly surroundings, look up at the sky, and wonder how all this takes place in the Creator's wondrous universe. Around the world, many religious and spiritual traditions have four words to describe the all-ness of God. *Omnipotent*: Omni in Latin means all and potent means powerful, thus describing God as all powerful. The second word is *Omnipresent*: God is all present, everywhere, in all things seen and unseen. The third word *Omniscient*, meaning God is all knowing. Lastly is *Omnibenevolent*, which means God is all loving, infinitely good.

Omnipotent is what I refer to as "power," Omnibenevolent is "love", and Omniscient is "wisdom." Omnipresent means, God's power, love and wisdom are always present. The Divine attributes of *Power, Love* and *Wisdom* are offered as tools for the soul's earthly existence. Souls through the human condition choose how they use these tools as part of their agreement. Power is offered so we may learn to create, to relate and to serve. Love is intended to provide the experience and learning environment for us to understand what we came here for, and to promote harmony through a peaceful existence within ourselves and all earthly inhabitants. Wisdom is attained when we've kept our minds on the higher path of spiritual growth. The soul seeks to experience and know who God is through these attributes, learning and discerning the right use of them.

During the course of my life, and in my deepening relationship with Jesus over the past years, I have come to realize with greater awareness and appreciation the importance of Acceptance, Courage and Discernment in order to attain spiritual awareness and personal growth. Spiritual awareness and personal growth are the natural results of acceptance, courage (to look and change from within) and discernment. These qualities are described in the Serenity Prayer and I believe correlate with the Divine attributes of *Power, Love* and *Wisdom.*

The Serenity Prayer, used by many 12-step programs throughout the world, was written by Reinhold Niebuhr, and adopted by Alcoholics Anonymous groups in the early 1940's. Here is the familiar version.

God grant me the serenity
to accept the things I cannot change;
courage to change the things I can;
and wisdom to know the difference.

It was the AA's intent to adopt this prayer as a means of assisting people who were struggling with alcohol addiction. It offers a pathway to inner peace and freedom from the grips of shame and addictive behavior. I believe this prayer forms a bridge from making self-destructive choices that come from our lower mind to choices that are more from our higher mind, thus more constructive. The prayer is useful for all of us attempting to overcome the human struggle of choices and change. It emphasizes the importance of acceptance, courage and discernment. It also captures the moment of choice—discerning whether to accept the reality of a situation as is or to change it. I've come to appreciate how this prayer weaves the attributes of *Power, Love* and *Wisdom* with the attributes of *Acceptance, Courage* and *Discernment.*

The Power and Serenity of Acceptance

The first part of the Serenity Prayer says: *"God grant me the serenity to accept the things I cannot change."*

Our willingness and ability to accept the uncertainties, and even the tragic events in our life will, in the long run, provide us with greater inner power and the spiritual peace and strength to move forward. Our personal power, inner peace and self-worth can be compromised by unfortunate life situations. When this happens, we can feel alone and powerless. Our lower self will want to control what is not ours to control. Our ability to tap into the Divine wisdom within is blocked by the attitude of non-acceptance. We can forget the presence and power of God. Yet, God and our higher self are asking us in circumstances that don't seem to make sense or seem unfair to accept the situation. It is normal for us to resist and ask, *"Why?"* We need to know. We want control. We need to make sense out of this. The answers are found through "acceptance" of the things we cannot change. Due to our limited perspective, we would benefit from realizing that some aspects of what we experience, and the "why" of it, may not be totally understood in a way that makes sense to us.

Resistance and non-acceptance will move us further from the answer, limiting our willingness to change what we can. Acceptance and trust in divine order are the answers to the question, "Why?" This is what makes acceptance so powerful. Acceptance generates a forward movement, overcoming resistance. The "why" doesn't matter now because we accept the things we cannot change. We surrender to the power and knowing that is greater than ourselves, letting go of the need to control; the need for a concrete answer. Recall that Divine Love is unconditional love and acceptance of the spirit in all that exists. The act of acceptance is an act of love; it moves us, arousing the spirit within us. With acceptance, we let go of conditions and limits and can view our experience from the higher perspective. Acceptance opens our heart to compassion; it illuminates the path to serenity and empowerment.

Acceptance comes from an open and willing heart. It's a sign and act of spiritual maturity. Acceptance calls us to spiritual surrender and trust (to have faith) in a power, love and wisdom greater than ourselves. An acronym for faith:

Full
Acceptance
In
Thy
Heart

Acceptance as spiritual surrender magnifies our connection to a higher power and to love. This restores faith and hope, allowing for a higher meaning of life experiences.

The ego mind can magnify problems through fear and worry. Contemplate the ancient wisdom of Santideva, an eighth-century Buddhist monk: *"If there is a way or solution to the problem, then what is there to be worried about. If there is no way or solution to the problem, then what is the use of being upset and worried?"* The solution or way is to let go of upset and worry to just *"be"* with what life is at this moment. There are times in our life when we are powerless. It is best to acknowledge this, and with humbleness, surrender to the Omnipotence (*all powerful*) God and the Omnipresence (*all present*) God. This surrender brings us into harmony with our Omnibenevolent (*all loving*) and Omniscient (*all knowing*) God. In times of accepting our powerlessness, we do have the power to change— from within. When I accept the things I cannot change, I then naturally change what I can—myself. In this, we empower our self; I change my perception and belief about "what is." I change from the inside-out. This is the embodiment of true, authentic power—this brings peace to the heart and mind.

Here's an example: I have prepared as best I can to take an important exam. The day of the exam, I am nervous and worried, and I hear that "critical inner voice" say, *"I have not prepared enough. I'm going to fail."* To counter this voice, I become aware of my breath. I quiet my mind, acknowledging my anxiety in this moment. I connect with Source and the part of me that knows that I have prepared the best I can and believes "I can" pass the test. I ask for guidance, strength and calm as I sit for the exam. I become more relaxed, and become that STAR—I *Surrender, Trust, Allow,* so I can *Receive* a passing grade. My perception, attitude and confidence are strengthened. I am calm and confident now; I do my best and trust that I'll pass the exam.

Our mind can and does get triggered in difficult situations, taking us back to times in our lives when we felt powerless. We bring these memories, beliefs and emotions into current situations. We can work through what's happening in the moment more rationally and effectively, when we go within, connecting with our higher power and higher self. When we practice the 4 R's in a situation, like this: *Recognize,* we're able to accept where we are in this moment, so that we can *Reconcile, Release* and *Reframe* our fears and connect to the "I can" within us.

True power and strength manifest the soul's desires to do the will of God; trusting and allowing oneself to be aligned with Source in order to co-create. True creative power is life force energy generating constructive results; using power to benefit our desires, through surrender, trust and acceptance. Acceptance is allowing; it's an act of acknowledgement and demonstrates the willingness to take responsibility for oneself in positive, compassionate and forward-focused ways.

Love Fuels the Courage to Change

God is Omnibenevolent, all loving, infinitely good. God's love is the primary Divine Attribute. It calls us to the yearning and mystery of love. Jesus in this simple phrase, *Just Be Love,* was calling attention to the importance and power of love in coping with and understanding life situations. Love is what called me to deliver these messages.

The second part of the Serenity Prayer asks for *"the courage to change what we can."* The only aspect of life we truly have the power to change is ourselves. It takes courage to change our perception, belief, attitude and behavior about our self within a situation and/or relationship. Love, acceptance and change starts from within. Courage is using our heart and higher mind to rise above our false and limiting beliefs in order to create a change in our life. It is through the energy of love that courage arises. To rise as love is to manifest the courage to change what we can. It's an act of courage to say "yes" to life and more importantly to say "yes" to ourselves.

In the 12-step program, I am asked to admit that I am powerless to an addiction and then turn it over to God. With this acceptance, I then need to do the inner work of working the 12 steps. Embracing and working these steps is an example of the courage it takes to change what I can. I have connection with, and faith in my higher power and higher self; I love myself enough to do my part toward overcoming the powerlessness of addiction, or other unfortunate life situation.

Earlier in this chapter, I mentioned about us asking the question "Why?" in our difficult times. I have found in my own journey the importance of, rather than asking, *"Why?"* or *"Why me?"*, asking instead *"**Why not me?**"* Asking this question takes courage and acceptance. It's a profound path back to love and soul understanding. It opens us up to a deeper level of surrender and acceptance, creating an awareness for greater possibilities in the perception that moves us through the things we cannot change. Asking "Why not me?" opens us to more deeply explore, with curiosity and innocence, the soul contract; the lesson that was meant to be learned from the experience. Courage is an important ally in transcending fear. It creates the willingness to be vulnerable when expressing love to ourselves and others. It invites us to step out of our comfort zone. By going beyond what we've known to be true about ourselves, we move to a higher state of consciousness to something better. Love creates the courage to overcome addictions, to reconcile a broken relationship or to walk away, if need be. Love generates the courage to admit our mistakes, speak our truth and strive for self-improvement. Love also fuels the courage to be of service to others.

The Wisdom to Know

Analyzing others is knowledge
Knowing yourself is wisdom.
Managing others requires skill.
Mastering yourself takes inner strength.
Knowing when enough is enough,
Is wealth of spirit.
Be present, observe the process,
Stay present, observe the process,
Stay centered and prevail. —Tao, 33

Wisdom is grounded in truth and understanding and aligned with divine principles. It is allowing the Omniscient, the wisdom of God, to flow in us. Wisdom is more than knowledge expressed with words—wisdom resides in the silence; it listens and holds a higher perception. Wisdom dwells in the soul-heart, and often arises in stillness, solitude and fasting, igniting the higher mind, where inner knowing and truth can be discovered and lived. It's the basis of the power of acceptance, and the courage to change; it values compassion to self and others. Wisdom is part of the Divine Attributes and the third aspect of the Serenity Prayer, *"the wisdom to know the difference."* The Wisdom to know the difference is *discernment.* In the process discernment, I come to understand what I cannot change and surrender to this, while generating the courage to change what I can. It's the ability to discern from our higher-wiser perspective, what to release to the higher power and what to take responsibility for. Wisdom is acceptance and responsibility in action.

Wisdom comes from awareness and detachment from our destructive thoughts, beliefs and behaviors. When we become attached to thoughts, especially negative ones, our energy is drained. Wisdom is detecting those inner negative thoughts and beliefs that block us from connecting to our positive thoughts which support and empower us. Our inner critic's use of judgment toward others or ourselves interferes with our ability to discern. Judging thoughts take us away from love, weaken us, and create a false sense of power and security. That's why judgment is paralyzing to the body and mind. The inner critic feels empowered by being the judge that has the final word. This is a form of power over, not power-with. Judgment creates irrational and limited patterns of perceptions and beliefs, which block our ability to view experiences from the higher perspective. Judgment, like fear and resentment, keeps us living in the past and stifles our potential and our spiritual growth.

Discernment is the ability to recognize which perceptions, thoughts and beliefs of past experiences no longer serve us, and the willingness to create new ones that do. This is the wisdom to know who we are and make empowering choices. When we are authentic, we elevate our thinking and gain clarity, which expands our possibilities and potential in life.

> *The essence of milk is butter, the essence of the flower is honey,*
> *the essence of grapes is wine, and the essence of life is wisdom.*
> —Pir-o- Murshid Inayat Khan, Sufi teacher

Wisdom connects us to the essence within us; our intuitive inner knowing. The Holy Spirit is the feminine aspect of God. Wisdom is the Holy Spirit, the Divine Mother, the heart knowing of God. The Bible's book of Proverbs speaks of wisdom as the feminine aspect of God, *"Wisdom has built her house. She has hewn (cut) out her 7 pillars."* (Proverbs 9:1, KJV). The Holy Spirit offers the ability of self-mastery through our hearts knowing and right action. The Holy Spirit assists all souls with discernment and trust to move forward on the journey.

With wisdom, God invites us to dance with the power of acceptance, as love is manifested by the courage to change. When love and power unite, wisdom is born. Wisdom gives the higher meaning to love and power. Love promotes wisdom, which inspires the courage to take right action; wisdom offers the right use of power and love. People who have power without love and wisdom become tyrants. Greed is power without love and wisdom. How we use power will be how we express love. How we use wisdom will determine how we use power and evolve as love.

> Jimi Hendrix said it well: *When the power of love overcomes the love of power, the world will know peace.*

Wisdom accepts "what is" and summons the courage of our inner warrior to engage in changing what truly is ours to change. The greater our strength and will are in alignment with the will of our Creator; wisdom will arise from within, expanding our soul evolution in human form.

Let us say "Yes," to God's knowing and use of power, love and wisdom. Let's say "Yes" to God and embrace the serenity when we accept our Creator's ways in our life struggles and tragedies. Let us pursue the courage and strength to change what we can, especially our self, and the wisdom to know the difference. This is our birthright and the higher, more expanded way to walk the Earth— rising as love and goodness.

25

Love and Compassion

Compassion is a mind having a single savor of mercy for all sentient beings. From compassion all aims are achieved. —Nagarjuna

Compassion is one important pathway to love and happiness as Lao-Tzu expresses here:

I have just three things to teach:
simplicity, patience, compassion.
These three are the greatest treasures.
Simple in actions and thoughts,
you return to the source of your being.
Patient with both friends and enemies,
you accord with the way things are.
Compassionate toward yourself,
you reconcile all beings in the world.

Simplicity, patience and compassion create ease and reverence in our life.

Compassion comes from the Latin word compatior, meaning: *"To suffer with or feel with."* To "feel with" is the ability to develop an expanding awareness, which leads to a greater connection with others. To "feel with" also means to have the willingness to get into the world of another person who is struggling, to feel with them and have a deeper sense of understanding. We can never truly experience and feel what the person feels, however, we can offer compassion, a caring and accepting presence. I don't believe the true intent of compassion is to "suffer with". To me compassion is being present to the suffering of another with an open heart and mind. It's to feel empathy for another's pain without losing yourself in their suffering. To support and encourage them, as they find their way back to love and inner peace.

The Buddha said: *"Compassion is that which makes the heart of the good move to the pain of others."* Chandrakirti, the sixth century scholar from India stated, *"Compassion itself is seen to be the seed of the rich harvest, water for growth, and the ripened state of long enjoyment. Therefore, at the start I praise compassion."*

Compassion, like love, is the fertile ground that enhances life. Compassion is the recognition of oneness with our brothers and sisters and all sentient beings. It moves us to assist others who are suffering, in physical, emotional, spiritual, social, or financial ways. Compassion is the act of caring and supporting each other as we walk the path.

> *The whole idea of compassion is based on a keen awareness of the interdependence of all these living beings, which are all part of one another, and all involved in one another.* —Thomas Merton

Compassion is fundamental to the human spirit and to our greater interconnection to life. An act of compassion creates a dynamic, powerful expression of love, understanding and acceptance. Expressing compassion indicates the ability to love and serve without expectations or attachments. It reveals our divinity within our humanness. Like reverence, compassion shows acknowledgment of the preciousness of life.

Compassion is about altruism, the act of unconditional giving and sharing. It flows freely from the heart, expanding the mind and creating acts of loving concern. Humanity and Mother Earth have the capacity to share, there is enough to go around. Scarcity exists due to the unwillingness and selfishness to share resources. Compassion is the cooperative spirit of caring and sharing. It's the willingness to serve, to make the world a better, more peaceful place. Compassion is the foundation of understanding, acceptance and forgiveness, and builds bridges between souls and hearts. It comes through as a listening ear, a gentle smile, a reassuring voice and a helping hand. Compassion is simply the act of loving kindness.

The Importance of Compassion for the Self

Compassion is love and grace in action. It is wise, healthy and loving to have compassion for ourselves, as much as for others. Self-compassion softens the inner critic and affirms value and concern to the self. The Dalai Lama has said: *"If you want to be happy practice compassion."* Love and happiness go hand in hand. People who are compassionate to themselves, have an increased sense of physical, emotional and spiritual well-being. They are more socially connected, with an appreciation for life.

Offering the self, love and compassion, creates space for inner happiness and peace to be remembered. Love and compassion for oneself, helps us understand how to love and offer compassion to others. When we are gentle with and express loving kindness to ourselves, it's easier to open our hearts and minds to others.

Self-compassion refers to a way of relating to the self—with kindness. It is not to be confused with arrogance, bullying or vanity, this indicates a *lack* of self-love and insecurity. Self-compassion, entails being gentle, accepting, supportive and understanding. In other words, being kind to ourselves in good times and especially difficult times. To offer self-compassion, you understand that your worth is unconditional, even when you make mistakes.

Give yourself permission to be imperfect, within your perfection. Self-compassion is about giving ourselves room to be human, to be flawed and broken, to have a bad moment or day. Many people struggle with needing to be perfect, needing approval. In God's reality, I believe we are seen and known as perfection and love. Because we come from the energy and thought of love and perfection. Recall, when we accept our imperfections therein lies our perfection. To be flawed is to be human. From the higher perspective, what our lower self views as "mistakes" are intended to be understood as opportunities for learning and growing.

Compassion: A Way to Serve Others

Jesus and other spiritual teachers emphasized the importance of loving our enemies; of having compassion for those who may bring harm to us or others. Compassion is an invitation to view the experience, and the souls involved, from a higher perspective and truth. Having compassion for others allows divine reverence and grace to work through us, so we can see the perfection in all that is without judgment or resentment. Recall, in spiritual terms, that the word perfection means *"to have compassion for."* Being compassionate is not rescuing a person from learning the soul lesson of a difficult experience. It's being present with that person—without expectations, accepting they may not be ready for learning and growth.

Compassion is born of the wisdom to access our wise self within. During times of uncertainty and hardships, that part of us, the wise one within, knows there's a reason for the situation and that it's intended to move us to greater awareness of our soul's journey. When we are open, gentle and empathic toward our self and others, the higher perspective is more accessible for guidance and understanding. Compassion should be part of our daily lives. We can help ourselves and others each day with simple acts of loving kindness. Examples include: being patient and accepting with ourselves and others, saying please and thank you, holding the door for someone, carrying a bag for an elderly person, visiting a disabled neighbor, or helping a child in need, volunteering at a homeless shelter, offering a person or dog a drink on a hot day. Acts of loving kindness happen when we listen without judgment to the concerns within ourselves or our neighbor. Simply picking up that piece of trash on Mother Earth is an act of kindness and compassion. Compassion toward ourselves and others is a part of the pathway to love and self-mastery.

Vietnamese Buddhist monk and peace advocate Thich Nhat Hauh wrote in his book, *Living Buddha, Living Christ.*

> *We often think of peace as the absence of war; that if the powerful countries would reduce their arsenals, we could have peace. But if we look deeply into the weapons, we see our own minds—our prejudices, fears, and ignorance. Even if we transported all the bombs to the moon, the roots of war and the reasons for bombs would still be here, in our hearts and minds and sooner or later we would make new bombs. Seek to become more aware of what causes anger and separation, and what overcomes them. Root out the violence in your life and learn to live compassionately and mindfully.*

Compassion is a bridge from fear, mistrust, loneliness and despair, to love, understanding, acceptance, connection and hope. Compassion embraces those in need, freely offering concern, encouragement and a way back to love. Imagine what a little more compassion would do for humanity and all that inhabit the Earth. Love calls us to the energy and dynamic of compassion. It is part of what we are here to experience. It's a basic and essential aspect to *Just Be Love.*

26

Love and Imagination

Love is not blind; it simply enables one to see things others fail to see.
—Unknown

As I begin this chapter, I would like to note the importance of the 4 I's of *Innocence, Intuition, Imagination* and *Inspiration*. I was guided to specifically write a chapter on Love and Imagination, as the other three I's and their significance are woven in this chapter.

Imaginative thought comes from the heart and our higher, intuitive mind. This fuels the soul's creativity, adding a sparkle to love and life. Imagination is the creative expression of the Divine in us. If we are made in the image and likeness of the Creator, we too can create. To imagine is to begin the creative process. Imagination is the mind opening to and aligning with the energy of our soul and our heart; the higher dimensions of ourselves, where the realm of possibilities is alive and vibrant. Through imagination we create a mental image that previously was not in our consciousness. Everyone has the ability to imagine. As with any other human ability, some people have greater capacity to use their imagination than others. The more our heart is open, and our mind is free, the more our imagination will flourish.

A true sign of intelligence is not knowledge but imagination.
—Albert Einstein

Imagination is a form of intelligence. To understand nature and the world, one must be able to dream as much as to think. Imagination is the creative power necessary for designing and building; it inspires inspiration. Without imagination life would be stagnant, and little would be created. Imagination plays a vital role in the direction and achievement of success in one's life. It is a form of innocent perception; letting go of judgments; exploring with childlike openness and wonder. The power of imagination arouses desire, allows us to visualize, and spurs us to action. Imagination is often the most overlooked and neglected self-help tool and inner guide. All great achievements start with our intuition and then imagining what is possible.

Imagination does not make us an idle and impractical daydreamer. On the contrary, it's a great tool for many aspects of our lives. We use our imagination more then we realize. We use it at work and play, to set goals, to solve problems, to plan our vacations and our retirement. We use it in our relationships to love or to hate, for better or for worse. We use it in spontaneous sexual expression for real or for fantasized experiences.

Imagination as part of the 4 I's arrives through our *Innocence*; it's sparked by our *Intuition* and *Inspires* us to act—to create. Imagination is the soul's expression in human form. Ideally, it's love and innocence in action that gives rise to possibilities. It's trusting and allowing our creative energies to see unlimited possibilities. *Intuition* and *Imagination* are both avenues through which we become *Inspired* to express ourselves. It's our childlike essence. When we're interacting with young children, we become aware of their active imagination. To give up on our imagination at any age is to accept shame and view love as conditional. The energy of unconditional love and acceptance fuels our imagination.

There can be many tragedies in childhood, yet perhaps the one often overlooked is the loss of the child's imagination. If imagination and creativity are stifled, so are love, innocence and understanding of soul awareness. An example is when a child is told they can't have an imaginary friend. Parents say, "What would others think of us?" Remember the adult who said to you as you were drawing, "Just stay in the lines." "Don't draw outside the box." Yet you were just expressing what you imagined. These are some of the ways we learn and begin to believe it's not okay to be who we are and to freely express ourselves. These are some of the ways the heart becomes fearful, guarded and closed, and our imagination shuts down. The traveled road of separation becomes our mode.

Many people discount imagination because their imaginations were discounted. The lost imagination turns into an increase in linear, black or white thinking, and the need for proof that something exists. We learn that if we can't see it, feel it, taste it, touch it, or hear it, then it doesn't exist. If we didn't experience it—it didn't happen. If I shut down your imagination and cause fear in you, I can control and manipulate you. Can you relate? Imagination is not about proof or convincing the five senses that something exists. It's about honoring and trusting the intuitive heart and 3rd eye, the higher self within. When we engage our imagination, we are in the higher dimensions of the self, and the quantum field of unlimited possibilities.

> *Imagination is everything. It is the preview of life's coming attractions.* —Albert Einstein

Our imagination can be a catalyst for a positive constructive purpose, or it can be used for a dangerous, destructive purpose. Walt Disney is a great example. His imagination was wild and free. It's what made Disneyland and Disney World and his movies so magical and full of joy and truth. Growing up, Disney had a stepmother who was very demeaning and controlling. That's one reason many of his movies have an evil woman in them. He was working through his trauma and pain, and perhaps projecting some. He took his painful past and made it into something magical and joyful for humanity. Disney was told he was crazy when he proposed building Disney World to his group. He didn't let his critics stop him because he said, *"We start tomorrow."* The rest is history.

On the flip side Adolf Hitler's dream was to be an architect. However, he dropped out of high school to help his mother, so he could not apply to an architectural school. He turned his attention to becoming an artist. He had his imagination, creativity and dreams stifled when, at age eighteen, the Vienna Academy of Fine Arts rejected his application and paintings. He was devastated by this rejection. He had lost his father at age thirteen and shortly after the Arts Academy's rejection, his mother died of cancer. He struggled through his early years with rejection and grief. Hitler unfortunately took his painful past and used his imagination toward the desire to create a superior race and nation. The rejection of his dream and his struggle with school were the main reasons why he had books and art destroyed during his reign of power and terror. In his grief of losing both parents and his dream, he projected his sadness into anger and the need for power and control. The rest was a tragic nightmare in world history.

Many innovative and joyful achievements over the centuries would not have come to pass had people given in to their inner (and outer) critics. I've complied a short list of people who displayed vibrant imagination. They include: Jesus, Buddha, Michelangelo, Ben Franklin, Martin Luther King, Mother Teresa, Albert Einstein, Thomas Edison, Edgar Cayce, Helen Keller, Maya Angelou, Nelson Mandela, Bill Gates, Steve Jobs, Louise Hay, Georgia O'Keefe, Oprah Winfrey, Michael Jordan, Dr. Gary Young, and Steven Spielberg—the above and many more all knew and used their power of imagination. They also all experienced having their imagination and talent rejected. Even though some of them knew it would cost them their physical lives, they kept their dreams alive, despite the odds and sacrifice. Look how we have benefited today from their "can do" spirit.

Consider that the Divine has a wonderful, wild imagination. Look around and see how imagination created the universe, you and me. It's a key to inner wisdom and genius. Given this, ask: Why are we so afraid of imagination? Why do we tell others, especially children, to turn it off? Why do we want to limit this positive potential?

As we begin to grow spiritually, we come to realize the importance of the 4 I's: *Innocence, Intuition, Imagination* and *Inspiration*, which all support our journey to seeking love and our higher consciousness. The 4 I's are keys to living our potential. Imagination offers us the ability to look at a situation from different points of view. It opens the door to possibilities. It offers us a miracle, because miracles happen when we shift our perception. It helps us heal from a painful past and offers us confidence in the present and the courage to step more fully into the unknown future. Imagination seeds our desires.

Like love, imagination, calls us to action, to create. Action brings what's been missing into reality, into form. It is healthy and vital to dream. However, too much wishing and daydreaming for something to happen without taking concrete and positive steps along the way can create a stagnant and unhappy life. Imagination without the will to act, neglects the higher self. Imagination and wishing without action will prevent growth or self-actualization. This can stem from the need to be safe and comfortable. Love always calls us to action from the inside-out.

Think of how many times your intuition and imagination were in high gear, yet you disregarded its message, only to regret it later. To have an imagination is great. To just sit in the bleachers with it is to be a spectator in life. It's subscribing to fear and doubt, not love. When our imagination turns into fear, self-doubt and avoidance, we are in the lower self, likely experiencing a limiting belief around a painful past experience. The higher self is the container and sustainer of our divine abilities. It's fearless and has the confidence to get us on the field of life, to take meaningful risks using our instilled gifts and see where it leads us. Connecting with our higher self is an act of love for ourselves and others who may benefit from what we have to offer. The divine gift of imagination frees us, assists us, in discovering our unlimited potential, creating the best version of our self and our world.

Human Development at the Expense of Soul Development

L ike love, imagination creates possibilities; it promotes learning, encourages growth, and provides social skills and builds connections. It helps us overcome fear, builds self-confidence, and connects us intimately with the pulse and wisdom of the higher and wiser self. These skills are the building blocks for children and their overall development of both their human potential and spiritual expansion. For adults, imagination is what helps us stay true, determined, focused and connected to our life purpose. It keeps the childlike (not childish) qualities flowing within us. Imagination, like love, is vital to create these possibilities and keep them alive, while making life fun and worth living. Imagination moves us out of the confines of our limited mind and into the infinite space of the universal mind. The wonderful thing about imagination is that it's free and always open and available to us. Imagination only asks for your invitation, opportunity, desire and willingness to reconnect once again. Go ahead; send your imagination an invitation to get together again. Notice how it feels and where it guides you.

In the beginning of this book I mentioned an experience I had with Jesus, the clouds, and the sunset. It was through this very real and powerful, mystical experience that my willingness to write this book came to be. I started to imagine the book as already written. From this imaging, I began to get more messages from Jesus, and I started to put words on the pages. We all have the potential for these experiences in which the elements of the divine realm communicate with us and through us. No matter our age, imagination and inspiration are always possible. It is always our choice what we do or don't do with the power of imagination.

When we reconnect with our imagination, we reconnect to our innocence, to our childlike qualities, and to love and joy. To paraphrase Jesus's line from scripture: *If you want to enter the kingdom, be like a child.* Imagination allows us to *Just Be Love,* innocent and free. Return to your imagination and you return to love.

27

Love and the Miracle

Miracles are not contrary to nature, but only contrary to what we know about nature. —St. Augustine

The word "miracle" comes from the Latin word *mirari* or *miraculm*, meaning to wonder, to behold. From our earthly perspective, miracles are considered acts of wonder for they seem out of the norm and beyond our comprehension. We don't understand how a healing could have happened or a person survived an accident, or a friend showed up when we needed them most. We say, "it's a miracle"— "divine intervention."

A miracle can be experienced when we align with the Divine. Miracles happen when we truly surrender to the consciousness and power of Source. By doing so, we create a conduit for God's energy, love, will and grace to flow through us, setting the miracle in motion. When we accept that God's love never wavers or diminishes regardless of our limitations and self-destructive choices, we can surrender our will and align with Divine will. A miracle begins to happen when we let go of our fears and doubts, when we no longer define ourselves by our wounds; we remember ourselves only as love.

Miracles occur naturally as expressions of love. The real miracle is the love that inspires them. In this sense everything that comes from love is a miracle. —Marianne Williamson

The universe thrives on miracles. To believe a miracle is to remember we are love—a part of a greater whole. All of life is a wonder, and we are part of this wonder, because we are an act of creation. It's amazing how fertilization occurs through the union of an egg and sperm and the pollination of plants. Think of how life is birthed daily due to this process. Every day miracles occur; it's the nature of the universe. It's up to us to align ourselves with the energy of miracles so they can manifest in our lives.

Having awareness of why we desire a miracle has value, however, how we might block its arrival with unconscious thoughts and beliefs is of equal importance. To promote healing, wholeness and create miracles consider the following:

- We love and accept our self.

- We face our fears and challenge our doubts.

- We seek to reconcile the struggles and pain of our past and to understand the spiritual meanings it holds.

- Practice patience, acceptance, compassion and forgiveness.

- Be more understanding—trust the process and unfolding of life's lessons.

- Express gratitude and appreciation within life experiences.

- Take a walk-in nature; plant flowers or a tree and watch them grow; hug a tree and a fellow human.

- Notice and appreciate the hawk circling high above, the squirrel or rabbit that crosses your path.

- Hold a baby, play with a child, pet a dog or cat.

- Love your neighbor and yourself.

- Get to know your neighbor and yourself.

- Pray, practice meditation, yoga, or other creative arts.

- Tell the truth to yourself about yourself; acknowledge the mistake and reconcile this within yourself and with another.

- Look up at the stars, howl at the moon, honor the rising sun and sit with the setting sun.

Miracles are not out of the ordinary in nature or the cosmos. Miracles are the very fabric of nature and the universe. To understand this and live this truth is to experience miracles. As we evolve spiritually, our awareness and acceptance of miracles grow.

> *We do not need magic to change the world; we carry all the power we need inside ourselves already: we have the power to imagine better.*
> —J.K. Rowling

Our power to create is vast and unlimited. A miracle arrives through our belief in it. A healthy, "can do" belief creates inspiration for a miracle to manifest. The willingness and power to imagine create the opening for the miracle. Our belief creates certainty, a conviction of the soul-heart. This generates a powerful and transforming force that communicates to the universe, like waves that ripple when a pebble is tossed in water. *"Ask and you shall receive."* Have faith and believe. They create the space and patience for the miracle to unfold. Faith knows the importance and value of its friend belief and belief knows the value and importance of patience.

> *The miracle is not to fly in the air, or to walk on water, but to walk on the earth.* —Chinese Proverb

A miracle happens when we are present with ourselves and others—when we let go of judgment and fault finding of others and ourselves. An act of kindness brings an opening for a miracle. The miracle replaces the struggle when we are like the candle flame, focusing on the light in our times of darkness.

Fear, ignorance, doubt, shame and blame keep us in the lower energies. They prevent the possibility of miracles. Self-responsibility, surrender, trust, acceptance, allowing and knowing ourselves as love, move us to higher energy. This opens us up to receive the miracle. As each moment unfolds, we choose the energies and the vibration we will be in and how long we will stay there. How you just reacted in perception, emotion, feeling and belief to this last statement determines (consciously or unconsciously) which energy vibration you live in. This is your created reality. This is the level of your awareness, your soul's maturity and growth at this moment. It's not right or wrong, good or bad, it "just is" in this moment. The next moment can be different; can be a miracle, if you choose.

> *Once all struggle is grasped, miracles are possible.* —Mao Tse-Tung

Lesson 77 in *A Course in Miracles* says, *"I am entitled to miracles."* I am entitled to miracles because I am one with God. We receive miracles because of Divine laws (see appendix). Experiences happen on a spiritual level, yet we experience them through ego perceptions, emotions and beliefs. Our experiences are not judged good or bad in our soul's reality, rather they are seen as the teacher, as opportunities to learn and grow. Our ego, our shadow personality would have us believe a difficult experience is a threat and something to fear and control, so it blocks the opportunity of miracles coming into our awareness. We alone decide if we are entitled to a miracle or if we will deny ourselves the possibility of them occurring.

We have two choices. One choice will align us with love, with our Creator and with the process of co-creation. The other choice will align us with fear, limitation and pain. No matter which choice we make, we are still loved by God. The Creator rides the wave of the soul's journey in the human experiences, with no attachment to an outcome or a time frame. Source lets us choose. Through the array of life experiences, opportunities are offered, and spiritual growth is encouraged from our higher self. We choose how we perceive, feel, believe and act. Getting out of our own way begins to move us in the direction God intended. Commitment, patience and discipline create the change within.

When we change our thoughts and perceptions, we begin to change the way things appear to us. This, in turn, changes the emotions and feelings we create around the experience, which then changes our belief about ourselves and the experience. This shifts our attitude more toward observing and away from judging, creating an opening for new possibilities and growth, i.e. a miracle.

When we shift our ego's perception and belief, we lighten up on our self. To say, "This is all I know," "I've always done it this way," "It's easier said than done" or "It's too hard" shuts the door on possibilities and miracles. We are trapped in the belief of our limited self. We are saying "no" to aspects of our life. Fear and unworthiness say "no" to life, inhibiting miracles, while love and worthiness invites us to say "yes" to life. When we say "yes" to life and ourselves, we create possibilities that open us to receiving miracles.

Who would you be if you shifted your belief about yourself? How would your life change? Would this shift manifest a different reality for you than you currently experience? Do you see the possibilities, the opportunities this shift can create for you?

The French poet and novelist Anatole France said: *"To accomplish great things, we must not only act, but also dream; not only plan, but also believe."* Change happens at the point of a shift in beliefs and we generate positive feelings around this belief. Miracles happen when we change our energy. Change your energy by creating uplifting and positive thoughts, perspective and a "can do" belief in a miracle. Then imagine how you would feel when the miracle occurs. Create and sustain this feeling daily, as if the miracle has already happened. The stronger our belief is that a miracle will happen, and the more we can relax and hold the positive feeling about the miracle; the higher the vibrational energy will be for the desire to become our reality.

To *Just Be Love* can naturally create a miracle, because what comes from love can be called a miracle. Remove the barriers of fear and doubt and replace with love and trust. Transformation happens from the inside-out, this is co-creating with the Divine. This will lead to remembering that we are what we come from love—the eternal spirit. Listen to and embrace the soft still voice within that says: *"Just Be Love—this is who you are. Welcome to the divine reality. Welcome to the miracle—Welcome home to love."*

28

Love and Abundance

Abundance lies at the edge, where the land, water and air meet.
—Unknown

I ask Master Jesus, what is abundance?

> *Dear David, the above quote about the edge, refers to the edge of nature, where the elements of land, water and air meet. This is where part of the abundance of life lies. The edge for human's, lies within their center. The edge is going beyond your comfort zone. There is an edge within where chaos dances with order, where fear meets love, and the fear is embraced by love; its then that fear remembers itself as love. It is here that your past and your future merge with your present, shattering duality, to manifest oneness. Yes, life does manifest anywhere and everywhere. Yet the edge, the center of yourself, truly displays passion and possibilities.*
>
> *Abundance is comprised of intention, belief, attention and will. All of this is energy you either create alliance or discord with your higher self and the universe. Having the correct insight about how the universe governs itself and how to align yourself with this information is crucial to manifesting abundance. Your response to abundance must be of spirit for this aligns your passion and focused action. You create abundance through the awareness of spirit and what the spirit in you desires.*

Abundance Is All Around Us

There are many ways abundance is experienced. It comes through our appreciation for all that makes up our life—like relationships, food, shelter and natural resources that sustain life. Abundance is experiencing and knowing we are part of a wondrous universe. Abundance is passion in doing what we love to do and living our purpose with integrity. It comes from developing self-mastery. There's abundance in the joy of seeing a child walk for the first time; in honoring the rising or the setting of the sun; in watching the parade of a trillion stars on a clear night; in serving others; in giving gratitude for a good harvest. Notice the wonder, the openness, the lushness of trees and flowers as you walk in nature. These are all examples of abundance, because they are energies that are freely exchanged through the giving and receiving of life. Acknowledging and cherishing this energy exchange is experiencing abundance. Yes, abundance is all around us and within us; to recognize and appreciate this brings joy and serenity.

> *Enjoy your health. Enjoy your happiness. Enjoy all the beauty that life has presented to you. Why not? Why restrict yourself? Keep opening. The sky is the limit. There is no limit to the infinite.* — His Holiness Sri Svami Purna

Jesus's message to all of us:

> *Dear ones, the universe is full of abundance, for it has everything it needs; and is the recognition of the fullness of life. Abundance is the understanding and acceptance that everything is always there in the field of awareness. This is the wisdom of knowing completeness, vs. separation. The universe is always creating, expanding and renewing through and with itself. Abundance is the acknowledgement and acceptance that the universe has provided you with everything you need, not only to sustain you, but so you will thrive. Accepting and knowing this truth eliminates need and greed. Realize there is enough for today, creates enough for tomorrow as well. Abundance, like all of creation, is a vibrant and moving life force energy that is given freely and received in gratitude. It seeks to be honored and not taken for granted or advantage of. You are gifted by the universe through acts of love and abundance. Acknowledging and honoring this demonstrates gratitude to the universe.*

> *Abundance, my friends, like all of my teachings, is about learning harmony and reconciling what you believe you don't have with what is always available and possible. The thoughts, interpretations and beliefs you hold around your life experiences create energy. This is what shapes your present and future experiences. If and when you choose to change these perceptions and beliefs from the past, you create new possibilities in the present, which begins to generate a new*

reality. The significance you attach to your experiences will support and empower you or will oppose and weaken you in spirit, body and mind. Abundance my friend, is the energy of love and empowerment.

We Won't Take It with Us

Abundance also means fullness, a fullness of spirit that spills over like a powerful, majestic waterfall. Simple abundance is eternal and of the soul's heart. Abundance is the willingness to receive with an open and grateful heart. Abundance is what accumulates in the heart, not just through the mind, our bank accounts or possessions. Abundance is wealth, and true wealth is so much more than money and material possessions. The word wealth comes from an old English word "weal" which means well-being and "th" means condition. Put these two words together and the word wealth means "well-being condition". Yes, we deserve to have money and the ability to acquire the finer things in life, to be secure and have comfortable, pleasing surroundings. The desire for money and material things is not the problem; the problem is more the "love of money" and "love of material things." It is our intention, belief, feelings, and attitude toward money and possessions that either creates true wealth and abundance or detracts from it. Being defined by and consumed with money and material possessions create an unhealthy attachment.

The love of money never creates true happiness and inner peace. When we experience our physical transition (death), what will our soul need from the physical world as it moves on its journey? Reality is, we won't be taking our money and material possessions with us when we die. You never see a U-Haul behind a hearse. The things we desire and have defined as abundance, are short-lived and perhaps more for comfort and to look good. There are many forms of wealth. Limiting our concept of wealth to just money and material things, limits our perception of true abundance. In the Gospel of Thomas, saying 111, Jesus said these words that apply in present day. *"For him who finds his true self the world of objects is of no worth."* True wealth is finding and knowing the self, which creates self-mastery and real freedom. True wealth comes through loving kindness, natural beauty, creativity, joy, fellowship and service. Many of the teachers, like Jesus who have spent time in our physical world, were not caught up with material possessions. They understood that the experience of the "I AM" within one's heart is true abundance. They had the wisdom, openness, ability and strength to allow their minds to cooperate with the wisdom and vibration of the higher self. They allowed their hearts and their higher mind to be the mediators for the lower mind, not the other way around.

The universal law of compensation is the law of cause and effect in action. This applies to abundance—the concrete effects of our deeds are given through friendships, gifts, health, inheritance and blessings. Paraphrasing from the Bible (Galatians 6:7), *"What we reap we shall sow."* True abundance comes through alignment with Divine love, power and wisdom. True abundance honors the four elements of earth, air, fire and water, the resources to sustain life, offered to us as an inheritance and a gift of love. When we show appreciation for these resources, we acknowledge this abundance. Humanity is charged with being stewards of these resources, not just consumers without respect for their value. Individually and collectively, we are the guardians when we become mindful and grateful for what is provided and entrusted to our care.

It is vital that we are aware of how our perceptions and interpretations of life's experiences either block or attract what the universe offers us. Who we believe we are, is often consumed by thoughts and beliefs of scarcity. The ego's need to be somebody creates an endless striving for recognition and fame. The fact that we are here, and breathing is enough. Just Be—we already are what we are striving to be.

> *Abundance is not something we acquire. It is something we tune in to.* —Dr. Wayne Dyer

There is a universal law of vibration which states: *"All things in the universe travel in particular patterns."* This law applies to our thoughts, feelings, beliefs and choices as well. Everything has its own unique vibration and pattern. In order to hear the music that is playing on a radio station, we need to tune the dial to match the frequency of the radio station channel. The same is true for human desire. We need to match our inner frequency to the frequency of what we desire. Our vibration and its corresponding frequency are greatly influenced by our perceptions, thoughts, intentions and feelings. Our frequency and vibration then become more pronounced, either in positive or distorted ways, by our core beliefs. We must match our thoughts, beliefs and feelings to the vibration and frequency of the source field. Like perceiving the glass to be half full or half empty, our perception, thoughts, feelings and beliefs create either abundance or scarcity, each having a particular vibration and frequency. The dance of our emotions, thoughts and perceptions, lead to our feelings, beliefs, creating an energy that attracts a like energy. The law of attraction simply means: *What I think about—I bring about.*

Our lower mind lives in a state of needing and wanting many things, such as, a new job, a new home, more money, a better relationship. To create what we truly desire we must let go of wanting or needing. The universe hears and answers our broadcast; it gives us what we are communicating. It is important to hold the intention of what it is we specifically desire. Unconsciously (some call it subconsciously), we often tell the universe only what we don't have or don't want. The universe hears this and then offers us the experience of what we don't have or want, because that's what we tuned into and broadcasted.

Remember consciousness is developed through openness and awareness. Most of what the Divine desires for us is understood and lived by us in the opposite way than it was intended. Until we recognize this error of our ways, we will continue to struggle with the concept and attainment of true abundance. Much of our restlessness and unhappiness is due to our misalignment with Source.

> *When we choose to focus on what is not missing from our lives but are grateful for the abundance that's present...we experience heaven on earth.* —Sarah Breathnach

A False God Called Consumption

In writing this section please note, I'm not an expert on the economy and I certainly don't have "the answers." I'm just offering observations and my personal viewpoint. Please take this in the spirit intended.

Much attention is paid to our economy here in the United States, as well in other countries throughout the world. This is creating one of the major blocks to true abundance. Our world has become increasingly driven by competition and accumulation of material things, buying into the illusion that materialism is the pathway to happiness and fulfillment. Where are the abundance, love and wisdom when our nation and our world are driven by the mind-set that if we don't spend money (buy things), our nation/world will suffer and sink into a recession or depression? This only feeds the ego's perception of lack, need and greed. It creates a world of *haves* and *have nots*. If you "follow the money," you discover power and influence of a few at the expense of many. It creates a world full of entitlement and co-dependency.

This is a powerful means of creating separation from each other, from our natural world and from our spiritual essence—Love. For some, consumption and greed have replaced respect and appreciation for natural resources and their purpose in our survival. The Mother-Father God is truly our supply chain—not our super stores, oil companies or drug manufacturers.

197

We have developed a need for and an expectation of instant gratification. This is not an economy based on Divine love; this is an economy based on ego. The main issues, during the United States presidential elections over the last hundred years, have been about war and the economy. I recall James Carville's famous political statement to the effect; *"It's the economy, stupid."* He mentioned this statement during Bill Clinton's successful 1992 presidential campaign. This quote underscores how so many are focused on the economy, and the importance of buying so they can "have," which they perceive buys happiness. I believe this focus has become oppressive, creating moral erosion and spiritual disconnection. My reply to Mr. Carville and the world about what really matters is—*It's our spiritual essence, my friends.*

The economy and all we have made of value and importance are not true abundance. Have you noticed that our financial systems, along with many other systems, are in disarray? We are trying to function through means that truly no longer serve and sustain us. The new cycle and energies that are coming to our planet are designed to assist us in finding more sustainable, loving means to have a global economy that maintains our spiritual essence. Some counties are getting the right idea about an economy based on spirituality and are taking steps toward this ideal. An example, in 2012, Iceland created a peaceful resolution to years of a corrupt government and financial intuitions by the arrest and incarceration of irresponsible parties.

Albert Einstein said, *"The world we have made, as a result of the level of thinking we have done thus far, creates problems we cannot solve at the same level of thinking at which we created them."* Our task is to embrace higher levels of being, thinking and believing in this world. We've got the wisdom and talent; we just need a more loving and determined will to get there.

Physicist and author Brain Swimme said: *"Humans gather together and learn the meaning of the universe, our cosmology. Now, we gather together and watch TV ads. Every ad is a cosmological sermon—the universe is a collection of objects to be fashioned into items for our consumption, and the role of humans is to work and buy objects."*

Since the Great Depression and then World War II, the United States has seen great economic growth and prosperity along with several other countries. The world has become consumed with consumption. The following are the words of retailing analyst Victor Lebow shortly after World War II:

> Our enormously productive economy... demands that we make consumption our way of life, that we convert the buying and use

*of goods into rituals, that we seek our spiritual satisfaction, our ego
satisfaction, in consumption... We need things consumed, burned
up, worn out, replaced, and discarded at an ever-increasing rate.*

The two quotes above are just as true today as they were seventy years ago.
Not much has changed except in the need to compete, consume, discard and
replace at even greater rates than was first observed. What would Mr. Lebow
say today about consumption as our way of life?

We are now experiencing the law of compensation and cause and effect
(see appendix) at a more rapid rate. Time is on the side of the Divine and our
higher, wiser selves. This will be a wake-up call as humanity is exposed to
needless, yet preventable hardships. We created it through our selfish acts, and
we will correct it when we wake up and align with the Creator's intent. Our
task now is to take responsibility for our beliefs and attitudes about money
without the game of blame and shame. What is needed now is a higher level
of awareness. It's not about working harder or faster; it's about aligning with
the principles of divine truth.

The following three statements reflect my understanding of loving
principles that reflect divine truth. An economy based on loving principals is
similar to how the natural world functions.

- Use ecological approaches with reverence and compassion for
  sustaining and empowering life.

- Takes only what is needed for sustenance.

- Honor the governance of the Divine in the spirit of cooperation and
  interconnectedness in harmony with the rhythm of nature.

I believe we humans have not evolved in consciousness to the level needed
to live in accordance with loving principals. Many of us continue to choose
the "me first" approach and thus disrupt the natural balance of a cooperative,
abundant planet.

All life is energy. The economy of money is an energy exchange. I envision
an economy of inclusion and collective sharing, bartering of resources with a
fair, cooperative, give-and-take exchange. The positive exchange of energy is
created by the willingness to do our fair share without dependency or greed.
The true economy is an economy driven by love, compassion, inclusion and
sharing. Like the four natural elements which benefit all, an economy based

on love would include and benefit all, not just a select few. This type of economy embraces the concept and ideals of true power, love and wisdom, not control, manipulation, scarcity and greed.

True Wealth and Spiritual Abundance in Action

True wealth is a form of spiritual abundance, it doesn't mean we have to be poor or live in a cave in the mountains. True wealth in a spiritual way sees money as good and a way to learn and grow as a spiritual being while living this human experience. Money can be a means of expressing love and concern, it's an energy exchange that provides resources and opportunities to help others and improve our planet. A few people of note leading the way spiritually are: Bill Gates, Mark Zuckerberg, J.K. Rowling, Orpah Winfrey and Barbra Streisand. They are making the conscious choice to hold a spiritual attitude with their wealth. All five of these individuals created advances in our world, Bill Gates, through technology, and his wife Melinda, through their foundation, have donated billions of dollars to causes that decrease poverty, world hunger and improve education. Author J.K. Rowling through her *Volant Trust* has donated millions to help people with medical needs and other charitable causes. Media executive and personality Orpah Winfrey has donated millions of dollars through, *The Angel Network, The Oprah Winfrey Foundation, The Oprah Winfrey Leadership Academy Foundation* and *The US Dream Academy*. Barbra Streisand, as an entertainer, organized *The Streisand Foundation*. Her foundation donates substantial funds to charities that impact women's and children's welfare, environmental issues and civil rights. Lastly, Mark Zuckerberg, through social media, and his wife Priscilla Chan, also donate billions of dollars to humanitarian causes across the globe.

An interesting side note about these three individuals who pursued their passions. Bill and Mark both left college before graduating, while Barbra never attended college. Over the course of human civilization there seems to be a correlation, between a person's spiritual passion and their ability to recognize their spiritual abundance. Thus, they seem to be more willing to give back to humanity.

Several of the wealthiest people around the world are currently involved in a movement called, "The Giving Pledge." The idea originated from conversations between Warren Buffett, Bill and Melinda Gates and other humanitarians. The concept was to invite the world's wealthiest individuals and families to commit to giving more than half of their wealth to philanthropic causes either during their lifetime or in their will. The Giving Pledge is an effort to help address society's most pressing problems. As of May 2019, The Giving Pledge has received pledges from 204 of the wealthiest individuals and families from 23 countries.

Some people have more to give than others, yet that's not the point. What is the point of giving, no matter the way or the amount? To give from the heart with our time, talents or money is true wealth and spiritual abundance in action.

Our world economy is an energy exchange between all that inhabit Mother Earth. Ask yourself: *When we create goods and provide services, does it enhance humanity and the planet, or is it just a way to make money, especially for a few at the expense of many? Is this product or service made and delivered with the intent of loving kindness, cooperation, appreciation and compassion? Or is this product or service created with the energy of fear, competition, greed, control and indifference?* I believe that the way these questions are answered reflects the energy from either our higher self or from our lower, shadow self. It also reflects the impact that product or service will have overall on the Earth family.

These times call us to break free from old habitual patterns of limited thinking. It is important that we stay positive and forward focused. When we change an unhealthy pattern of thinking, we shift our paradigm and we shift our world. This opens us up to see the abundance in our life.

Ted Jones wrote this when questioned why he was not interested in taking the investment company Edward Jones public and becoming a multimillionaire:

> *I'm the richest man in America. I have a wife that loves me in spite of all my faults, I have four dogs. Two love only me; one loves everybody. One loves no one but still is very loyal. I have a horse I love to ride around the farm, and best of all; she comes when I call her. I have too much to eat and a dry place to sleep. I enjoy my business. I love my farm and my home. I have a few close friends and money has never been my God.*

Creatures of Habit

We have many habits; some move us forward, while others keep us stuck and block our potential. We create our habits and our habits create our future. Spiritual teachers say that even our soul has habits that it carries from lifetime to lifetime. We are all creatures of habit. Changing habits is essential to changing our life. Everything we repeatedly think, say and do is a direct result of our habits. Habits are the product of our conscious and unconscious beliefs. They are those actions or reactions which are on autopilot, which you do without consciously having to think about them. The success we enjoy in life, or the lack thereof, is directly related to the nature of our habits, and the result of our beliefs.

A way of viewing abundance is moving from the habit of focusing on what I don't have, to what I do have, thus creating the state of gratitude and the energy of possibilities. What we focus our mind on is what we will attract. If our need to protect our old patterns and habits is stronger than our desire to create unlimited possibilities within the field; we will stifle our ability to actualize our higher awareness and potential.

> *We are what we repeatedly do. Excellence then, is not an act but a habit.* —Aristotle

It's important to learn how to break out of old patterns, such as the habit of negative, self-defeating thinking that limits our perception and potential, and instead rekindle the "I AM" and "I Can" spirit within us. This will naturally make it easier to create abundance in life. This is our true nature and the true nature of love within this abundant universe. When we can naturally shift and expand our perception, we expand our realm of possibilities. When we can allow ourselves to experience novelty, we go to the edge of ourselves to challenge our fears and assumptions. When we allow ourselves to experience this, we grow. When we step out of our comfort zone and experience life in new ways, we create a higher vibration, becoming aware of our true and unlimited self.

Change and Abundance

> *The secret of change is to focus all of your energy, not on fighting the old, but building the new.* —Socrates

When humans experience change, fear and resistance are common thoughts and behaviors. I believe they are the main obstacles toward spiritual growth and abundance. Many subscribe to the belief that change is difficult and full of uncertainty. Yet change is the makeup of the infinite universe; it's happening all the time, all around us and within us. In the dynamics of change, we struggle with uncertainty and the need for control. I've come to realize that the degree of uncertainty we can tolerate is directly related to the quality of our lives. Can we face our fears while embracing change? Rather than resist change, can we let go of the old in order to create and build on the new?

In the process of change, the pendulum of our thoughts and behaviors can swing from one extreme to the other. For example, we go from living a very unhealthy, unhappy lifestyle, until we have a wakeup call, i.e. a heart attack, cancer, mental breakdown. So, in order to live, we compensate. We may go to the other lifestyle extreme, perhaps to the point of obsessive thinking and behaviors of health for fear of being sick again. In time we realize we may be going overboard with this change because there is no joy or peace in this lifestyle either. Many people can relate to the trap of this dynamic, recognizing it is driven by fear and assumptions. The key is to find a healthy balance as you focus on your "process" and move through the changes brought on by your life experiences, lifestyle choices and behaviors. This takes awareness and patience. Each of us will find our own unique point of balance on the lifestyle continuum.

Change is not new, but it does seem more accelerated and life-altering now. It's important to build on the new and improved you and the world you're creating. Stay loving, grounded and supporting to yourself and others. We are all in this grand experience of higher learning together. You are me and I am you. There is abundance in change. Keep focused on what can be, not what has been. Our experiences offer opportunities for learning and expansion. Through the process of change, pathways to Divine love and true abundance are developed.

Six Steps to Accepting Change:

1. Cultivate awareness that life is impermanent—things change.

2. Accept and embrace the new "normal." Life today is not like it was yesterday.

3. Be open and willing to acknowledge and unlearn your misperceptions, false beliefs and created habits, so you can learn anew and expand.

4. Notice your fear and resistance to change, and who you become because of this. Ask yourself: Is this change causing me to think and act from fear or love? How does this fear and resistance assist and empower me in creating opportunities?

5. Feel and admit the fear and say yes, to the change anyway. Accessing your "courage to change" helps to say yes, when feeling the fear.

6. Focus on the benefits of change not what you believe you will lose or need to give up. Look for possibilities in the uncertainty. Trust your higher self and the universe; otherwise you will be consumed by the wave of change.

When we move out from under the lower self's perception and beliefs and embrace those of the higher self—change is accepted more freely.

Gratitude Naturally Cultivates Abundance

Love is the way I walk in gratitude. —A Course in Miracles, WB-195

Gratitude is an expression of love and the foundation of abundance. The attitude of gratitude naturally cultivates abundance. Like love, the expression of gratitude carries a high frequency. It opens our hearts and moves us from the fear and limitations of the ego to love, appreciation and greater potential. Gratitude is part of our purpose for being. It keeps us in the present moment, where love and abundance happen. Gratitude is a stress reducer, helping us experience life with more grace and ease. It cultivates self-worth and strengthens our connection to Source and others. Establishing a conscious habit of gratitude brings meaning to our lives and can be transformative. An attitude of gratitude, sparks desire, fosters commitment and drives our determination.

With gratitude comes acceptance, which demonstrates that we see the gift and lesson in life's struggles. It allows us to see with the eyes of the soul and moves us to view our experiences from the higher perspective, acknowledging that, despite the hardships and uncertainties of life, the universe always has our backs. We are always cared for and loved. A key to happiness is the willingness to be more grateful for your life and your experiences, rather than sorry for your life and your experiences. Abundance comes from trusting that all life experiences ultimately have a purpose. The willingness to serve others and feel the abundance of life, within what appear to be struggles and uncertainties, is one of the highest forms of gratitude. The expression of gratitude is a choice and like love, calls us to action. John Kennedy's quote speaks of the importance of gratitude, *"As we express our gratitude, we must never forget that the highest appreciation is not to utter words, but to live by them."*

Generosity, The Pathway to Abundance

Our Creator is always giving, so when we give, we become an expression of God and creation in action. The energies of caring and sharing, are acts of loving kindness. Generosity and service to others opens the heart and expands the soul and the mind. Giving creates abundance. When we freely give, we naturally receive. To give is to love. To give is to say yes to abundance. Scarcity distracts the mind and closes off the heart. *Generosity is the servant of the heart and the pathway to abundance.* When we give from the heart, we are coming from the energy of unconditional love. There is no greater energy and vibration than unconditional love. Giving creates joy and the feeling of joy brings the sense of abundance.

> *Discover the joy of giving and you will discover the reason for living.* —Mark Hansen

Generosity is a way of going beyond the self, giving without considering any loss. Joy comes from giving and offers meaning and purpose to life. When we are generous with our hearts, our time or our talents, we are giving as much as we would if we were giving our money or our possessions; we are aiding another, while expressing love and gratitude to God. We all have a need for love. To freely give love is to feel love. A part of The prayer of St. Francis says it well, *"For it is in the giving that we receive."* When we touch the life of any sentient being on the Earth by offering assistance, we are expressing love.

Father Sky and Mother Earth are always giving abundantly. Even things we view as dead are still in a form of giving, such as fallen trees and leaves, fish washed ashore, and rotten fruit or vegetables tossed to the ground. All these are still living in their soul energy state. They are giving to the Earth by decomposing and releasing nutrients into the soil, allowing more vegetation to grow and animals to feed. Yes, this process takes time; patience is part of abundance. The design of nature here on earth is pure abundance, infinite intelligence and grace. Nature's interactions demonstrate the energy of love, acceptance and beauty; of giving and receiving. Be grateful to Mother Earth and Father Sky for how they freely and lovingly teach us about the abundance that comes from giving. To *Just Be Love* is to give and be in the abundance of the Divine.

29

Love as Stillness and Movement

The secret of creation is known in silence. When you do nothing you are the most active. —Swami Amar Jyotius

In Psalm 46:10, NIV it says, *"Be still, and know that I am God."* Stillness is a silent transforming energy through which our I AM Presence is revealed, and the essence of love is experienced. It is from the void of stillness that we come to heart awareness and hear that soft still voice within; calling us to our divinity, calling us to the Divine Mother-Father—calling us to love.

When we let go of "doing" and move to the center of ourselves in stillness, we become aware of our "being;" we hear the soft voice of spirit through our soul's knowing. It's here that truth is heard, questions are answered, desires and dreams revealed, and intentions made.

Where there is stillness, there also is the energy of movement, created as form, which emerges from stillness. Stillness creates love, movement creates life. Movement is the universal hum and vibration. This creates a rhythm as it comes and goes, like the cycles of life that run throughout the cosmos. Movement is the expression of life and love in action. It is through the energy of movement that the Divine creates, expanding and renewing all that is. It has flow and rhythm, like waves in the ocean. With movement answers are lived.

Stillness and movement are two halves that make up the whole. They are the desire of the spirit and the fuel for the soul. Stillness and movement honor each other, knowing they complete the whole. They weave and dance with each other, seamlessly and effortlessly in their expression; creating balance to sustain life as love.

Stillness and movement have their own unique pulse and rhythm. They connect us to the oneness and the remembrance of the love that we are. In stillness there is the quietness and acceptance of life. In movement there is the constant flow of life changes. When we accept the movement, the rhythm, and the cycles of life, there is a sense of stillness, peace and love.

Our holy breath creates movement with each inhale and exhale. Yet, there lies a still point between the inhale and exhale. Be still in this moment and notice your breath. Notice that still point within the movement of your breath. In meditation we use the breath to quiet the mind, while moving to a higher state of awareness and peace. With each inhale we go deeper into the self and with each exhale we expand outward, moving to the potentiality of life.

In stillness we move toward the Divine; the awareness and presence of love. In stillness we are called and inspired to contemplate the realm of possibilities. In movement we create what is possible.

Be still in your movement and observe where it guides you. Move into your stillness and notice what comes through you. With this unity we find deeper connection and contentment with life. We find greater understanding about the energy of love. We become aware of love's depth and the breadth of possibilities.

Be with the stillness of love and observe life in all its forms. Be with the movement of life and notice love revealed. Be with them both and notice how they connect us to our Source. Be in stillness and movement and notice yourself. All is well.

30

Love and the Homecoming

Don't you realize that the sea is the home of water? All water is off on a journey unless it's in the sea, and it's homesick and bound to make its way home someday. —Zora Neale Huston

When we think of flowing water in a creek or river, we can ponder its desire to get somewhere. Water is a great metaphor for describing our spiritual journey—our way home.

From the smallest spring to the grandest of rivers, water seeks its way home. It faces many obstacles, twisting and turning, bending and weaving, over, around and through; it flows and adapts as it finds the way to its Source. Water flows with consciousness and in alignment with the Divine. Yes, water is conscious and alive; it has energy, a soul and a purpose. Water is made up of hydrogen and oxygen, the basic elements of creation, and an integral part of Mother Earth. Seventy percent of the Earth is water; over 60 percent of the average adult body is water; an adult brain is nearly 80 percent water. All of life on Earth, could not exist without water.

Water, like many other forms of creation, just is. Its purpose is to flow and adapt as needed. It can be fluid or solid; it can be warm or cold; it can be a part of great energy and power, as well as great beauty and grace. It can be very calming and soothing, or it can create destruction, chaos and loss. It can be fresh and pure or become polluted and toxic. No matter how it expresses itself, it is a vital part of life.

As humans we too have a yearning for home. Love calls us to the sacred unity with our Creator and within ourselves. Coming home in this case is not about our physical transition. This homecoming is about remembering the love that we are, while still experiencing this earthly journey.

What makes a river so restful to people is that it doesn't have any doubt - it is sure to get where it is going, and it doesn't want to go anywhere else. —Hal Boyle

Water is void of fear and doubt. It has no attachment; it just is and does not lose itself or its essence within the ebb and flow of its life course. It seeks the way home, to unity with its Source.

Like water, we too have many obstacles to overcome on our journey in the sea of life. Our fears, doubts and unhealthy choices create painful turbulence, which can lead to suffering; preventing us from being in flow with Divine love. It seems the more we attach to outcomes in the twists and turns of life, the more resistant we become to life experiences. The less we flow with life, the more we can become toxic and stagnate, causing us to forget our essence. When we are "in the flow", we celebrate the journey; the journey home to our true selves—to Love.

Who would you be if you followed those inner promptings from your higher self that offer guidance along the way? How might your life be different if you stayed true to yourself and to the flow of life? What would your life be if you decided to learn from the obstacles and the turbulence of experiences, rather than resist, get stuck, even consumed by them?

Water inherently knows where it needs to go and how it needs to flow. It is mindful and trusting of the process. It seems to know it can, and will overcome what's in the way, and will always make its way home. Can you be more like water? After all, over half of your physical make up is water.

In this moment relax and observe your breath going in and out. Make the choice to be in the flow and rhythm of your breath and your life as you journey home. Be flexible and confident, knowing you can and will get there by acceptance and the courage to change what you can, as you move through what comes your way. Learn from your experiences by looking deep within yourself for the wisdom of the answers. Rather than blaming yourself, others or God, counter negativity, fears and self-doubt, with love, listening to and flowing with your inner guidance.

As water empties itself into the sea, it knows it has come home and is embraced by waters of the ocean as they become one. When we can *Just Be Love*, we awaken to the all-ness and oneness of this homecoming within our self and with the Source of all that is.

Spend time observing the water; a creek, river or ocean; it doesn't matter. Notice it, listen to it. Let it speak to you and teach you. Let it show you how it moves through the obstacles of life. Pay attention with your inner eye and ear to its flow, to its message. Love is in the water, as love is in you.

The I Ching says: *"You can't push the river, nor can you hold it back, no matter how hard you try."* The water that leads to the sea of life is abundant and knows the energy and the ways of its Creator. It knows where it's going, and nothing can push it or hold it back; it has its rhythm and purpose. Be like water, for you are the water. Be like love for you are love. You can't be pushed off the path or held back unless you allow it. Love is waiting for you to join itself.

> *Love is like a river, peaceful and deep, love is like a secret no one can keep.* —Darlene Lemus

Love is like a river; it runs deep and flows with life-force energy. It has twists and turns and times of greater speed and turbulence. Love, like water, contains the fullness, the all-ness of life; it is always creating, expanding and renewing, and is always seeking its way home to its beloved.

Love, in its giving and receiving, keeps us in the flow of life and returns us back home to ourselves and to our Source. The waters of the Earth all call us home to love. They whisper to us, for they know us by our vibration and our flow. When we truly listen and accept their calling, we know we are one with the energy and thirst of love. Our choices are never the same when we come home to love.

31

Love as the Sun Rises

And he shall be as the light of the morning, when the sun rises,
even a morning without clouds; as the tender grass springing out
of the earth by clear shining after rain. —2 Samuel 23:4, AKJV

The Energy and Magic of the Sun

An anthropologist once went to an indigenous tribe in a faraway land. In his journal he wrote that every day, just before dawn, the members of that tribe gathered outside to perform a strange ritual. They started to yell and crash objects in order to make a lot of noise. Only when the sun finally rose above the horizon did the Indians stop the rite. *"This helps the sun win the battle against darkness and rise again,"* someone said.

Astonished, the anthropologist asked the tribal leader if they really thought that the sun only rose because they made all that noise, which seemed a bit irrational. The leader smiled and answered, *"You are so silly! Of course, the sun will rise, regardless of our rituals. The Sun already won this fight against the dark night a long, long time ago. The sun inside each of us, however, still has to struggle to win the fight against our lower instincts and this is why we make all this noise, to help our inner suns triumph over our dark side."*

This story synthesizes much of the symbolism of the Sun in ancient cultures. Our inner sun is a mirror of the sun we see in the sky. By watching the rising of the Sun, we are also watching the rising of our souls toward spiritual ascension. This is why the Sun is honored in many cultures.

If I had to choose a religion, the sun as the universal giver of life
would be my god. —Napoleon Bonaparte

The Sun symbolizes the Creator's light and love for us. It represents our connection to Source and our higher self. The sun can be seen as a reflection of the divine light. We must realize that this light remains within us, and hold on to it, especially during dark and difficult times. Our ability to sustain this light keeps us in the awareness and presence of Love and our I AM Essence. Jesus, other spiritual masters, and native cultures valued and honored the energy of the Sun, using it to commune with God. An example of this is the Bible passage in Psalm 113:3 that speaks of the spiritual significance of the Sun, not only as a marker of time, but also as a symbol of the Divine to be praised. *"From the rising of the sun to its setting, the name of the Lord is to be praised."* The Sun represents perseverance. Its light and love are always there and symbolizes determination, strength and power-with.

All life on Earth is dependent on the energy and light of the Sun to sustain itself. Healthy doses of sunlight help boost our mood, creating a natural high. Studies show that being in the sunlight helps increase the production of the brain's natural mood chemical serotonin and hormone melatonin. Sunlight is also a source of vitamin D, helpful for bone growth and other body functions.

Throughout human history, there has been a rise and fall of human consciousness. The movements of the Earth with the Sun, and the cyclic wobbling of the Earth's axis of rotation, create an alignment with the zodiac constellations through the 26,000-year cycle. This is called the "Precession of the Equinoxes "which create substantial effects on individual and collective consciousness and behaviors. Research is showing that our galaxy, in particular our Sun, has significant influence on the Earth. The Sun's current solar cycle is sending an increase of solar winds and flairs that are producing an increase of charged particles. These are weakening the Earth's magnetic field. This affects our spiritual, physical, mental and emotional bodies, the Earth's crust and inner cores, our climate, our weather patterns, and even our man-made electrical and communication systems.

The sun is the microcosm of the soul. —H. Koppdelaney

The Sun calls us to the awakening of life; to our soul. The Sun beckons us to explore the mysteries of love and life offered with the dawning of each new day. It inspires us with yet another fresh start on life's journey. The morning light of the Sun asks us to be open and allow life, with its infinite insights, to "dawn" on us as we rise through the process of inner awakening and ascending.

The rising sun signifies the start of a new cycle; a rebirth. The darkness of night is followed by experiences of light. It affirms to us that our periods of darkness and struggle are followed by light, awareness and resolution and new possibilities. As a new day dawns, we are offered an opportunity to let go of what no longer serves us to begin this day free and refreshed.

My Experience with the Rising of the Sun

I spent ten days in the Yucatan in Mexico touring the Mayan ruins and celebrating the winter solstice on 12-21-12 in a *connote* (natural pool of warm water). I arrived at Chichen Itza to experience the early morning sun; one of many gatherings in fellowship and celebration for the ending of the Mayan calendar and welcoming in the new age of Aquarius.

The following description is from my journal, as I watched the rising sun on the beach in Cancun, Mexico.

It's now 5:30 a.m. on 12-23-12—walking the beach and taking in the sights and sounds of the ocean, awaiting the sunrise, I sit at the ocean's edge for a time, to experience the rising sun and give praise.

I look out at the ocean and the sky as they meet, creating an edge—the horizon. The horizon announces the imminent arrival of the sun as it reflects a soft orange color; the sky just above is a medium blue, turning darker farther up. I look. I ponder how light and dark call us to honor the weaving of each in balance and harmony, both intended to be sources of the known and the unknown. Could it be that the horizon (the edge) is the meeting place of love and unity?

Above the horizon, the planet Venus, the Goddess of love, beauty and relationships appears, projecting her light as the morning star, welcoming and embracing the first rays of the sun as it begins to transform darkness into light. The rising sun symbolizes the masculine (yang), embracing the darkness, the feminine (yin). This is Divine love, the merging of the feminine and masculine energies in sacred unity to create—Mother Earth births a new day. God's love embraces both light and darkness. Like the rising sun begins a new day, life begins with love.

The sunlight moves up the horizon; it turns a yellowish orange and the sky above becomes a light purple. There are a few small gray clouds floating slightly higher up from the horizon. The sight and sound of the ocean waves and the changing colors of the sky bring a majestic feeling of awe to this moment. The Sun, not yet visible, projects its rays, a preview of its radiance and beauty. Up from the water's edge, intense rays of light display their brilliance and a feeling of joy wells up within me. Before my eyes, the clouds suddenly transform themselves into whitish orange glowsticks, floating in the dawning sky. The ocean now seems darker as the sky in front of me displays its fiery presence. The edge of the cloud's glows with a bright white light. I recall my experience a few years earlier with the Sun, the cloud and Jesus. Again, this day, the Divine painter, with palette of purple, white, yellow and orange, uses the sky as a canvas to create a breathtaking portrait of the rising sun.

The Sun shows itself now, rising from the water's edge; greeting the ocean and me. A faint line of clouds along the horizon divides the sun as it continues its ascent. The sun projects three rings around itself, each ring offering a different shade and intensity of its radiance. The inner ring is a bright, vibrant white, the next ring pale yellow, and the outer ring is soft orange. As the Sun moves upward, it projects short and intense rays into the sky, which then begin to reflect on the ocean's surface. A line soon appears as the sunlight reflects on the water; a divine line as it were, for it seems to be connecting the Sun, the ocean and me, as if we are one. The sky above the horizon now transforms from its earlier purple color to blue. The Sun's brightness gets more intense now as it embraces the morning sky with fullness and warmth. I welcome the sun this new day in praise and gratitude for its life force energy. I welcome the Sun by chanting *"HU,"* an ancient word for God—a love song to God.

In the presence of the Sun's energy and majesty, I experience a state of reverence, feeling my body warmed by its energy and glow. I am in awe as to how a star's energy that is ninety-three million miles away can so quickly light up and warm this space, as this part of Earth moves into the Sun's path. If that isn't infinite intelligence and love in action, I don't know what is! I praise the Father for this light, warmth and life-giving nourishment for the Earth Mother. A new day has begun. I am reminded of the passage: *"Yesterday's the past, tomorrow's the future, and today's the gift. That's why they call it the present."* Watching the rising sun is surely a gift, for it announces and celebrates itself only in the present. It speaks to our souls, warms our hearts, and illuminates our path. I hear it boldly say to me: *"Let the sun light from within you, my beloved David, rise and shine this day. Just Be Love on this sunny day I give you!"*

The cycle of life has spoken and revealed itself once again, as the Sun has enlightened and transformed the darkness. The rising sun reminds me of how I am to live my life. Be like the star Sun and: *Surrender, Trust, Allow* and *Receive*. Know that my times of struggle and darkness, will be transformed to light, growth and joy. I accept the natural cycle of life and death, not with fear or resistance, but with love, acceptance and compassion, knowing new life comes from death. This is how grief is turned to joy, depression becomes gratitude, despair turns to hope, suffering to freedom, tears into laughter, and the caterpillar transforms into the butterfly. Likewise, the lower self transcends into the higher and wiser self, as the unknown becomes known. Like death/transition, darkness is the great teacher and opportunity to learn about ourselves in relationship to life. The light is the acceptance of what is and the choice to learn with openness and willingness the lessons offered by the "dark night of the soul" experience. Reach for the strength and courage to stay in Divine love and light. The rising of the Sun teaches us there is no right or wrong, good or bad. It only asks us to rise as love, to a grander perspective and awakening toward the higher dimensions of the self.

In this experience of the rising sun, I feel closer and more connected to my soul, my Creator and my life. This morning, the Sun reveals the love and essence of the Divine to me and I acknowledge and reflect my love and gratitude back to the rising sun.

My prayer to you this moment was written in my journal that morning of the sunrise: *May the love, light, power and peace of the rising sun ignite your soul, warm your heart and illuminate your way, this day and always.*

32

Love as the Sun Sets

Those who live at the ends of the earth stand in awe of your wonders. From where the sun rises to where it sets, you inspire shouts of joy. —Psalm 65:8, NLT

I believe the cycles of the Sun provide opportunities for reflection about endings and beginnings. Ancient Egyptians believed that the setting sun was about death and saw the sun's decent to the "underworld" as the act of regeneration, re-emerging as the new dawn. Death was not feared in the ancient world. They viewed death as a bridge between different lives; a time in which consciousness, without the physical body, could explore the spiritual realm and recover from the hardship of the physical world. The ancients saw the spiritual realm as represented by the sun's encounter with the night on the other side of the planet.

The sunset can be a reminder about going within to explore our darkness, to see what's gestating or what needs releasing. It's about going to the edge of ourselves and exploring what we don't want to know, touch, or feel; yet we know it and feel it so well, because it haunts us and keeps us unhappy and unfulfilled. Joy is the result of going within; going to the edge of ourselves, exploring and reconciling our darkness.

I long for the evening to come but now I am terrified of the dark.
—Isaiah 21:4, NLT

The setting sun can be a time of introspection about our daily life and of life in general. What's life all about? Who am I? What's my purpose for being? These are life-changing questions, and their answers come from the soul. These are the questions of our "dark night of the soul" experiences. When we enter our depths in search for answers, they can be an exciting yet, difficult and unnerving quests. We long for the answers to these questions yet we can be terrified of where they may lead us and what they might reveal. They are buried like a treasure in the depths of a turbulent sea, where darkness and loneliness reside, and few dares to explore. Our intuition is there to assist us in this process, to find and reclaim the treasure of the true self and the deeper meaning of love and life.

Near my home at dusk one September evening, I looked to the west as the Sun began its descent into the horizon. Colors of bright yellowish orange filled the western sky; clouds lit up to bid the sun farewell. Rays from the Sun pushed through openings in the clouds which seemed to bring the message of God's light. I heard the words, "I send you rays of love and compassion." The size of this glowing fireball seemed so much bigger than usual. As it neared the edge of the horizon it seemed to say. *"My light and energy are always more vibrant and abundant when you meet me at the edge within you."* As the Sun descended into the horizon, I heard it saying: *"What did you learn this day? What did you give to others this day? Did you make this planet a better place today? What may have kept you from loving yourself or others this day?"* In parting, I heard the sun say: *"Thank you for honoring my energy. Remember my love and light is always with you. I bid you good day, my friend."*

Light and Dark—Enchanting Lovers

As the day begins to transform into night, the planet Venus appears once again, this time as the evening star. She emanates the mystery and intimacy of love as she welcomes both the light and the dark as necessary parts of the cycle of life; the unity of masculine and feminine energies. She shines forth her energy of love, and yearning for union, only this time, her darkness and void embraces the light. It's a farewell of sorts, yet she knows the light is always with her. Divine power, love and wisdom are balanced in both the dark and light cycle of life. The setting sun creates a desire for the light to linger, drawing the global family closer to each other and to our Source.

The setting sun, releasing into darkness, reminds us that the light of divine love never fades. This is why many spiritual teachers and seekers spend the beginning and the ending of their day with the Sun; it offers them the experience of Agape love with their beloved Source. Perhaps that's why the rising and the setting of the Sun are so powerful and beautiful. It's one way we can see, feel, and understand the loving presence of the Creator through our physical senses. To witness and honor the rising and/or setting of the Sun offers us a deeper awareness and communion with God and our I AM presence.

I reflected within myself on this day, where I'd been and what I'd done. Who touched me, and whose life I may have touched? It seems the setting sun provides a time for introspection, assessing what is there for me now? What is no longer needed? What may need to be released?

The Suns Cycle of Rising and Setting

The beauty and majesty of this cycle of the Sun's rising and setting hovers on the horizon—the edge of love, wonder and life force energy. Witnessing the Sun's rise and descent is to witness the power and grace, the love and wisdom of our Source.

The east and west horizons, both carry a message. Both call us to life and love in their own unique ways. One leads to the other as only divine intelligence and unity can do. They speak to our soul, open our heart and inspire our mind. Their message and insights need to simmer deep within us for a time and then be practiced. To witness the rising and the setting of the Sun is to experience the splendor of the Divine and to know love—its gifts and its spirit.

33

Love as a Snowflake

*Like us, snowflakes are one of God's most beautiful yet fragile
things and look at what they can create as they join together.*

A snowfall can be very beautiful and captivating, or it can be very
unnerving and dangerous. Many of us have experienced both sides of
winter's duality. The following is my perception of the beautiful side of a
snowfall and how it too is an expression of love from the Creator.

As the snow is falling this winter night, I feel Divine grace falling upon
me. Standing among all these gentle, carefree flakes coming from above, I
can't help but look up and notice with wonder and awe. Snowflakes are like
miniature stars falling to the ground; vast in number with no two alike. These
crystalline water creations hold the love and mystery of the Divine, just like
the stars. I open my hands to catch the snow as it falls from the backdrop of
the darkness and I smile, knowing that love, beauty and grace is touching me.

I'm in awe at how each flake is unique and how they all, separately yet
with harmony and grace, just descend from the night sky—softly cascading
and twirling their way downward through this earthly space, landing and
merging into oneness. In this moment, I have a greater understanding of
the miracle of love as the individual flakes embrace and merge and seem to
know how to be with each other. They never lose their identity, connection,
beauty, and peace as the Divine sends them on their descending journey to
sacred Mother Earth.

Love as a snowflake, how simple and free the Divine intends it to be.

Snowflakes feel cold and wet as they touch my face, but I don't mind,
because I'm standing under a canopy of angels descending from the heavens.
The cascade of snowflakes puts me in that childlike state of innocence and
wonder. I let my imagination go into full swing, twirling around, and then

laying on the ground, moving my arms and legs, making that angel of love like I know myself to be. I use my tongue to catch the cold, delicate white-water crystals falling from the night sky. I get a taste of heaven, feeling carefree and loved, noticing the simple beauty that surrounds me in this moment.

As the snowflakes pile up on each other, I notice the light of the moon revealing itself through the moving clouds. Tiny sparkles appear on the snow-covered ground that looks like glittering diamonds. On this magical night, it may be cold outside, but my heart is warm, radiating peace all around. I know I'm surrounded by love, for the beauty of this snowy night feels like God is wrapping me in a blanket of love and grace. How peaceful and free love intends to be.

34

Love as a Raindrop

Life is not about waiting for the rain to pass. It's about our willingness to be in the rain, to dance in it, to make love and to play in the rain.

I invite you to participate in an exercise to experience love as a raindrop. Remember the 1969 hit song: *Raindrops Keep Fallin' on My Head*? In this moment, recall, and if you choose, sing the words of this song. Notice how you feel as you hear the music and sing the words. As this song rings through your mind, do you notice that your problems don't seem quite so bad? Let me give you a line of the song.

"But there's one thing I know the blues they send to meet me won't defeat me. It won't be long till happiness steps up to greet me."

Imagine yourself standing in a gentle rain. Notice the freshness of the air and the sound of the raindrops as they fall upon your head. Notice how the drops seem to penetrate your skin to cleanse and wash away the stress and worry of life. Yes, nature has a way of renewing itself and us, making vibrant that which seems dreary and weary.

Raindrops are another form of Divine love and grace, descending from the heavens; the drops bring a freshness and renewal to life. No, you won't stop the rain… or God's love by *"complainin'."* Like the raindrops, you are already loved and already free. So, what's the *"worryin'"* really about and what's it really going to do for you? The raindrops teach us to be in the process, to allow ourselves to grow, to become whole yet again. The Divine always offers us this gift, just like we are offered raindrops, sunshine and rainbows.

Again, imagine the raindrops falling upon your head. Notice that the drops flow from your head down throughout your entire body. See the raindrops cleansing and renewing you, for this is what love seeks to do. Know that the light of the Sun lies just beyond the clouds, the raindrops and the worry. There is no need to despair. The rain will stop, and the clouds will pass. The worry will lift; love and light will shine once again. That's the beauty and mystery of love as a raindrop.

So, the next time those raindrops fall on your head, don't complain or worry. Let the raindrops fall on you and see them as God's infinite love, caressing you with tender care. Can you see the raindrops having the same experience of tenderness and love as they touch you? In your heart and soul, you know that there is no separation from the Divine—the raindrops come from Source and so do you. This is the nature of God's love, expressing itself as a raindrop. Yes, love is like a raindrop. So, dance in the rain and *Just Be Love* in the rain.

35

Love and Laughter

Before God we are all equally wise and equally foolish.
—Albert Einstein

Now, for the lighter side of love. Warning: Corny humor ahead.

Funny how life works, isn't it? I've struggled in life with finding the right job. When I was younger, I wanted to be a doctor, but I realized I didn't have any patience.

I was a musician for a while, but I soon realized I wasn't noteworthy.

After many years of trying to find steady work, I finally got a job as a historian until I realized there was no future in it.

My last job was working at a coffee shop, but I decided to quit because it was always the same old grind.

I'm working at being less selfish and improving my self-confidence. A friend commented on my improvement. I told him thank you, and that I felt I was making good progress. Then I said: "You know I may not be much, but I'm all I think about." My friend abruptly said, "So much for your progress."

Humor comes from a Latin word, *Humors* which means body fluid. I also take it to mean to be fluid, flexible or to flow. By playing with the word a bit, you can discern that the word *Hu* is the ancient name of God, and *Amour* in French means love, and in English means love affair. So, *Humor* can mean God-loving or having a love affair with God.

The question is sometimes asked: Does God have a sense of humor? My response to this question is yes, and for one simple reason—from the time we are an infant to the time we pass on, we can smile and laugh. Studies of animal behaviors are revealing that even some animals show emotions and express smiles and laughter. We laugh when a child giggles and smile at their innocent use of imagination and play. We smile and laugh at the physical features and antics of a pet or some animals in nature; at the shapes of rocks, trees and cloud formations. When we have an embarrassing experience, we might not initially laugh at that moment, but after time has passed, we may look back and find it amusing. The Divine has a playground, that we call the universe. Yes, it's true that God has a wonderful sense of humor and loves to create and play. A part of love is the ability to laugh, to find joy, not only in the good times, but more importantly, during the not so good times. A part of love is the ability to laugh, especially at ourselves. Yes, you and I have done and will do foolish things; we will have embarrassing moments and make wrong turns, intentional or unintentionally. The key is to learn from them, with an open heart and a spoonful of acceptance and grace.

In our fast-paced, crazy, upside-down world, we can get so preoccupied and stressed that we can mentally and/or emotionally snap. I often say to others that see me in the heat of my stress, confusion or overload, "I don't know about you, but of all the things I miss, it's my mind I miss the most." If I can't laugh at myself, live in the moment, and see myself as human, doing the best I can, my inability to accept and adapt will likely create more stress and struggle.

When life locks you in your room, simply go out the window.
— Unknown

Two of the biggest barriers to happiness are the fear of looking foolish and taking oneself too seriously. Life has gotten so complicated, and we are getting so busy and preoccupied, that we seem to be shutting ourselves down in many respects—filtering our thoughts and words, judging ourselves and second guessing our choices. We can become so stuck and closed, that when we experience our physical transition (death), we may wonder why we took life so seriously; why we didn't laugh and play more; hug and dance more; say I love you, please and thank you more; follow our dreams and intuition more.

Peace begins with a smile. Every time you smile, it's an action of love, a gift to that person, a beautiful thing. —Mother Teresa

Being too serious, negative, resentful or angry takes energy and work. When we frown, we use sixty-two muscles in our face alone, but when we smile, we only use twenty-four. It takes more work and energy to frown and be miserable than to smile and be happy. Have you noticed people who are often sad, but when they give themselves permission, have beautiful smiles? At times we laugh so hard we start to cry and can cry so hard we start to laugh.

Both are divinely given emotions and expressions merging into each other; one of the many continuums of opposites we experience in life. Laughter and tears are powerful ways of connecting to our deeper self, reframing our life, and creating pathways to healing. The line between life being very serious and very funny is really very thin, and only a matter of one's perception.

A smile or a laugh helps us lighten up on ourselves and can move us into one of three different states of consciousness. Warning, more foolishness ahead with a bit of truth...

Most of us first move to the state of *Denial.* While in this state you will often feel like you are peacefully floating down an enchanted river near Egypt. This will take you to the next state of consciousness, the frustrating state of *Cahoots.* There, it seems you secretly lived with a partner for a week one day. After spending time in the state of Cahoots, you can rest assured you will end up in the beautiful state of *Confusion.* I myself have spent most of my life in this state of consciousness. As you can tell by now, it's done wonders for my ability to laugh at myself, and it's heightened my sense of reality and connection to all that is; my ability to love myself and others.

> *We do not cease playing because we grow old. We grow old because we cease playing.* —Joseph Lee

Love and laughter call us to the childlike qualities of ourselves. This is the part of us that is innocent, spontaneous, playful, unconditional, creative, and full of wonder, wisdom and love. Throughout our life we're challenged to keep our childlike qualities free, open, and expressive, while taming the childish part that is selfish, demanding, whining, conditional and needy. Research on humor, shows that laughter is like a tranquilizer with no side effects. It can change our perspective and mood. A ten-minute laugh is equivalent to thirty minutes of meditation for relaxing and reframing our thoughts. Laughter releases the brain chemical endorphins known for their relaxing, feel-good effect. Laughing 100 times a day is a good physical workout; it's equal to ten minutes on an exercise machine. Yes, humor and laughter are universal solvents for the abrasive experiences of life.

We need at least twelve laughs and five hugs daily to stay healthy. Children laugh an average of 300 times a day; many adults struggle to laugh much at all during their day. Laughter helps ground us and keep us in the moment by bringing love and joy back into our awareness. Laughter helps bring people together. It connects people, because when we start to laugh, others naturally join in the laughter. The energy of laugher is contagious and part of the dynamic of love. I encourage you to check a short video on YouTube entitled "Buddha on the Train." This is a powerful example of how laughter can combat stress and loneliness.

> *A cheerful heart is good medicine, but a crushed spirit dries up the bones.* —Proverbs 17:22 NIV

Over the years, I've offered presentations on humor and health. I dress as a nerdy looking doctor, like Patch Adams (with all due respect to real doctors). My character's name is Dr. Feelgood. He's not a real doctor, but his message is very real; full of insight and fun—"a couple fries short of a happy meal" is how Dr. Feelgood likes to describe himself. He wears a blue wig; black framed glasses complete with white tape on the bridge. He also has reading glasses that have a banana attached at the nose. He has a colorful patterned shirt and equally colorful uncoordinated tie, all topped off with a white lab coat and stethoscope that doubles as a plunger. Parts of his presentation are very "moving."

I would like to share two powerful experiences that the good "doctor" has had.

One, I was giving a presentation at a church and was invited for coffee and cake afterwards. I enjoyed the fellowship and interaction with the attendees. While I was chatting with some folks a woman came up from behind me and pulled off Dr. Feelgood's wig. As I turned around to find out what was happening, the women started putting my wig on her bald head. She had a big smile on her face, as she handed me her wig, I put it on my head, and we all had a wonderful laugh. This woman shared with me that upon learning of her cancer diagnosis 6 years prior, she was only given 2 years to live. She said, "I've been living the message you gave us tonight about humor, health and love, and it's a big reason why I'm still here." I told her that her childlike courage with me tonight spoke volumes as to the healing power of laughter and the love it generates. We hugged and shared a teary smile, expressing joy and gratitude for the moment.

Another magical experience showed me the power of attitude and choice as part of the human condition. This time Dr. Feelgood was at a nursing home. After I did my presentation for the residents who came to the dining hall, some nurses asked if I'd be willing to visit a few residents who were still in their rooms. Of course, I agreed. When I entered the first room, the women immediately started laughing. I didn't even say anything, but she took one look at me and laughed uncontrollably. My very presence was antics enough to get her funny bone tickled. We had a delightful 5-minute visit. As I walked out of her room, the nurses looked at me in awe, saying, "How did you do that?" "Do what?" I asked. They replied, "That women has been here nearly 2 years and she rarely smiles, let alone laughs." I told them, "It was likely my blue hair and banana nose glasses." I then went into the room right next door. A woman was sitting up in her chair looking very sad and frail. I walked up to her and extended my hand to hers. As I was holding her hand I said, "Hi ma'am, I'm Dr. Feelgood, what's your name?" She did not give me her name, she just glanced at me with a very sad and tired expression and said, "I want to die." I said, "I understand, go in peace." I also said, "I'm blessed to have been with you." And I walked out. The nurses just looked at me and looked in the room of this dejected women and said, "Talk about two extremes with these two people." I said, "Yes, life has its extremes and choices; we just witnessed the power of perception and attitude and its impact on our life." They agreed as we walked to another room.

I often ponder the experiences with those two residents, as well as the women with the wig; the significance of the perception, attitude and choices each individual displayed. The same character, Dr. Feelgood, elicited two completely different responses and each person made a choice about who they would be in that moment. These stories are examples of how our perceptions, beliefs and attitudes impact our choices, either enhancing the quality of our life or depleting it.

When you look at some of the great comedians in the United States, many came into prominence because of difficult times in our country's history. Some would say that the Depression and World War II gave rise to some of our greatest comedy acts. It was "comic relief" for coping and dealing with the uncertainty and struggles of the time. After that tragic day of September 11, 2001, many comedians took time off from their jokes showing respect for the families affected, as the entire country dealt with the shock and grief, we all were experiencing. In time the laughter returned, and we used it once again as a way to cope with and move through the pain of that horrific time. The ability and willingness to laugh, while still respecting and honoring the pain of difficult times, is a very powerful and effective coping skill. Humor and laughter, when used with proper intent, are effective tools that reduce stress, bring hope, resilience, confidence and a sense of connection with each other, helping to ride the waves of life's struggles and uncertainties.

Many of the great comedians, past and present, had tragic, tormented personal lives. As we've learned, laughter can be a very effective way to cope with what life brings or it can be an unfortunate and unhealthy mask to cover up the wounds within. The tragic loss of the comic genius and compassionate soul, Robin Williams, was an unfortunate example of how humor and making others laugh was a way to cover inner pain and torment. Humor can also be used negatively at the expense of another, wounding through humiliation—there's that continuum of opposites again and how we are at a point of choice in many ways. Like love, humor and laugher are part of our true, divine nature; however, they are to be used with discernment, loving intent and respect.

> *Love ignites our soul, opens our heart, frees our body, and expands our mind. Laughter brings joy to our soul, warms the heart, tickles the body and reframes the mind.*

Do you know why angels can fly? Because they take themselves lightly. Aspects of our life can be a serious endeavor. I believe we would do ourselves a favor by choosing to travel lightly, like the angels. We can make life experiences more difficult and complex or we can choose simplicity and grace. *Which choice would help you move through life with more acceptance and less struggle? Which choice would help you learn from your experiences and bring you to a higher perspective? Which choice would allow you to experience more joy, gratitude and peace? Which choice could you make to Just Be Love?*

36
Love as a Rose

Parts of the rose reflect parts of life. There is strength and resilience in the stem and in us. There is pain in touching the thorns and there will be pain in touching life. Let us not forget, however, that the essence and beauty of the rose mirrors the essence and beauty of ourselves.

I like to think of the rose as a metaphor for our life. The stem of the rose is about our groundedness, being rooted and connected to the Earth, learning to take in its nourishment and energy for our strength and growth. On the stem are thorns, representing the boundaries needed to protect the rose from being handled carelessly. Like the rose, it's important for us to set healthy boundaries to protect our self along life's journey. Like the touch of the thorns, life hurts at times. Our painful times are part of what makes us human and working through them helps us grow in spiritual maturity.

Then there is the blossom of the rose, with its soft, beautiful petals and lingering fragrance. This blossom is the essence and beauty of the rose. The stem provides the strength, the resilience and protection; the masculine part of the rose that endures the hits of life. The blossom is the inner strength, grace and beauty; the feminine side expressing its essence. Both parts are needed. Both parts are what make up the completeness and fullness of the rose. The blossom emerges from the stem's grounding strength and demonstrates the balance of softness, beauty and the life force energy. The thorns ensure protection so that the rose can reach its divine potential. This balance of softness, strength and beauty, if bottled, could be labeled love.

Just as the caterpillar struggles in a cocoon to become a butterfly, nature develops a necessary means of protection that brings struggle and sometimes pain so that it may transform into its true essence. The same goes for us. The thorns of the rose are healthy and necessary for protection in order for the rose to thrive. In our own lives setting limits and using "tough love" is healthy and essential. Saying "no" to others when needed, is saying "yes" to ourselves and shows that we value ourselves enough to protect ourselves. Boundaries (tough love) can hurt others. It's painful for us to say "no" at times, yet we realize it's the healthy and constructive thing to do, because we care. This may be why we get frustrated and angry at God. We experience "no" and we don't understand "why?"—it seems unfair—yet God is still there, still caring, still loving us.

> *And the day came when the risk to remain tight in a bud was more painful than the risk it took to blossom.* —Anais Nin

Just like the cocoon holds the caterpillar as it struggles to become the butterfly, the bud of the rose stays closed, holding back the blossom until it's ready to open and display its true self. Our loving Creator provides mechanisms with the desire that all living beings have what they need to grow in spiritual maturity. The day comes for all living creatures to blossom, break free and live their true potential. For many, it may appear safe to remain in the bud of our created comfort zone. However, in divine reality this is more painful for us. We are not free to experience our true and vibrant self.

The next time you look at a rose, notice its stem; feel the energy of unwavering strength that pulses through its green fibers. Notice the reminder of the need for protection offered by the thorns; the pain felt as they are touched, yet the learning and growth that occurs. Observe the bud as it seeks to be open and free, releasing its essence through its beauty and fragrance. This is the fullness of the blossom, so soft to touch, pleasing to the eyes, and so gentle on our hearts. This is what Divine love does for us.

Come and embrace the totality of the rose and the totality of life here on Earth. Know that you are part of this totality, for you are the rose and the rose is you. This is experiencing oneness—experiencing Divine love.

I close this chapter with a beautiful poem written by a dear soul sister, Patricia McShane-Gearhart.

The Rose

> *I see the Rose and the Rose sees me.*
> *Our core strengthened,*
> *by risings through resistance;*
> *Answering Creator's call*
> *to grow up, to open, to trust.*

Life's storms stretch us, teach us,
and nourish us, into the fullness of our essence.
From bud to blossom she brings her singular scent,
whispering "be who YOU are."
Love's fragrance present,
even as seasoned petals respond to nature's nudge;
letting go of what was;
releasing into the journey back toward
Earth's embrace, and beyond,
to the Oneness, to the beginning,
where rebirth awaits.
I am the Rose and the Rose is me.

37

Closing Thoughts with Just Be Love

We are on a journey, a search for love, acceptance and peace.
Humans have a desire to love and be loved.

We have a desire for acceptance and connection. We have a desire for healing and peace. Our higher self knows that we are all the same despite our individual makeup and preferences. The Divine in us knows we are all connected and that we are a part of something greater. The lower self wants to be separate and see itself as special. The focus on differences can be a form of judgment, thus the absence of love. The way to love and peace is to focus on similarities, while honoring differences.

The following prayer for peace is compilation of peace prayers from fourteen different faiths around the world. I've created one prayer using a few lines from each of these identified faiths. I honor these faiths and how each expresses their understanding of our relationship with the Creator.

As you read, notice the similarities, the oneness within the different expressions; observe the shared beliefs. These peace prayers can also be called unity prayers, for they are expressions, not only of peace, but also unity. They are one voice speaking through different cultures, faiths and beliefs. They each express a truth from the higher perspective. They are collective souls speaking as one heart and mind, expressing love, peace and unity. The quest to *Just Be Love* is accepting and living in this unity and peace, individually and collectively.

Prayer for Peace

Baha'i: Be generous in prosperity, and thankful in adversity. Be fair in judgment and guarded in thy speech. Be a lamp unto those who walk in darkness and a home to the stranger.

Buddhist: May all beings everywhere, plagued with suffering of body and mind, quickly be freed from their illness. May those frightened cease to be afraid, and may those bound be free. May the powerless find power, and may people think of befriending one another.

Christian: Blessed are the peacemakers, for they shall be known as the children of God. But I say to you that hear, love your enemies, do good to those that hate you, bless those who curse you, pray for those who abuse you.

Hindu: Oh Lord God almighty, may there be peace on earth. May the waters be appeasing. May herbs be wholesome and may trees and plants bring peace to all. May all beneficent beings bring peace to us.

Jainist: Peace and universal love is the essence of the Gospel preached by all enlightened ones. The Lord has preached that equanimity is the Dharma. Forgive do I creatures all, and let the creatures forgive me.

Jewish: Come let us go to the mountain of the Lord, that we may walk the paths of the most high.

Muslim: In the name of Allah, the beneficent, the merciful. Praise be to the Lord of the universe who created us and made into tribes and nations, that we may know each other, not that we may despise each other.

Native African: Almighty God, the Great Thumb we cannot evade to tie any knot. You are the one who does not hesitate to respond to our call. You are the cornerstone of peace.

Native American: O Great Spirit of our ancestors, I raise my pipe to you. To your messengers the four winds, and to Mother Earth who provides your children. Give us the wisdom to teach our children to love, to respect, and to be kind to each other so that they may grow with peace in mind.

Shinto: Although the people living across the ocean surrounding us, I believe are all brothers and sisters. Why are there constant troubles in this world? Why do winds and waves rise in the ocean surrounding us? I only earnestly wish that the wind will soon puff away all the clouds which are hanging over the tops of the mountains.

Skih: That truth is above everything, but higher still is truthful living. Know that we attain God when we love, and only that victory endures in consequence of which no one is defeated.

Sufi: O Almighty Sun, whose light clears away all clouds, we take refuge in you. Guide all people, God of all deities, Lord of all angels, we pray you to dispel the mists of illusion from the hearts of the nations.

Tibetan Buddhist: May you be at peace; may your heart remain open. May you awaken to the light of your own true nature. May you be healed; may you be a source of healing for all beings.

Zoroastrian: We pray to God to eradicate all misery in the world: That understanding triumph over ignorance, that generosity triumph over indifference, that trust triumph over contempt, and that truth triumph over falsehood.

Let there be Love and Peace on Earth and let it begin with Me.

I thank you for taking this journey to *Just Be Love*. Much love and God's peace. Namaste, David

Appendix

Divine/Universal Laws

These laws help guide and direct us through life. Our soul journey in human form, is too effectively learn the positive use of these laws, through the energy of our thoughts, beliefs and behaviors to expand in love, potential and abundance.

Law of Love: Love is the primary law that governs and drives the universe. All of creation is manifested from the energy and intent of love.

Law of Oneness: Everything in the universe is connected to everything else.

Law of Vibration: Everything in the universe vibrates. All of creation has its unique vibration.

Law of Perpetual Transmutation of Energy: Higher vibrations consume and transform lower ones.

Law of Rhythm: Everything vibrates and moves to certain rhythm. These rhythms create seasons, cycles and stages of development and patterns.

Law of Giving and Receiving: It is through giving that we receive and when we receive, we give.

Law of Correspondence: As above so below.

Law of Obedience: Obedience means to respect. Out of respect, understand and obey the laws of the universe, not just humanities laws. What we as humans may define as normal doesn't mean natural. What is natural is what creates harmony.

Law of Action: Action creates motivation, which creates more action.

Law of Thinking: If the ruling mind is positive and clear in thoughts, you create positive and constructive pathways. This is thinking that creates, expands and is inspiring. It's purposeful, motivating and energizing.

Law of Supply: This is the law of goodness and unlimited supply. Ask and you will receive, seek and you will find. If no demand is made, no supply will appear. If we don't ask and seek, the answer will always seem to be "no".

Law of Cause and Effect: Nothing happens by chance or outside of universal laws. Every action has a reaction or significance. What we reap we sow.

Law of Attraction: What I think about, I bring about. Our thoughts, beliefs, emotions, words and actions produce energies, which in turn attract like energies. Positive attracts positive, negative attracts negative.

Law of Compensation: Is the law of cause and effect in action. This applies to blessings and abundance; the visible effects of our deeds are given to us in gifts, money, inheritance, friendships and blessings.

Law of Increase and Praise: To speak and act in the mindset and attitude of gratitude activates this law. Giving praise and gratitude draws us closer to the Divine and the abundant universe.

Law of Forgiveness/Reconciliation: The act of forgiveness sets us free from a self-imposed prison. Forgiveness and reconciliation are a cleansing of the heart and mind.

Law of Benefit: To benefit means to let go of the lower self (ego) for the growth and benefit of the higher self (soul). It's to let go of what no longer serves us to create (gain) something better.

Law of Non-Resistance: What we resist will persist and has power over us. True power comes through non-resistance.

Law of Relativity: In life, each person will experience a series of problems and lessons i.e. (test of initiation) for the purpose of strengthening light and love. Put problems into perspective, knowing "it's all relative."

Law of Polarity: Everything is on a continuum and has an opposite, except God.

Law of Gender: All of creation has masculine (yang) and feminine (yin) qualities.

There are 29 human traits that align with these divine laws:

Aspiration to a higher power, Unconditional Love, Acceptance, Understanding, Compassion, Joy, Courage, Dedication, Determination, Discipline, Trust, Forgiveness, Generosity, Grace, Honesty, Hope, Kindness, Gratitude, Openness, Patience, Praise, Respect, Responsibility, Reverence, Self-worth, Surrender, Allow, Curiosity and Imagination.

Bibliography

Bourbeau, Lise. *Heal Your Wounds and Find Your True Self.* Les Editions. E.T.C. Inc. 2002.

Brigham Young University. *Medical Research: Strong Relationships with Friends/ Family Decreases Risk of Death.* www.pr.com/press-release/251477. 2010.

Carroll, Lee. *The Twelve Layers of DNA: An Esoteric Study of The Mystery Within.* Platinum Publishing House. 2010.

Douglas-Koltz, Neil. *The Hidden Gospel of the Aramaic Jesus.* Quest Books, 2012.

The Giving Pledge. *The Giving Pledge 2019 Report.* Press Release. https://givingpledge.org/PressRelease.aspx?date=05.28.2019.

Fisher, Helen. *Why We Love: The Nature and Chemistry of Romantic Love.* Henry Holt and Co. 2004.

Holy Bible. ESV, KJV, ISV, NIV, NLT, NSV.

Holmes, Leonard. *Loneliness Impairs the Immune System. www.mentalhealth. about.com/od/research/a/lonely/flu.htm.* 2005.

Institute of HeartMath. *Science of the Heart: Exploring the Role of the Heart and Human Performance.* www.heartmath.org/research/scienceof heart/ head-heart-interactions.html.

Legatum Institute,.*2018 Legatum Prosperity Index Report.* www. li.com/media/press-release/2018-legatum prosperity. 2018.

Noll, Shaina. *Songs for the Inner Child.* Singing Heart Productions, 2011.

Orme-Johnson D.W., et al. *Preventing terrorism and international conflict: Effects of large assemblies of participants in the Transcendental Meditation and TM-Sidhi programs.* Journal of Offender Rehabilitation 36: 283—302, 2003.

Ross, Hugh McGregor. *Spirituality in the Gospel of Thomas.* Bright Ten Book, 2010.

Souledout.org. *World Peace Prayers.* www.souledout.org/newworldreligion/worldprayers/preaceprayers.html

Suzuki, David. *Sacred Balance: Rediscovering our place in nature.* Graystone Books, 2007.

The Foundation for Inner Peace. *A Course In Miracles.* Text and Workbook. Penguin Books, 1996.

Twitchell, Paul. *Stranger by the River.* Quality Books, 1987.

Yogiraj Siddhanath. *Yoga in Life.* www.yogainlife.net/hamasyog.htm 2007.